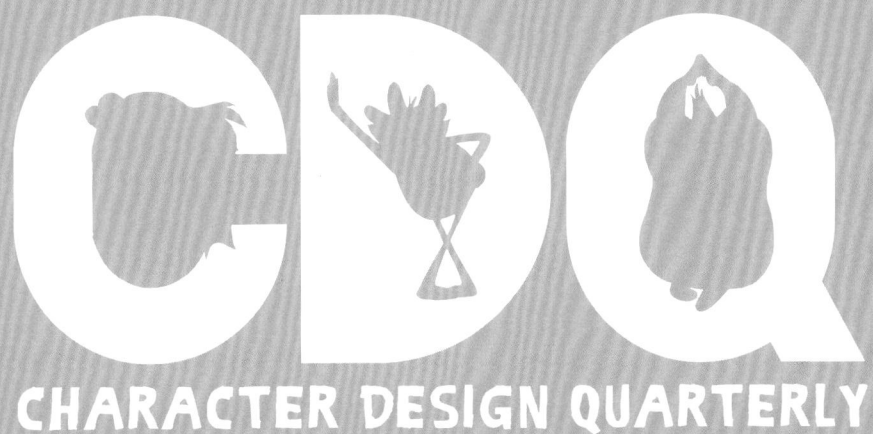

CHARACTER DESIGN QUARTERLY

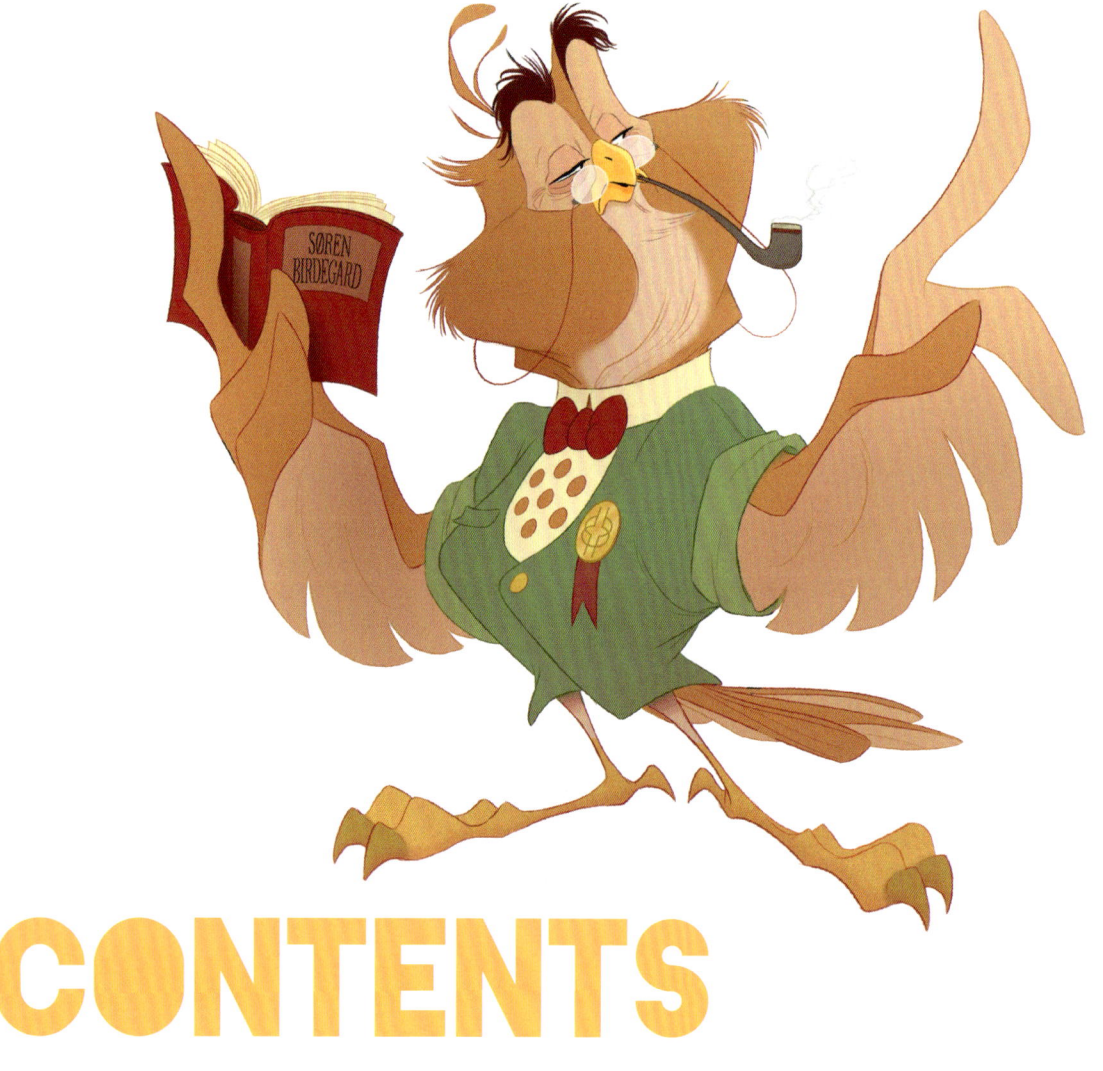

Image © Roger Pérez

CONTENTS

04
BEHIND THE COVER ART
We speak to Lynn Chen about her art and learn how she made this issue's colorful cover

18
CIRCUS DU SOLEIL
A circus family head off on vacation in David Navarro's in-depth tutorial

30
THE KNOW-IT-OWL TAKES FLIGHT
Roger Pérez creates a feathered friend from the prompt "brainy bird"

34
ARTIST CATCH-UP
Simone Grünewald returns to *CDQ* for a chat about the secrets behind her character designs

44
CHARACTERS WITH A STORY TO TELL
Alex Relloso talks about the inextricable link between story and character

48
HOW I STYLIZE
Jennifer Voigt shares tips for getting the most out of your character designs

52
THE GALLERY
A selection of stunning artworks from Eunbi Kang, Ben Eblen, and Shannon Halstein

WELCOME TO *CHARACTER DESIGN QUARTERLY 25*

Character design is not only a fun and rewarding craft to learn, it also opens up a whole host of different opportunities. In this issue we have many great examples of artists on varying and interesting career paths. Our vibrant cover art was crafted by Lynn Chen, who speaks to us about working in animation and video games, and takes us step by step through bringing her corgi Mochi to the cover of the magazine.

We speak to Cam Kendell who has been creating fantastical characters for a whole host of board games and to Simone Grünewald who works as a freelancer and creates online tutorials. Alex Relloso shows us how integral story is when designing characters.

We also have our usual collection of in-depth, step-by-step tutorials, plus mini features with invaluable artist tips. David Navarro shows us how to create three related characters, Roger Pérez brings a brainy bird to life, and João Moura adds a touching narrative to a character and sidekick tutorial.

However you plan to put your character-design skills to use, there's something to learn from every artist featured in this issue. Turn the page and get creating!

SAM DRAPER
EDITOR

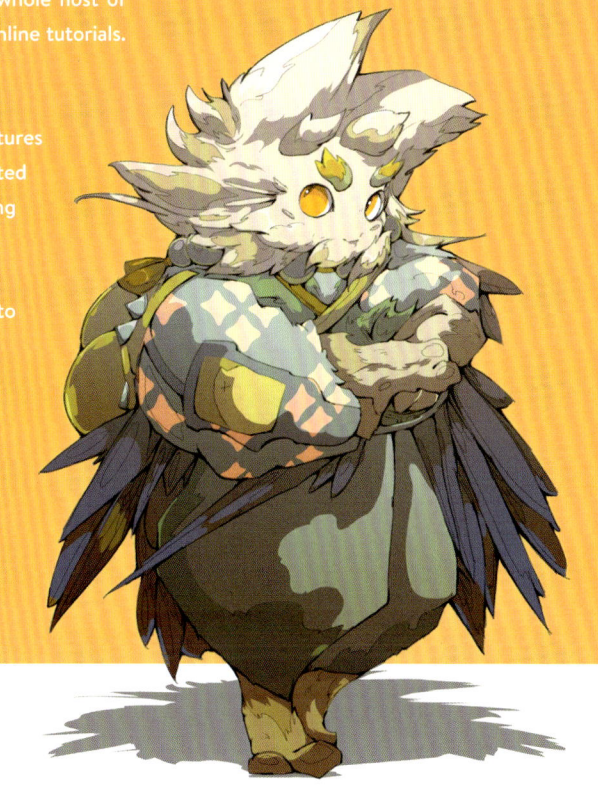

Image © Jennifer Voigt

60
STING LIKE A BEE

Anastasiia Platoshyna tackles our classic Random Word Generator feature

72
MEET THE ARTIST

Board-game artist Cam Kendell talks with us about his career and character designs

82
SETTING THE MOOD

Aurélie Lise-Anne shows us how light and shadow can affect your character designs

86
ONE FINAL ADVENTURE

An old man and his sidekick discover an artefact in this tutorial from João Moura

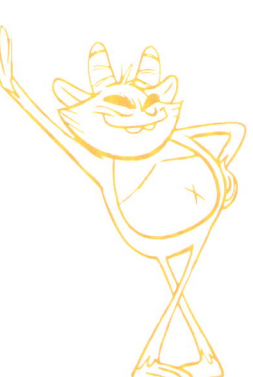

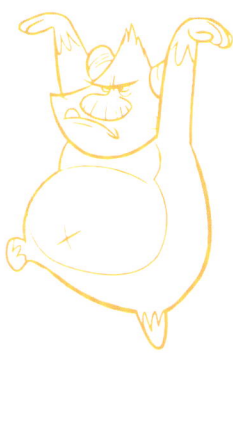

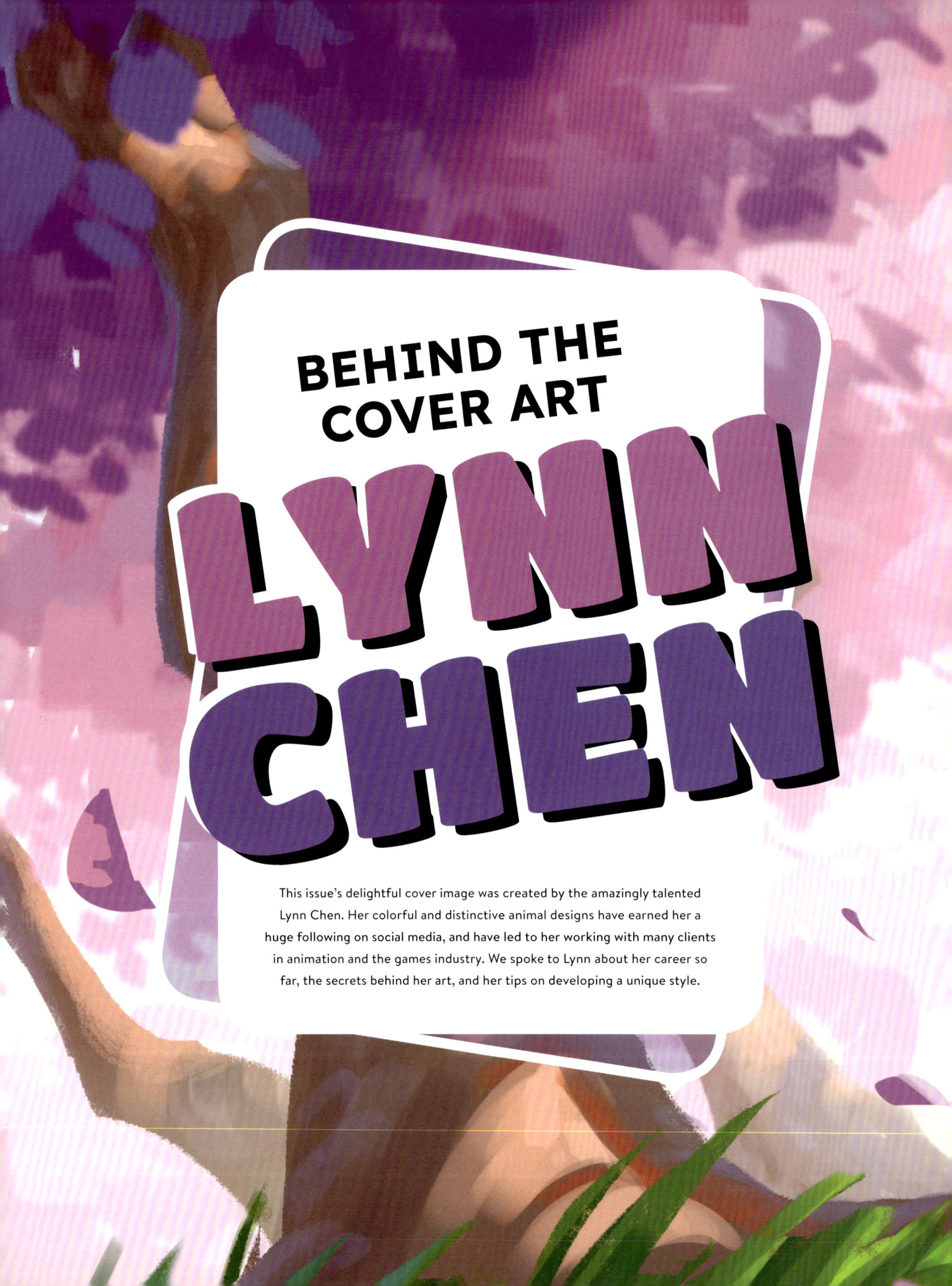

BEHIND THE COVER ART

LYNN CHEN

This issue's delightful cover image was created by the amazingly talented Lynn Chen. Her colorful and distinctive animal designs have earned her a huge following on social media, and have led to her working with many clients in animation and the games industry. We spoke to Lynn about her career so far, the secrets behind her art, and her tips on developing a unique style.

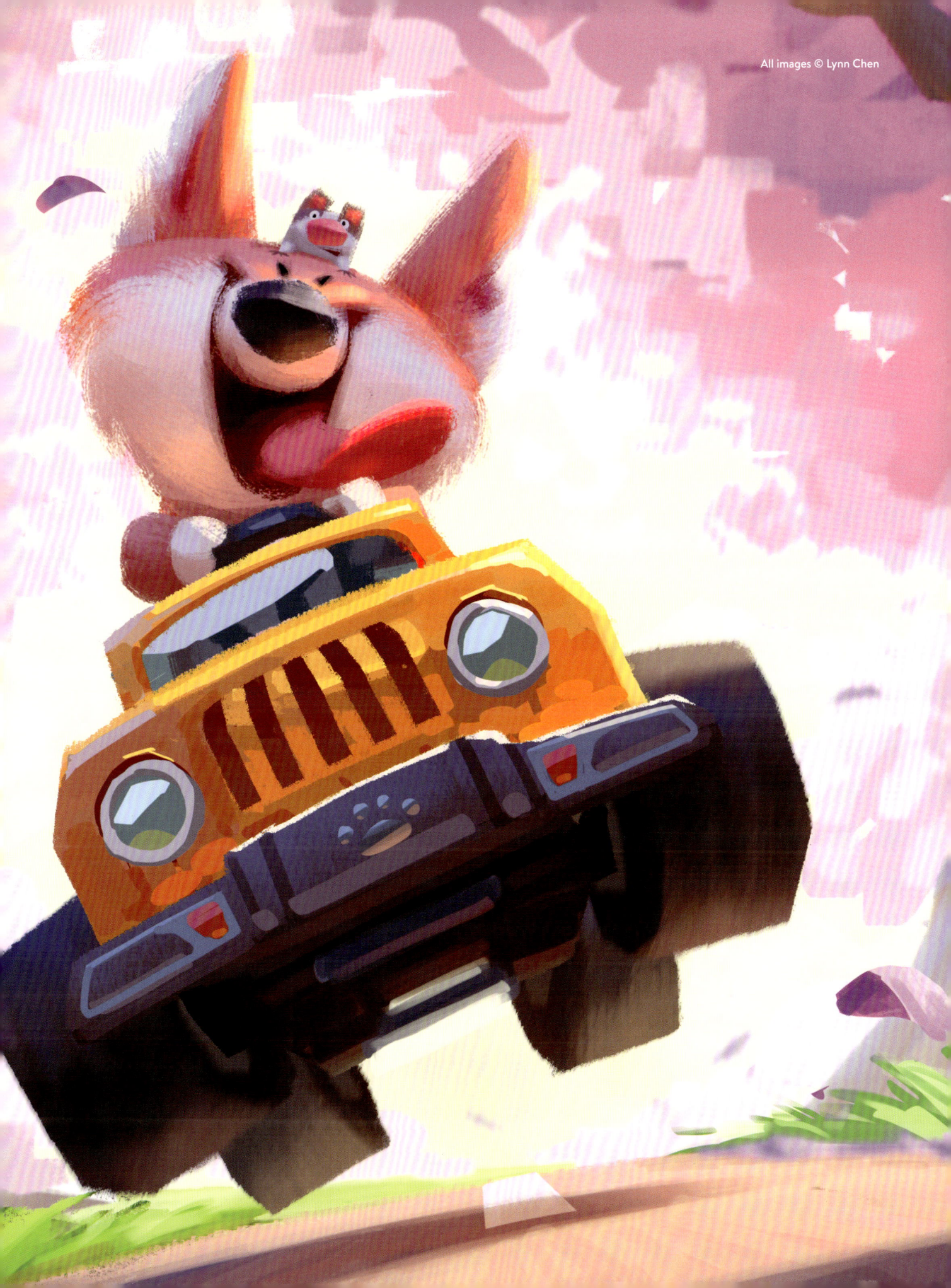

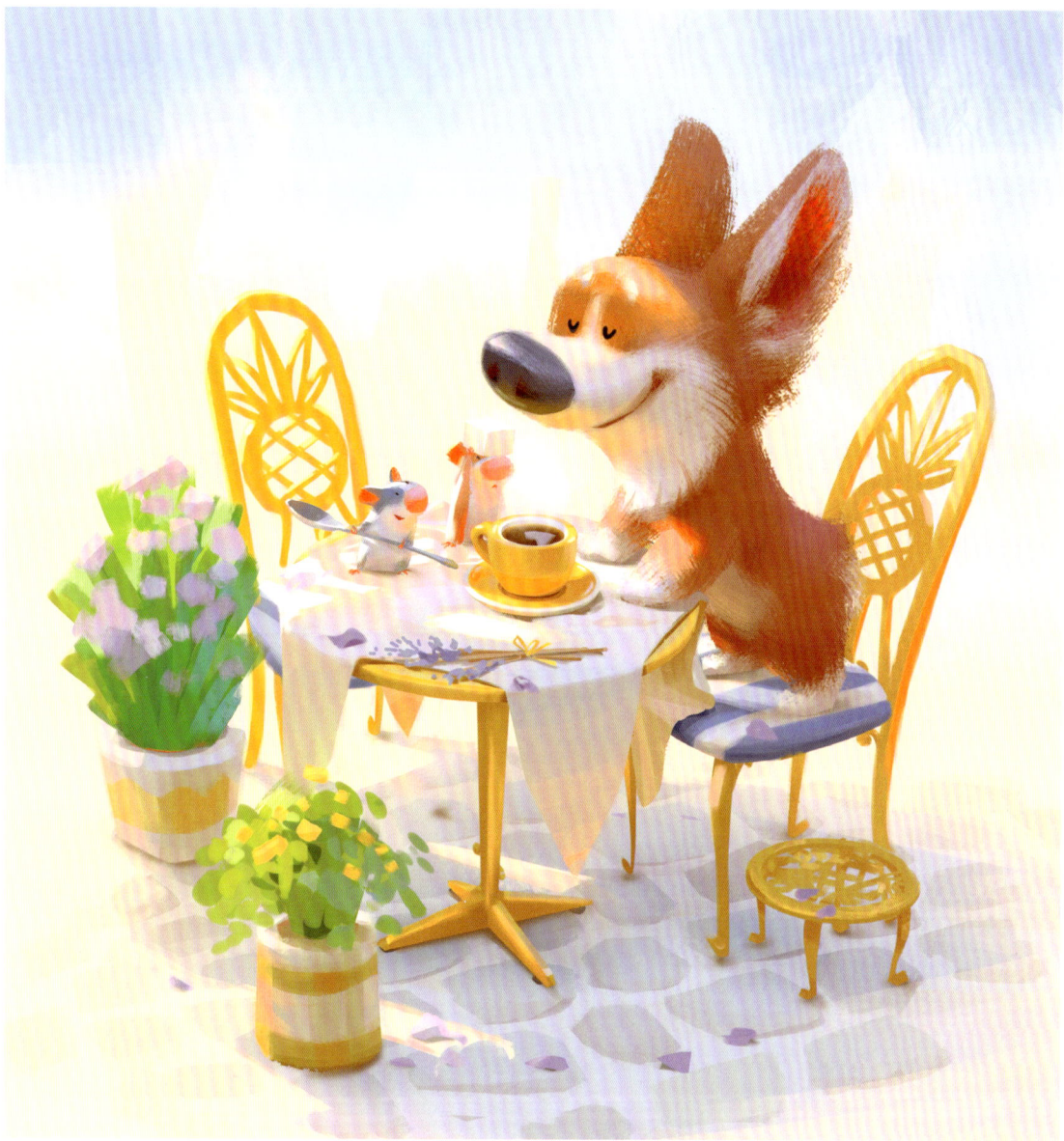

This page: Enjoy a morning coffee with friends

Opposite page: Chillax with friends

Hi Lynn, thanks for returning to *CDQ* and creating this issue's cover! Can you let our readers know a little about yourself?

Thank you for inviting me back – it's always fun working with *CDQ*! I'm originally from Chengdu, China, a city mostly famous for cute pandas and spicy food. I have an MFA in Illustration, a BFA in Animation, and through both found my passion for design and painting for game and animation projects. Currently, I work at Moon Active as a Lead Artist. My other clients include Warner Brothers Animation, FunPlus, DreamWorks Animation Television, Illuminations, Wacom, and more. During my free time, I love painting my dog, Mochi. He is a Pembroke Welsh corgi and loves to go on adventures with his little hamster friends!

Do you prefer working in games or animation?

I do love working in games a lot. In animation studios, you get to work on either the environment or the characters. In my experience, working in games gives you an opportunity to work on a much wider variety of tasks – not only characters and environments, but also splash paintings, promotional art, and much more. I love the range of jobs I get to do and find I learn a lot from doing all sorts of different bits and pieces. I do love working in animation too – I hope I get more opportunities to design for movies in the future.

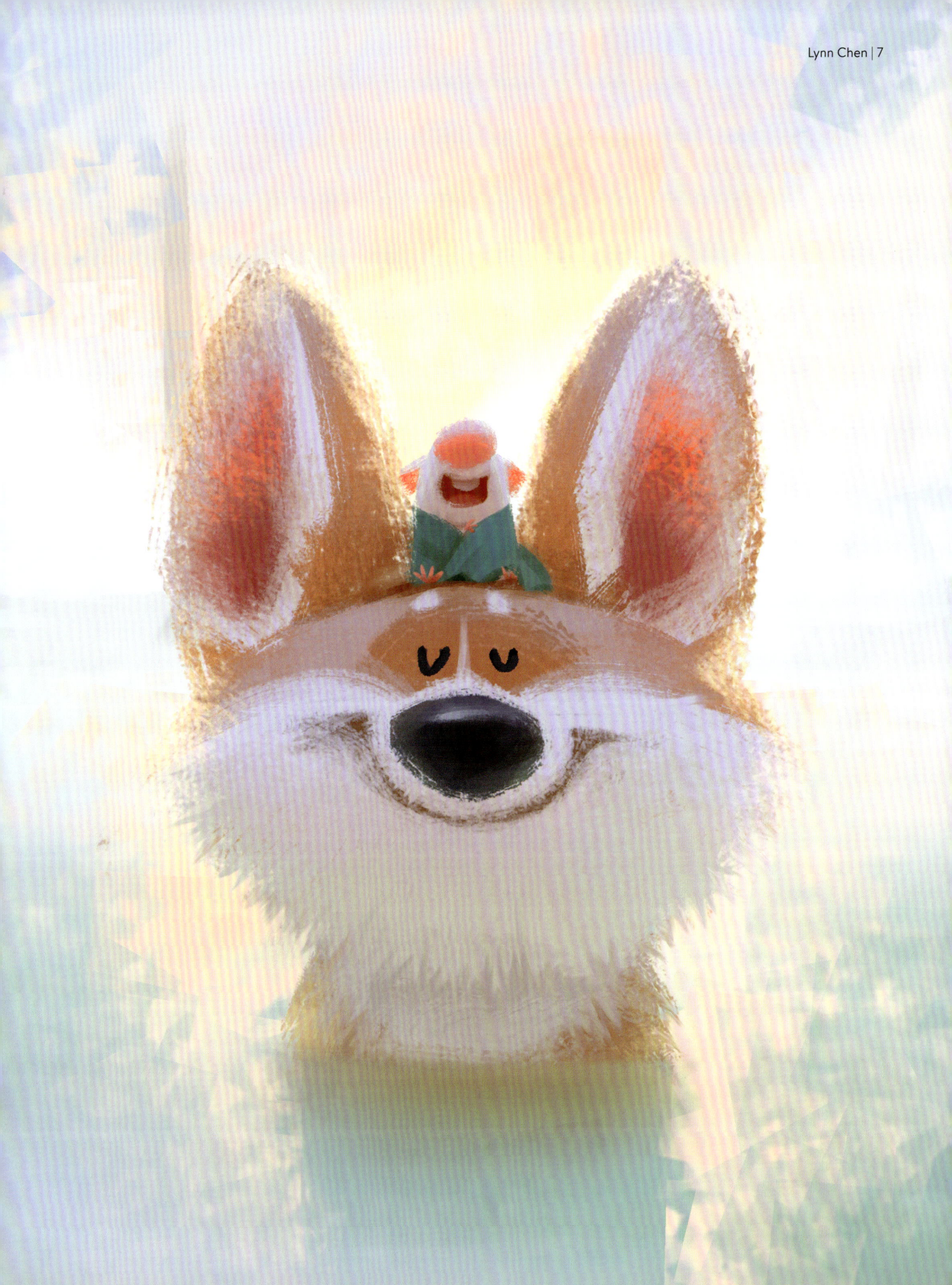

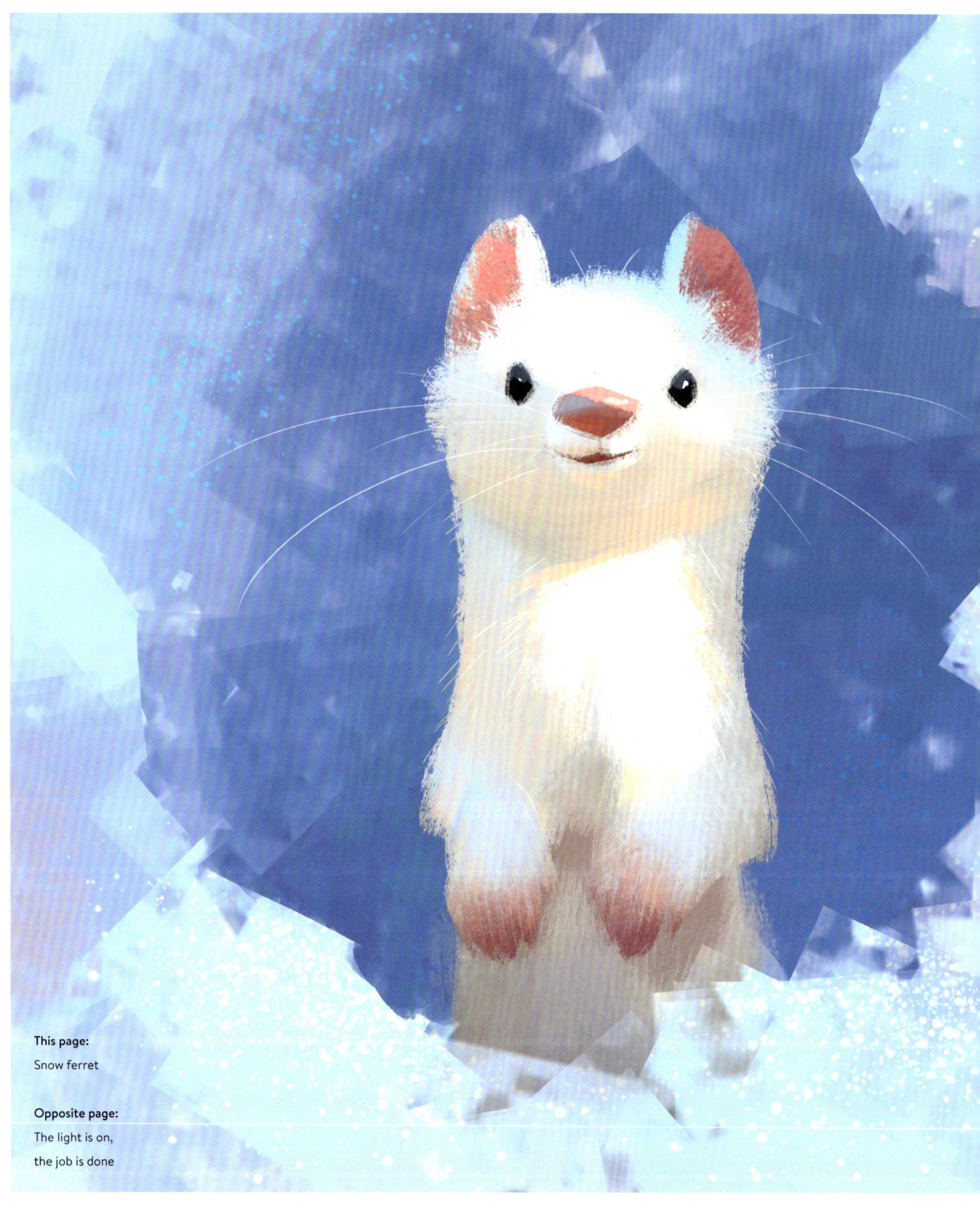

This page:

Snow ferret

Opposite page:

The light is on,
the job is done

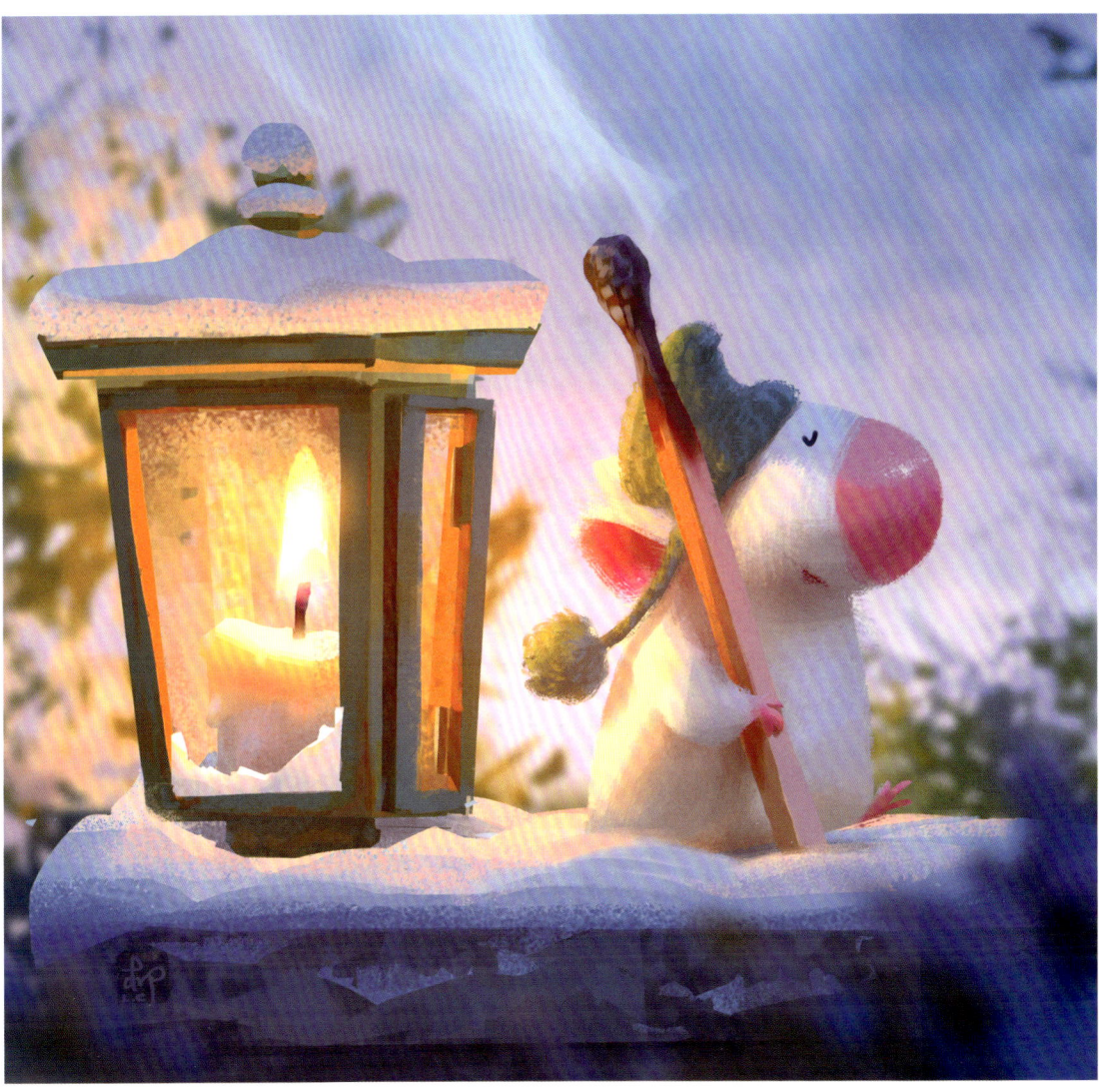

Your animal designs are so full of life and personality – how do you approach the challenge of showing emotion on creature's faces?

When I draw an animal character, although it's not a human face, the way I design the character is already humanized. The placement of the eyes, eyebrows, mouth – all the elements are just the same as human characters, so we can push them and see how far we can go in order to get the expression and emotion on our animal character's face. Another tip is to act the emotion out. I used to have a big mirror next to me while I was working – if I was drawing a sad character, for example, I could look at myself making weird faces in the mirror to try and find the right expression.

Your characters have such a distinctive look. How long did it take to develop your own unique style?

I would say my entire life has contributed to my style. Everyone is unique – we all have different experiences, different interests, and different inspirations, and everything that makes us unique contributes to our creations. For the style that I have right now, I benefitted from doing personal work every single day for a year, or maybe even longer. Completing daily exercises really helped me loosen up and focus on the story I wanted to tell. Certain painting techniques and habits started to form while I practiced often – it's from here that a style is born. So, practice more and your own style will come and find you!

This page:

Snack time

Opposite page:

Workout

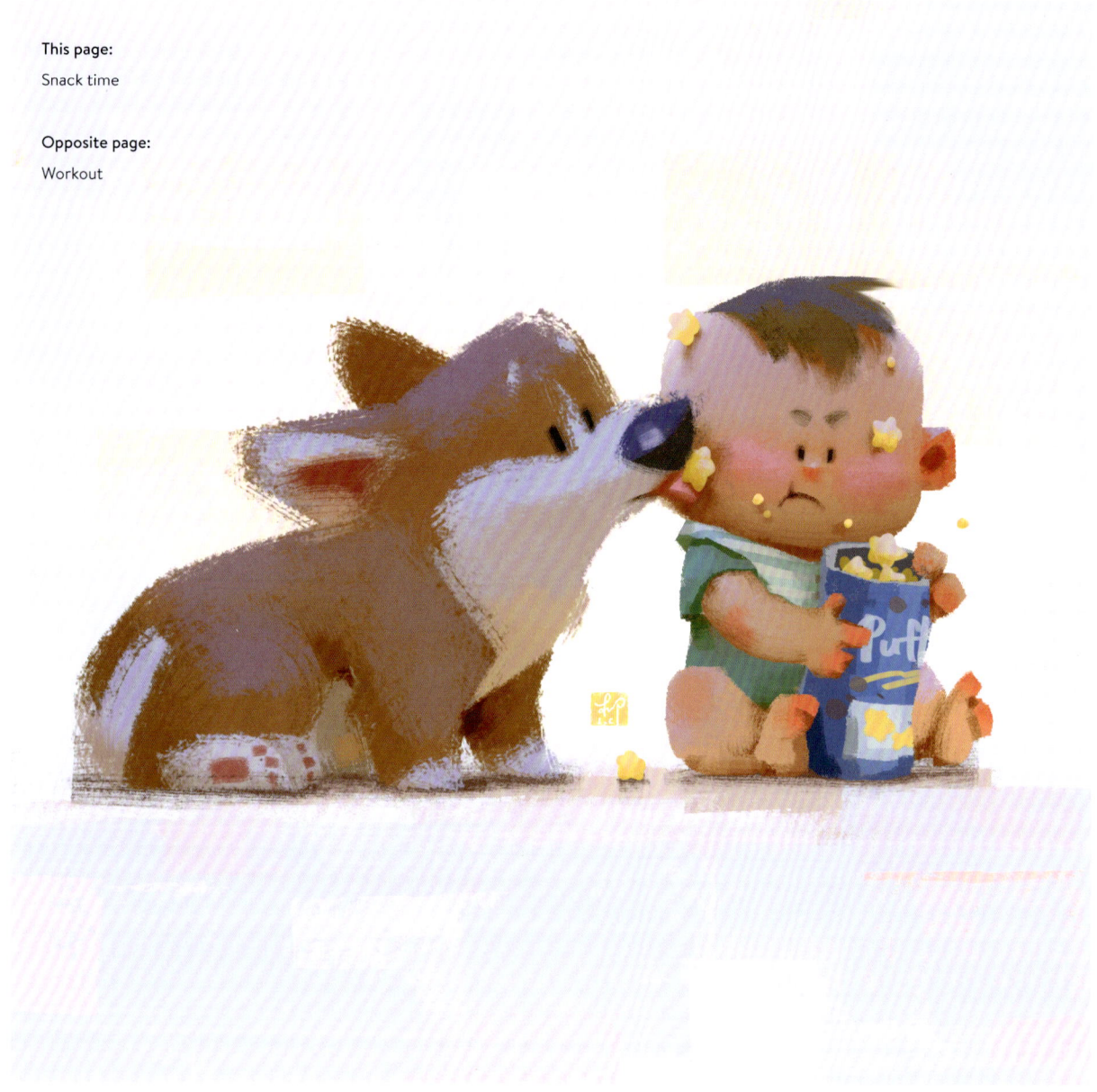

Do you have any tips for our readers for breaking into the industry?

It's great to have an online presence on social media, such as Instagram, ArtStation, or any platform that's good for visual images. While you can choose how often to post depending on your schedule, it's important to be consistent. Of course, you should still submit a portfolio to companies that you like, but do it while also keeping up with your drawing exercises. Over time, opportunities will arise that are suited to the type of work you create. One more thing – be careful not to fixate too much on social media. Don't worry how many likes you have or if someone is being rude. Focus on putting your art out there and then move on to paint some more.

Are there any upcoming projects we should be looking out for?

Hah, that's a good question! The movie I worked on at a very early stage (*Minions: The Rise of Gru*) has been out for a while – if you haven't watched it, don't miss it! I don't have any major projects coming up since we are expecting our little girl this year. But hopefully after that, I'll be able to start working on a new art book.

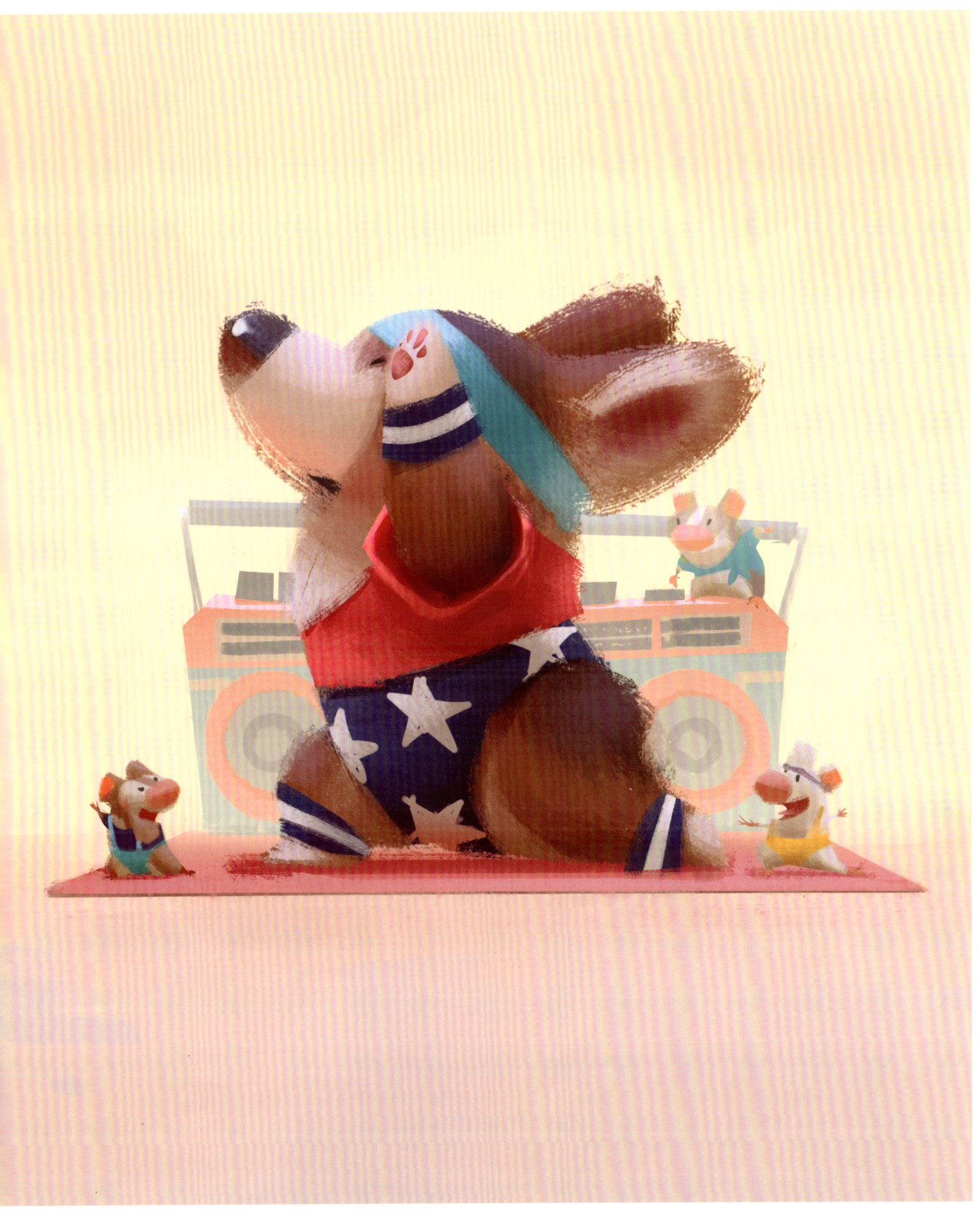

CRAFTING THE COVER

In this tutorial, I'll walk through my process for creating the cover image, from gathering references to the final rendering. The most important step is to sketch out ideas and figure out the composition. Then, gradually we'll block in shapes and paint in light and shadow. Although creating an image might seem like a big task, we can break it down and enjoy each step in the process. I work mostly digitally, so for this cover image, as usual, I used a Wacom Cintiq and Photoshop.

Starting with sketching

I usually start by gathering references online and then sketching. I keep my sketches very rough and simple. My major focus is on finding a composition that works for the cover but also feels dynamic. I'd also like to show my characters enjoying the environment. For sketch A, the yellow flower field, the character is sitting down, relaxed, while a gentle breeze kicks up some flower petals. For Sketch B, I choose a completely different setting. It's much more energetic, the character having fun driving a toy jeep around. Once I have a version of both ideas I'm happy with, I move on to creating a color rough.

> "MY MAJOR FOCUS IS ON FINDING A COMPOSITION THAT WORKS FOR THE COVER BUT ALSO FEELS DYNAMIC"

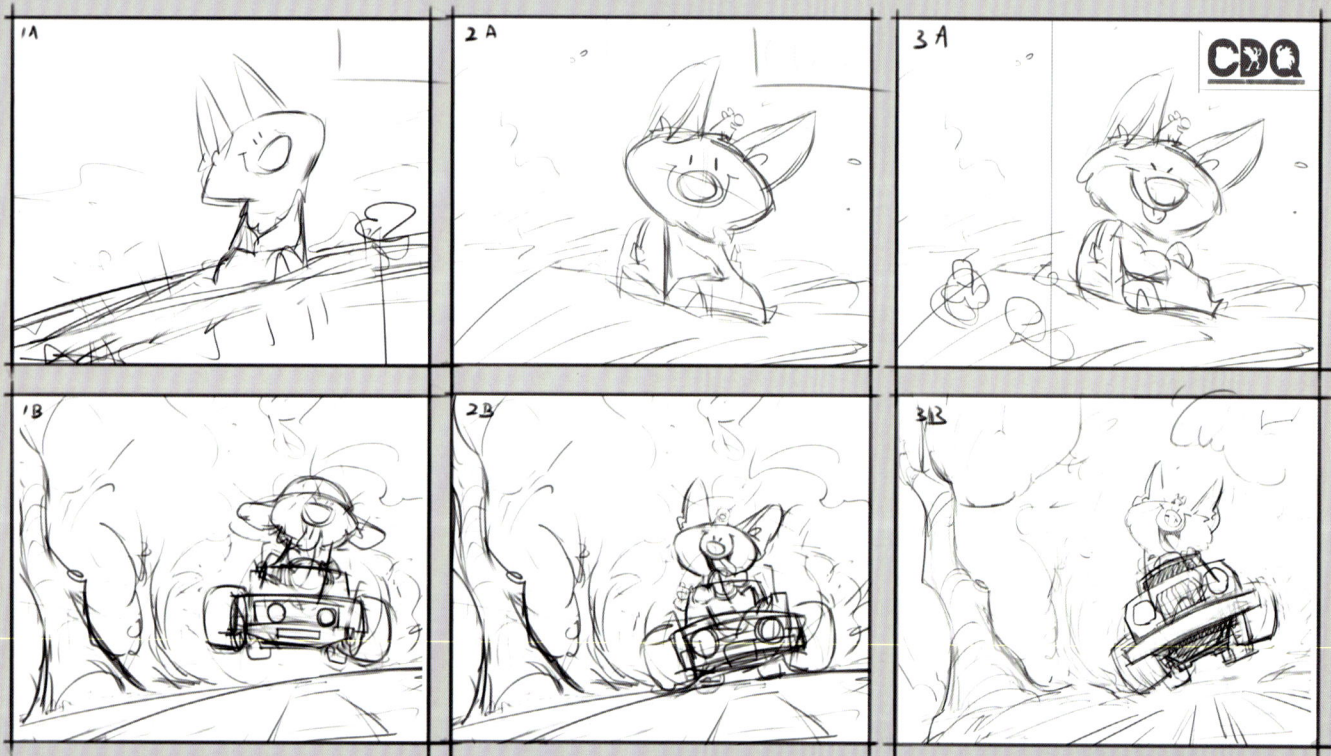

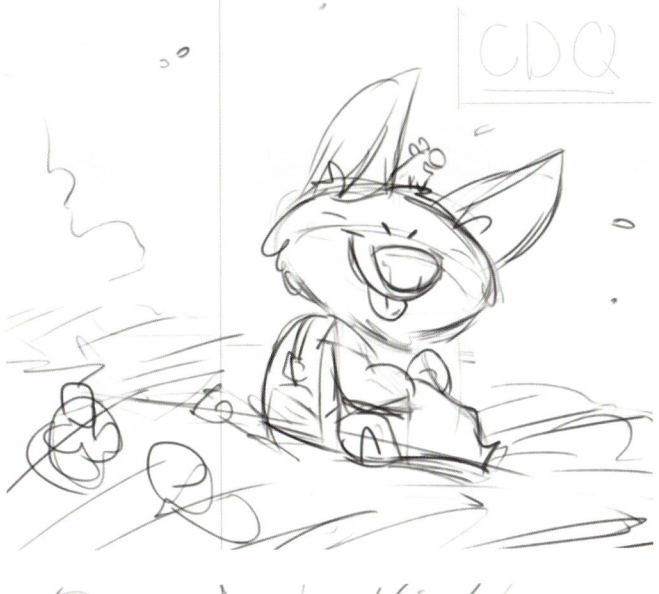

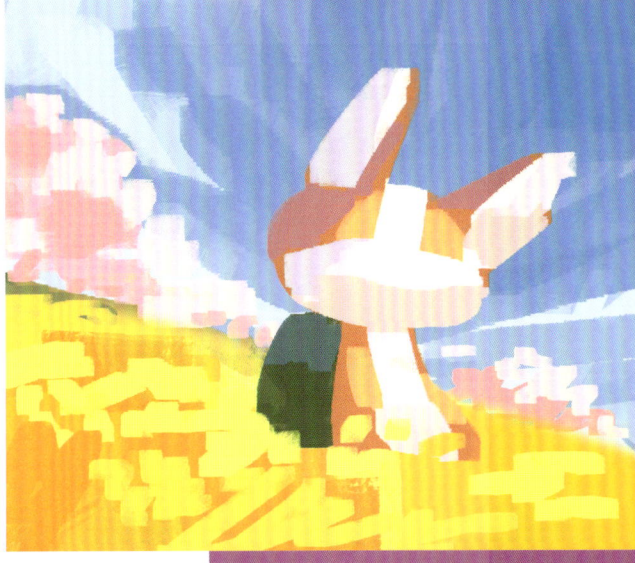

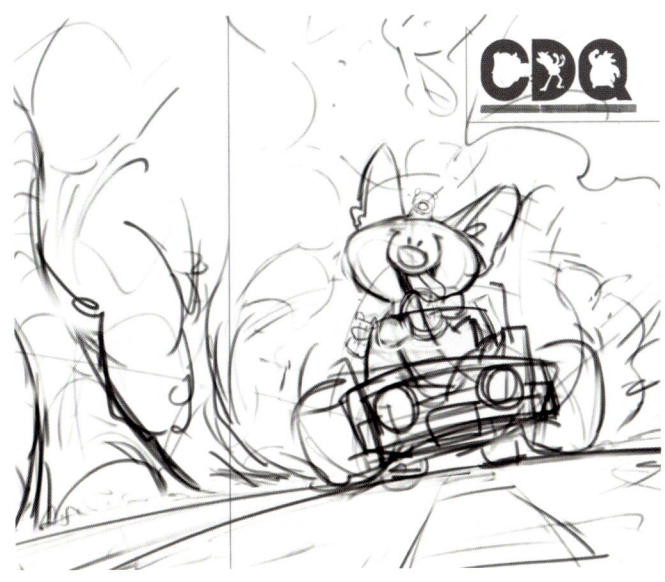

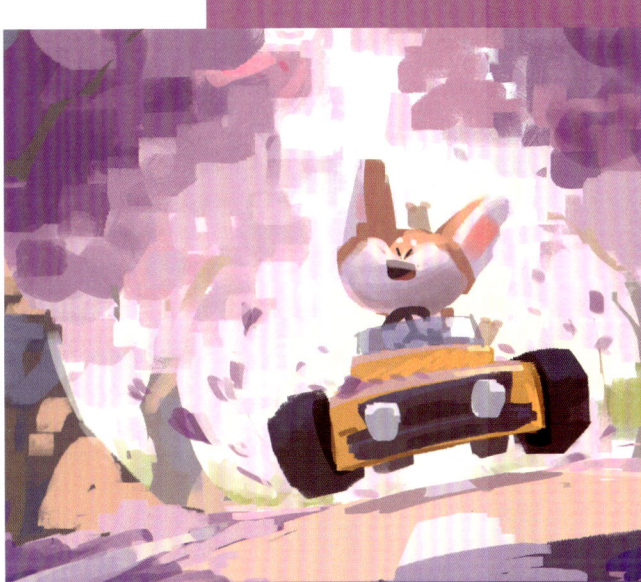

Rough and ready

At this point, I feel the purple flower tree idea might work better as the cover image. But I still want to give the other idea a try, so I make quick color roughs for both. As you can see, I keep everything very loose and simple. I use a blocky brush at a bigger size so that I don't paint in too much detail. These sketches are really quick and rough. I keep moving and changing the images until I find the lighting condition and mood that I'm looking for.

Opposite page: Rough sketches of both A and B versions of the cover image

This page: Rough color keys for both versions of the cover

This page: Use flat colors to block in shapes

Opposite page (top): Adding the fill light and surfaces it affects

Opposite page (bottom): Painting light and shadow information

"I START BY DRAWING BLOCKS THAT MATCH THE GENERAL SHAPES OF THE DRAWING"

Start to take shape

I decide to move forward with the second image and begin to polish the design. I start by drawing blocks that match the general shapes of the drawing, with flat colors. It helps to clean up the rough line drawings with a clear silhouette. I also roughly set up the values of the image, making sure I have a good contrast between my character and the background. I keep the initial pass of base color more in shadow, which is a bit darker and cooler. Not only does this give me a better silhouette, but it also leaves me enough room for adding in sunlight later on.

Light and shadow

With most of the shapes blocked in, I start painting the fill light which, in this case, is the ambient sky light. The cool, blue light coming from the sky affects almost everything that's not hit directly by sunlight, so I usually paint it first. It's important to only paint the surface that's facing toward the light source. So, the top of the character's head, ear tips, top of the toy car, and everything in the image that's facing up, all get a little bit of a cooler bright color. I also use some darker, warmer colors to indicate the contact shadow. This gives the subjects in the image a better volume.

Here comes the sun

Next, I move on to painting the key light. In this image, I'd like to have the sunlight coming through the leaves, so I only paint in dappled lighting. Sunlight is much stronger than the ambient light from the sky, so wherever the sunlight hits, the blue sky light gets washed out, and we see a much brighter, warmer color for the lit area. The next step is to add bounce light. Bounce light is usually warmer and less intense, but it adds life to the image. Here, we have it under the character's nose, chin, and any area close to surfaces that are lit by sunlight.

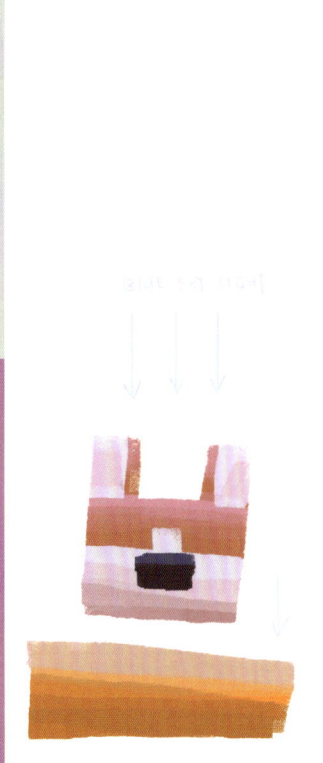

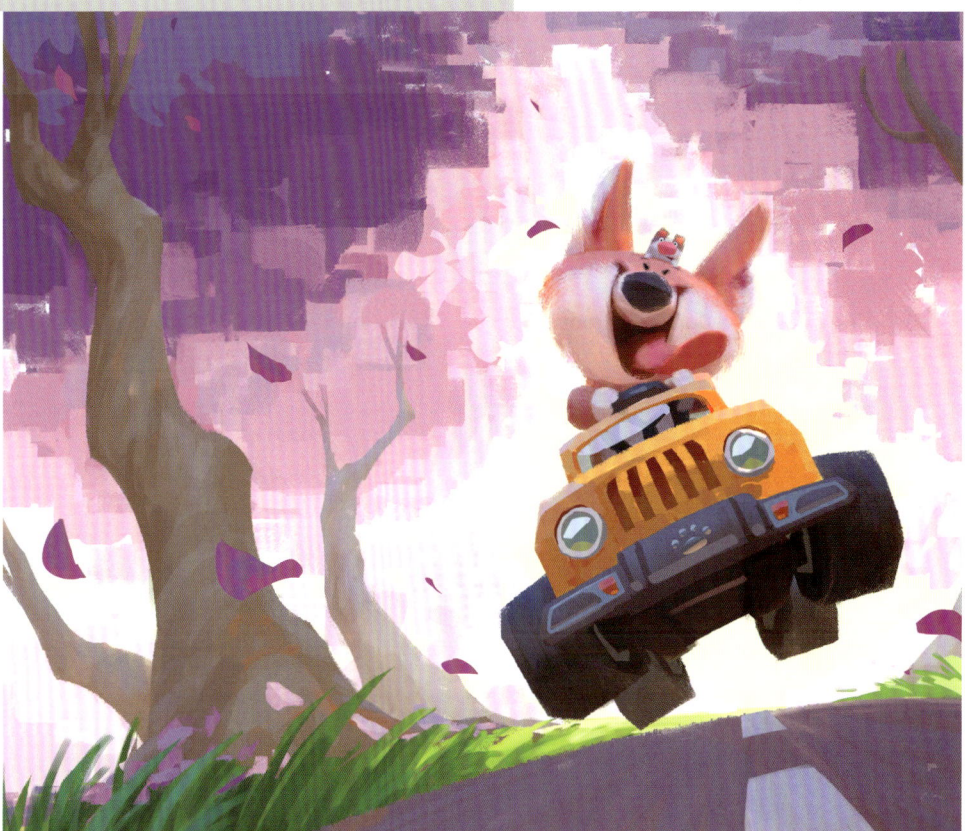

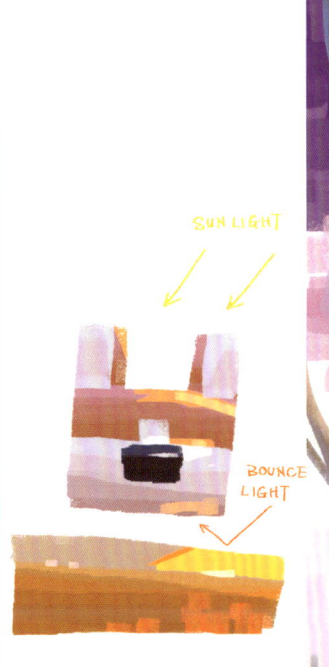

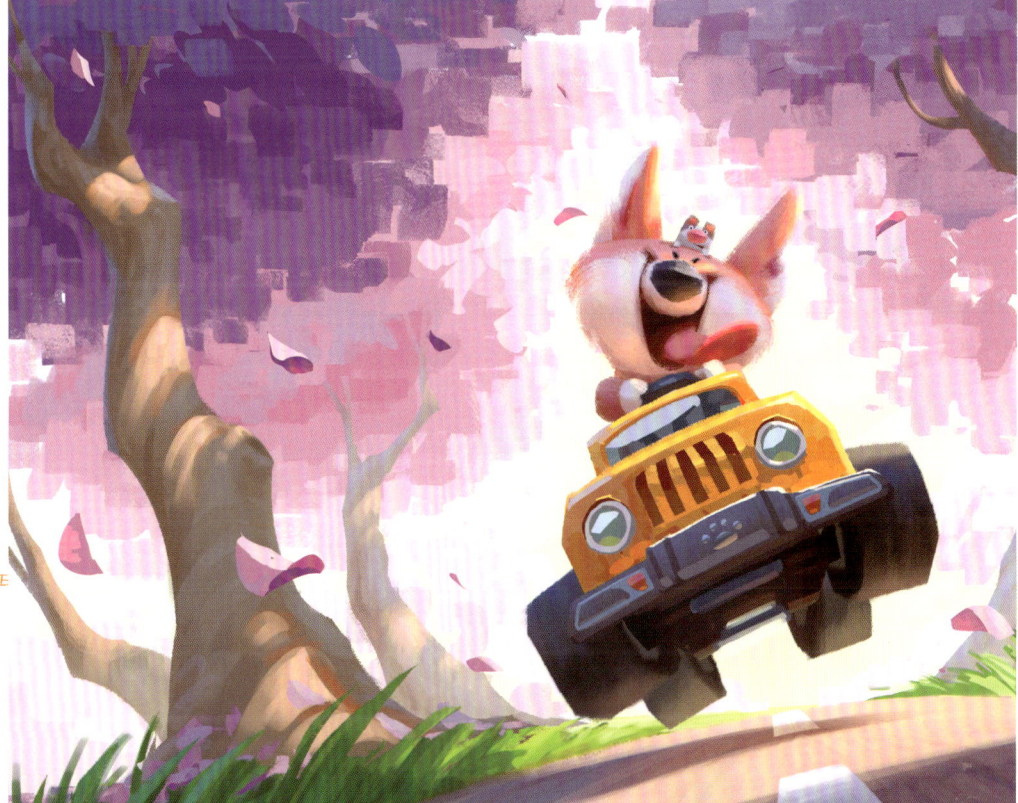

"I BRUSH IN SOME LIGHT BEAMS AND ATMOSPHERE, SO THAT OUR CHARACTER STANDS OUT MORE AGAINST THE BACKGROUND"

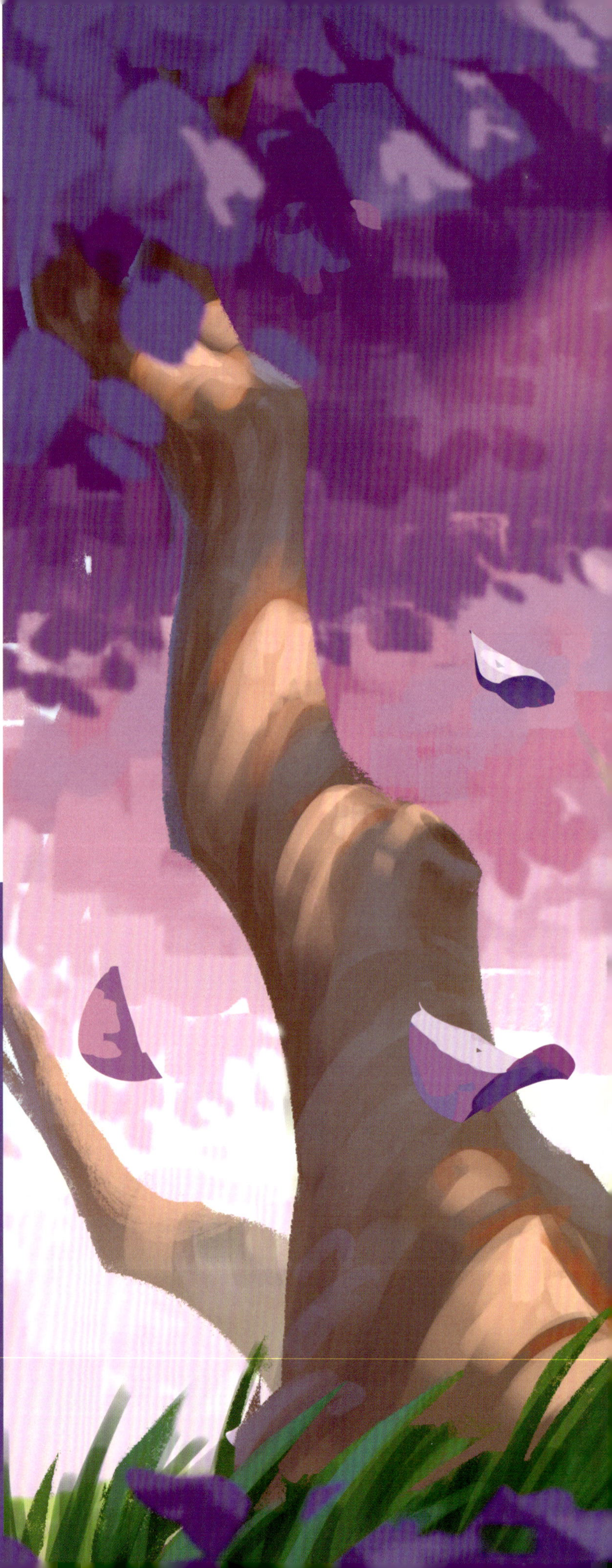

Finishing up

All that's left are the final touches. I go through the image and fix some of the value issues. For any of the details that aren't in the focal area I either reduce the contrast or blur them out, if needed. Next, I brush in some light beams and atmosphere, so that our character stands out more against the background. I often get asked the question: how do I know when an image is finished? For personal work, I think as long as we got our ideas out, we hit the mark of the overall mood, and there's no elements in the image that jump out as distracting, then I'd say we can save a high-resolution copy and move on to our next idea!

These pages: Final image © Lynn Chen

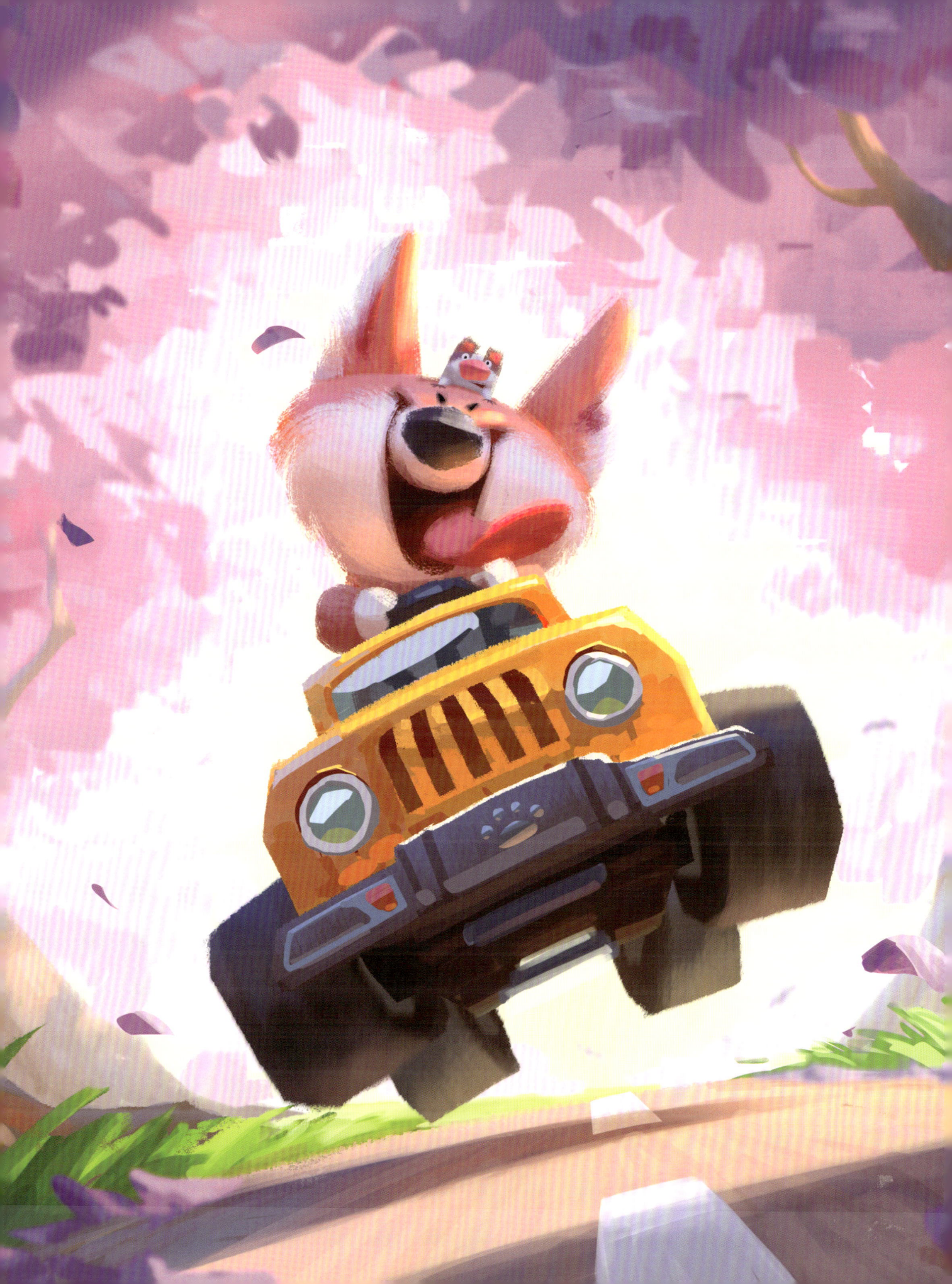

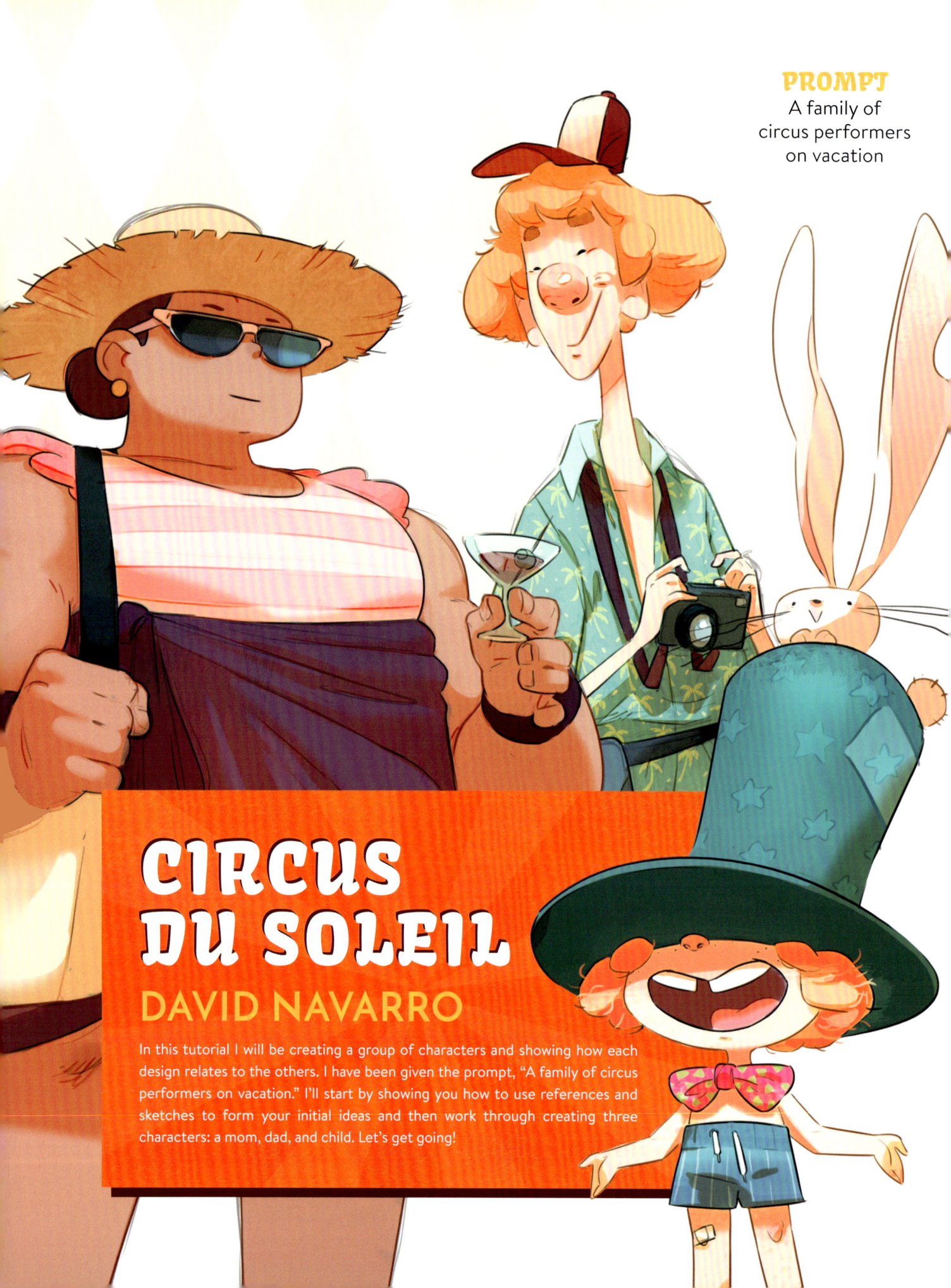

CIRCUS DU SOLEIL

DAVID NAVARRO

In this tutorial I will be creating a group of characters and showing how each design relates to the others. I have been given the prompt, "A family of circus performers on vacation." I'll start by showing you how to use references and sketches to form your initial ideas and then work through creating three characters: a mom, dad, and child. Let's get going!

THE WARM-UP

With your prompt in mind, start to gather references. Pictures, videos, movies – any type of information you can get your hands on can contribute to your theme. Next, start drawing free sketches. Don't try to make anything beautiful and don't be too strict about adhering to the topic. This stage is about mixing references with your style of drawing to create something that's truly unique. Try to draw fast without over thinking – focus on the theme and let the ideas flow. And most of all, have fun!

DRESS REHEARSALS

Once you have your first sketches, you probably have some idea of what you want to draw, or at least you already know the theme and have done a first warm-up. Try to keep doing things freely – don't get too obsessed with creating something beautiful or even particularly good! We are still just trying to get to know our characters.

Play with your designs, experiment mixing and matching different elements, and eventually you will find a look you are happy with. As we are drawing a group, working on each character at the same time will help keep a consistent story and style across each design. Think about how they each complement each other – for instance, if one character is big, you can make the other small. Contrast will always help to make the characters more appealing.

This page (top): Explore the theme and let your ideas flow

This page (bottom): Sketch the characters side by side to ensure their overall design is consistent

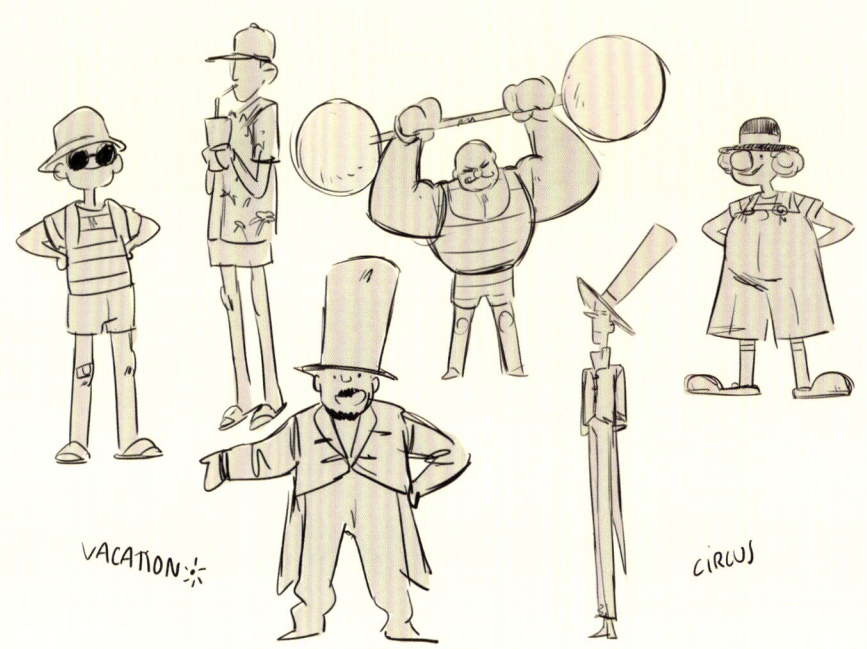

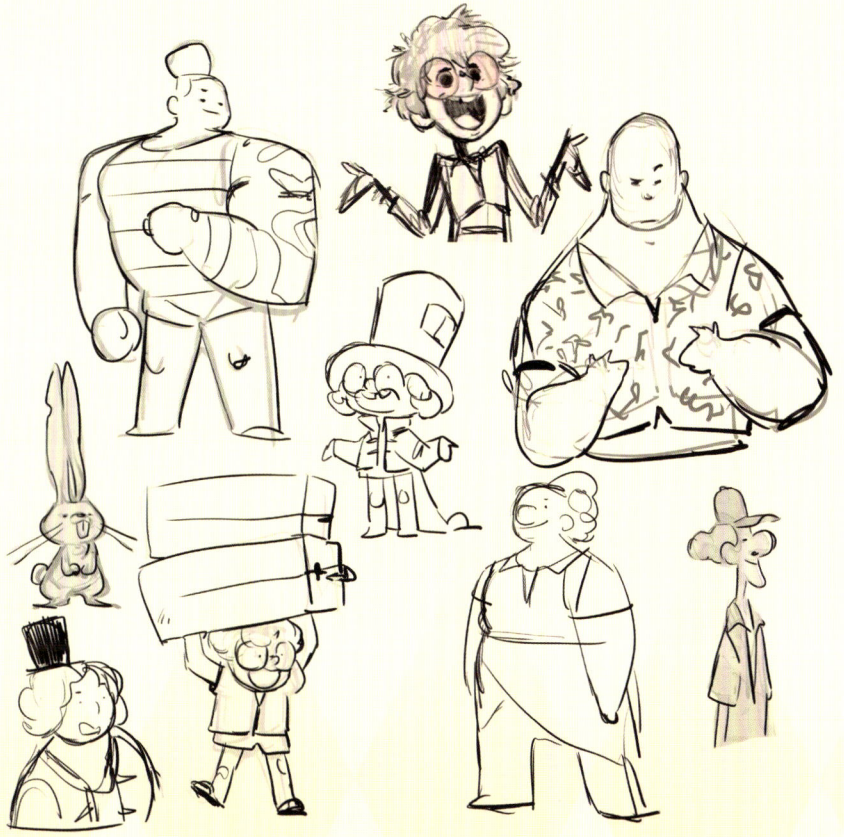

"EXAGGERATING DESIGNS IS CRUCIAL FOR YOUR AUDIENCE TO UNDERSTAND WHO THEY ARE LOOKING AT QUICKLY"

PERFORMERS ASSEMBLE!

By now you should have the general idea for each character sketched out. Be fearless and make changes to their initial design. Try to exaggerate each element, pushing to the limit and then pulling back if necessary. In drawing, exaggerating designs is crucial for your audience to understand who they are looking at quickly. As you experiment, the ideal forms will start to take shape. Think about who each character is and how they would want to be seen by others. Try different clothing and hair, too.

It's not necessary to draw the full body each time. In fact, sometimes just drawing the face can help you get to know the character better. Why not try adding some funny gestures and expressions?

With a rough idea for each of the family members sketched out, it's time to focus on each one individually.

This page: Push the designs to their limit and find out what works

Opposite page: How you choose to pose a character can help tell a story

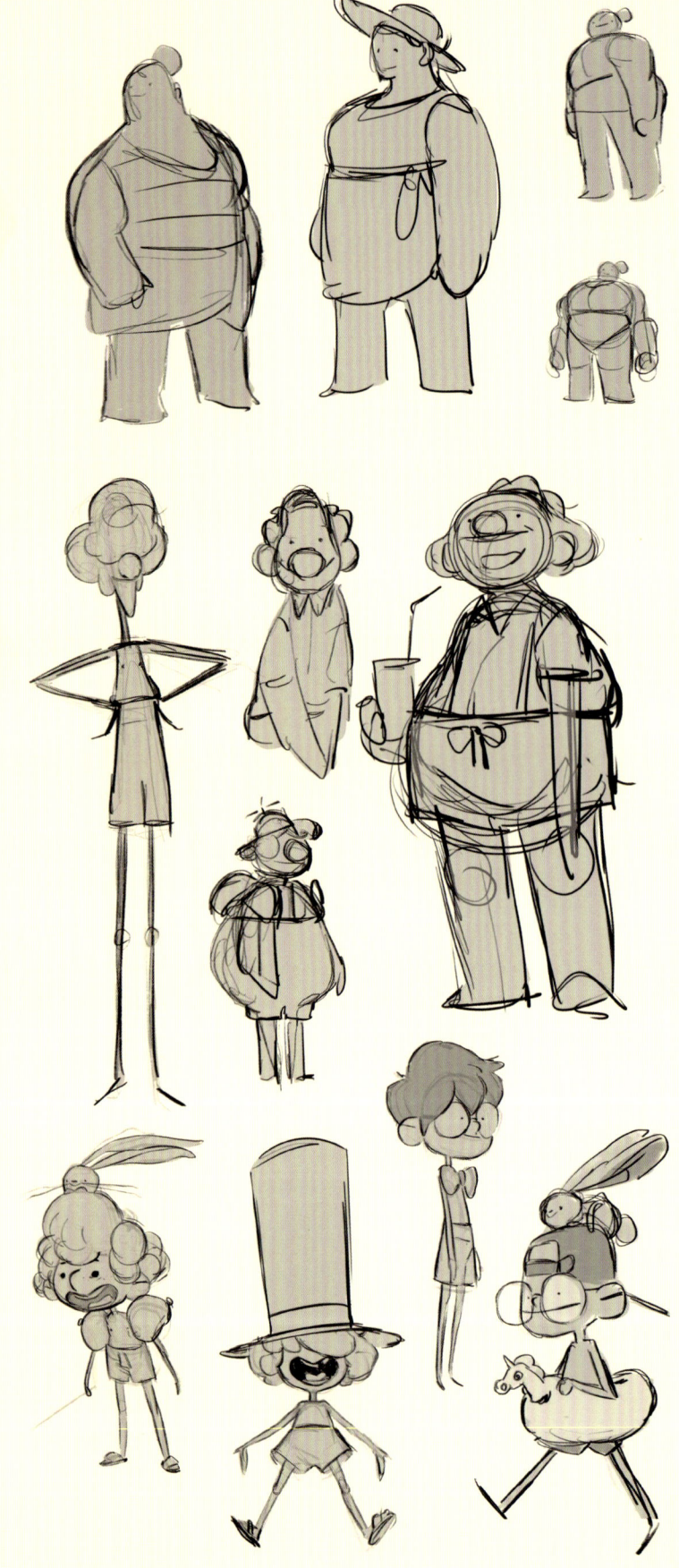

THE DAD

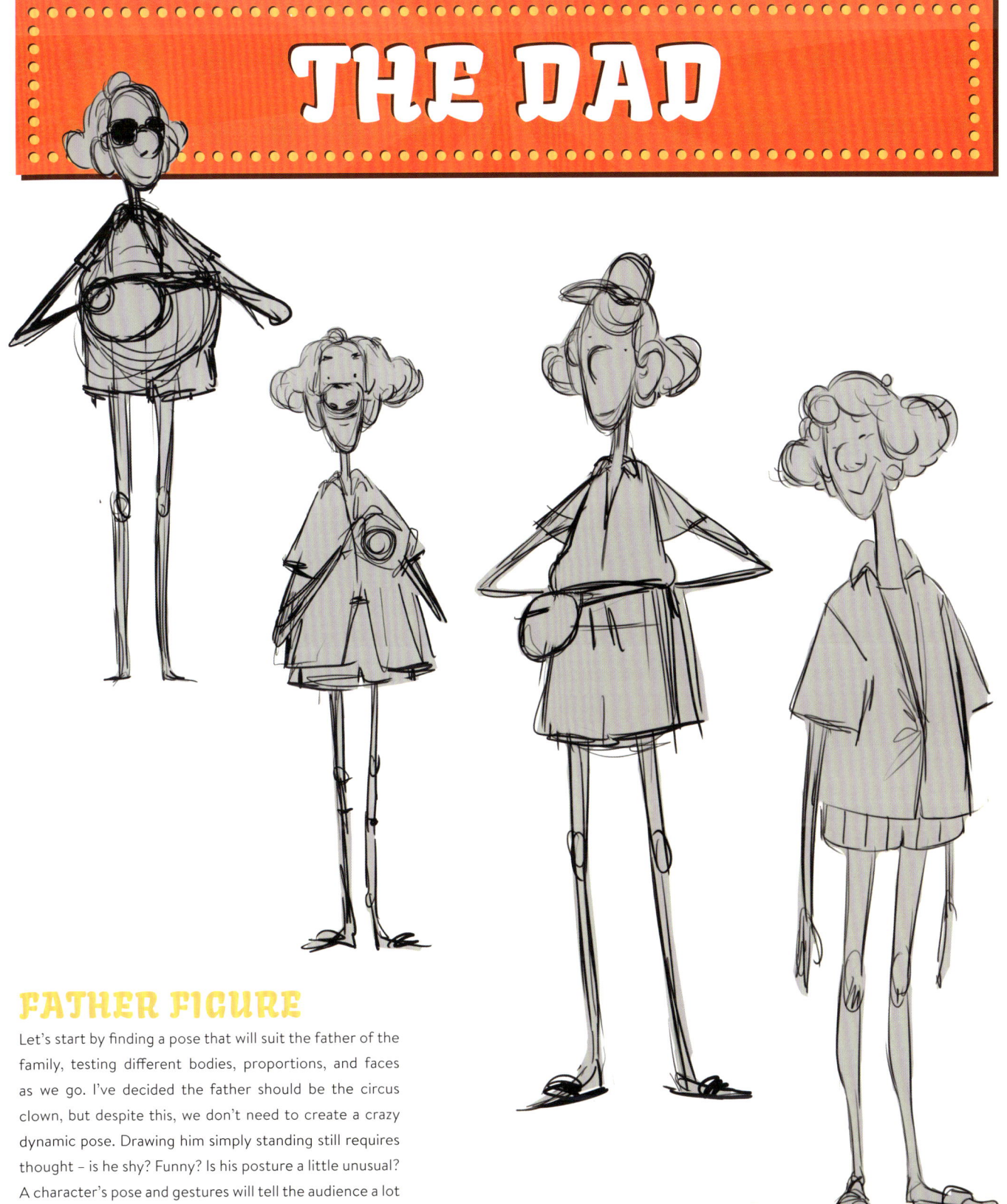

FATHER FIGURE

Let's start by finding a pose that will suit the father of the family, testing different bodies, proportions, and faces as we go. I've decided the father should be the circus clown, but despite this, we don't need to create a crazy dynamic pose. Drawing him simply standing still requires thought – is he shy? Funny? Is his posture a little unusual? A character's pose and gestures will tell the audience a lot about who they are, so don't rush this step.

ADDING DETAILS

With a clear idea of the character, we can now clean up the lines, being careful not to lose any detail along the way. Remember, shapes are important and define personality as much as expressions. Once your design is well defined, think about what details will bring more personality to your drawing. Remember your brief and think about the character's past experiences and what clothes they may wear. Add objects and details that help show the audience who he is. Don't be afraid to do more than one round of cleaning up your ideas. If you think of a fresh approach when inking, try it out on a separate layer.

COLORFUL COMBINATIONS

We have our character, so now we need to consider our next important topic: color. Think of coloring as another tool to help us define who our character is. Different colors and shades will express different emotions. As you try out different color combinations, think about how they change the mood of your piece and how you perceive your character. Always try out several versions – don't just stick with the first thing you do.

This is a great time to add even more detail to the design. For instance, subtly changing the look of the clothes can make them seem worn or new and further influence how the audience sees your character.

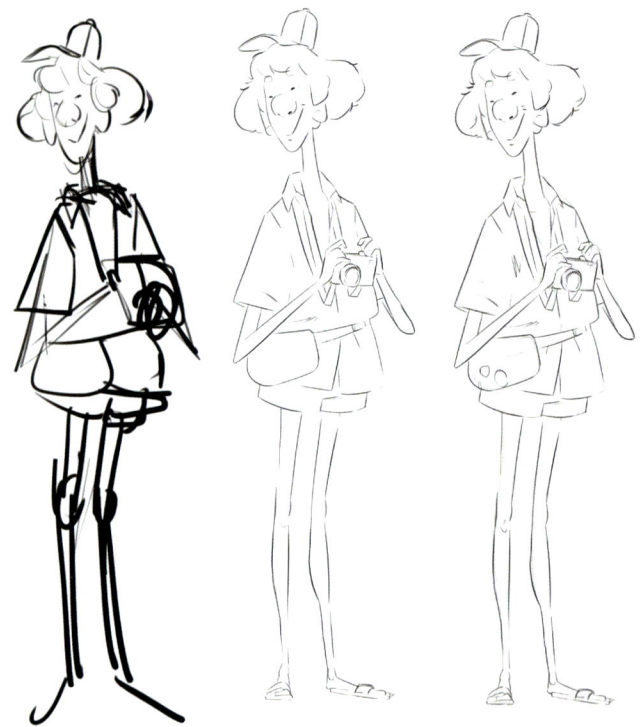

JUGGLING VOLUMES

Now that you've settled on the local color, it's time to make magic happen! By adding shadow and light we can give our circus-clown dad some volume to make him look 3D. Adjusting the light also allows us to control the temperature of the color, which influences the atmosphere of the overall picture. Warmer colors will make our character feel more affable and kind, whereas colder colors suggest a distant and serious attitude. Think about the texture of materials and how they would cast shadows. Finally, use the light and contrasts to focus on the important areas of the character and to direct the audience's attention.

This page (top): Cleaning up the clown dad's design

This page (bottom): Experiment with color to find which combinations work best

Opposite page: Adding shadow instantly makes the character feel more alive

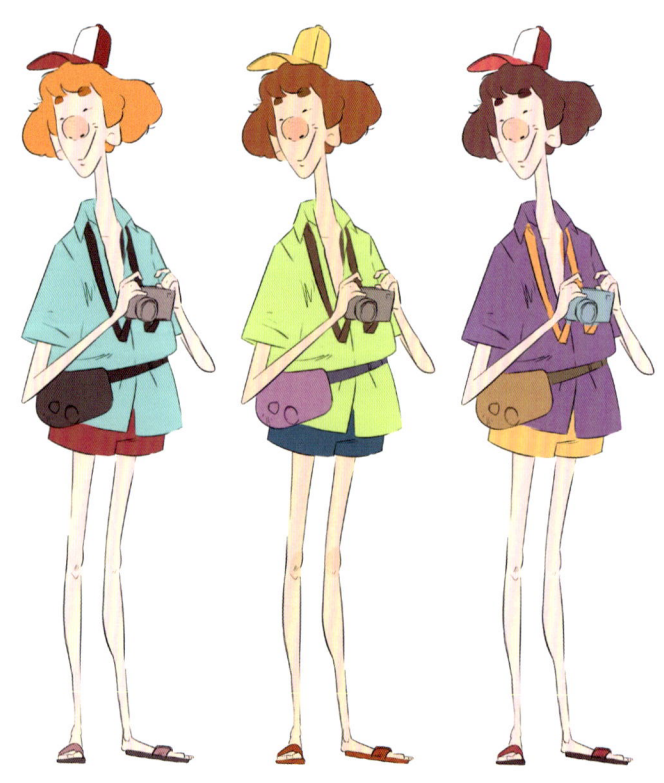

"WARMER COLORS WILL MAKE OUR CHARACTER FEEL MORE AFFABLE AND KIND, WHEREAS COLDER COLORS SUGGEST A DISTANT AND SERIOUS ATTITUDE"

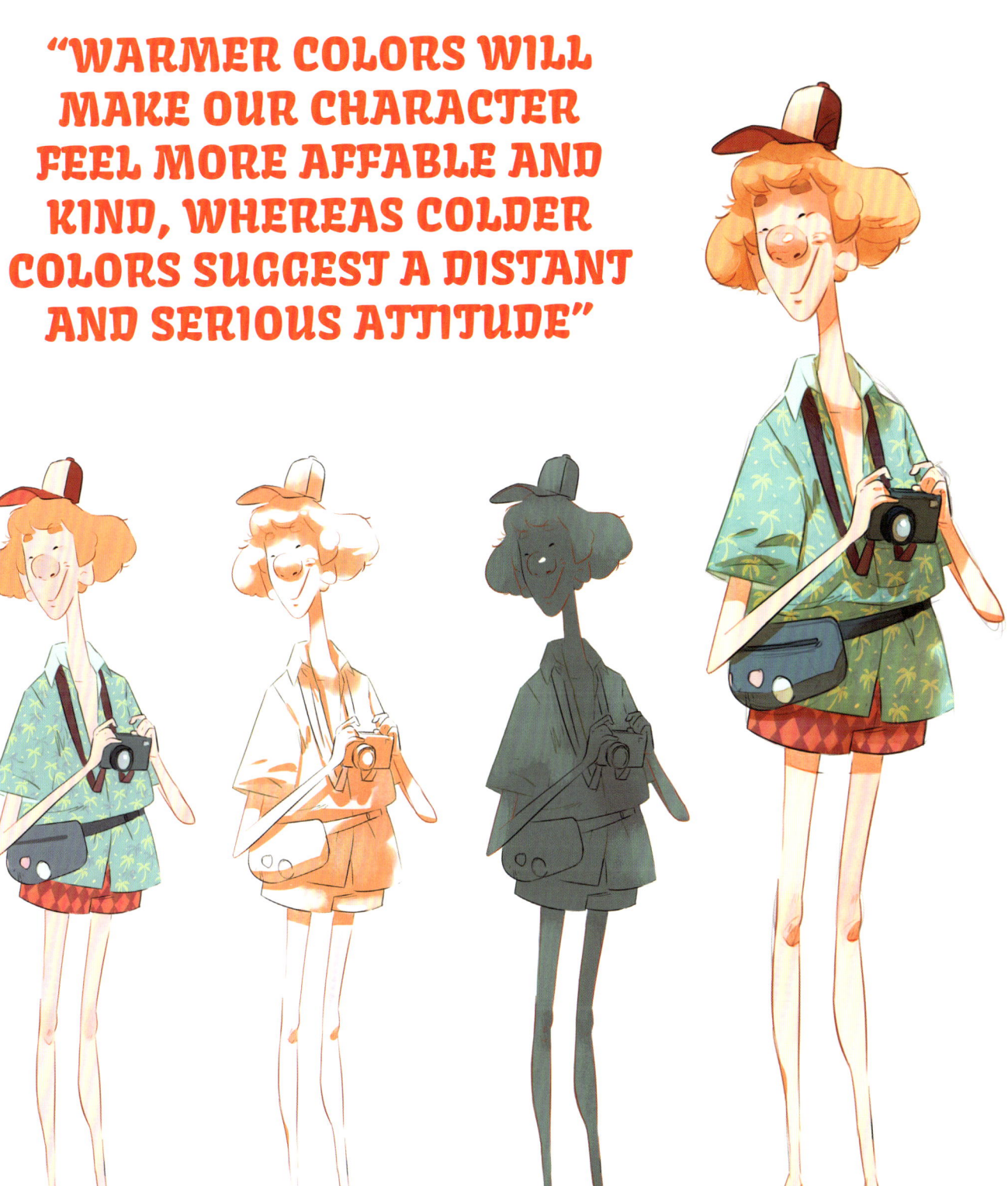

THE MOM

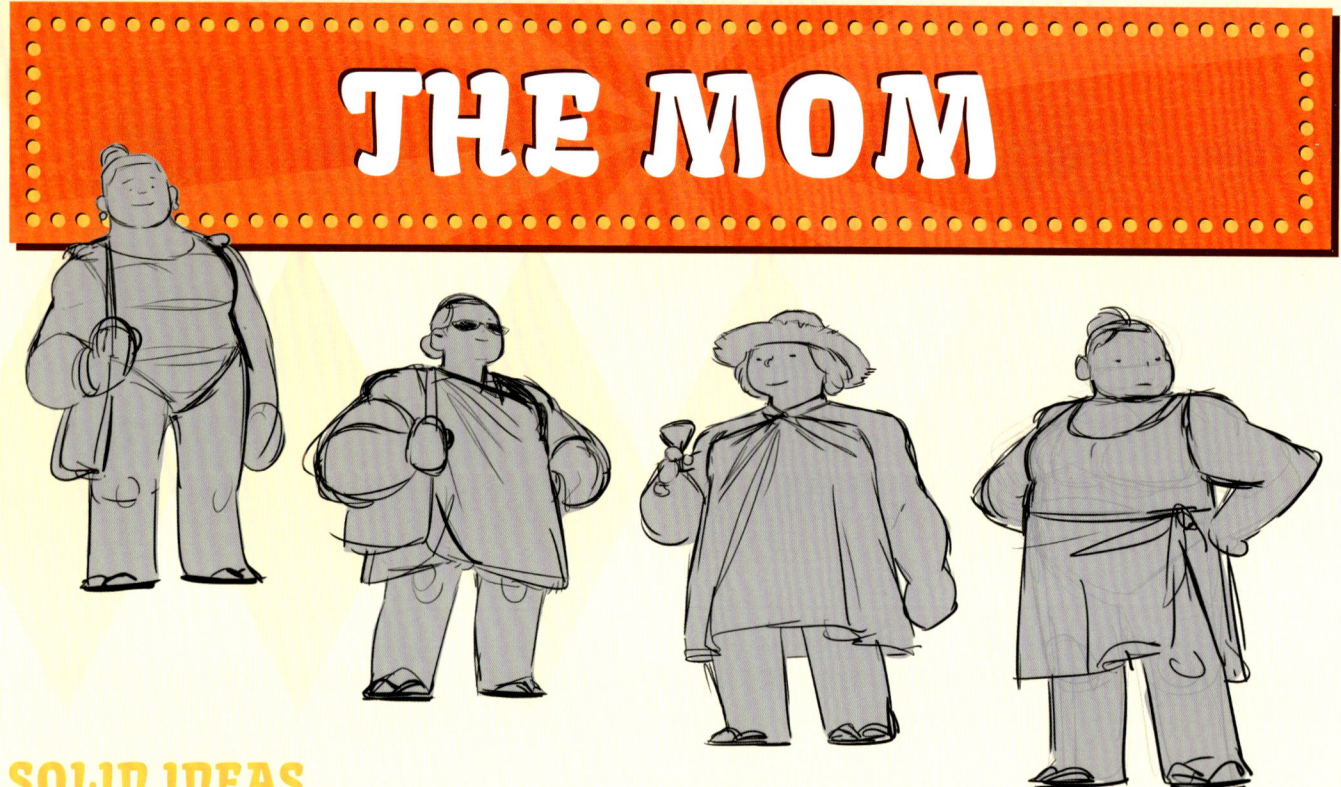

SOLID IDEAS

Next, let's focus on the mom of the family. She's the strongwoman of the circus, lifting weights and showing off amazing feats of strength for the crowd. With our sketch, we've already established the role she plays and the structure of her body, more or less, so let's play with the rest of the design. Remember, clothes can change the shape and contrasts of a character. Think about what elements will emphasize the role the character plays – maybe exposing her arms will make her look stronger. And what about the pose? She might look more serious or rude, depending on how you decide to position her.

LINE LIFTING

Now we need to patiently simplify the lines. Remember, it's important not to lose the pose and the qualities that define her character. Start with the bigger lines and then, little by little, work on the smaller details. Working on the longer lines first should also warm up your hand, so you'll be more accurate for the more fiddly work. Think again about the clothes, defining any wrinkles or imperfections that will make the character feel more alive. Finally, work on defining the expression on her face. Take your time – this is one of the most important areas of any design.

This page (top): Different clothes say different things about your character

This page (bottom): Start with thicker lines and move on to detail afterwards

Opposite page (top): The choice of clothing colors should be strong, without being too dark

Opposite page (bottom): Use contrasting shadow to highlight parts of the design

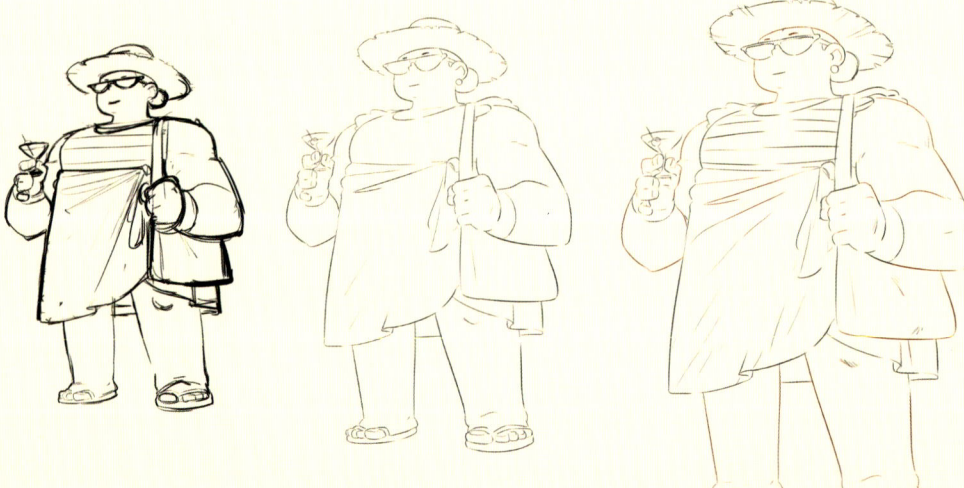

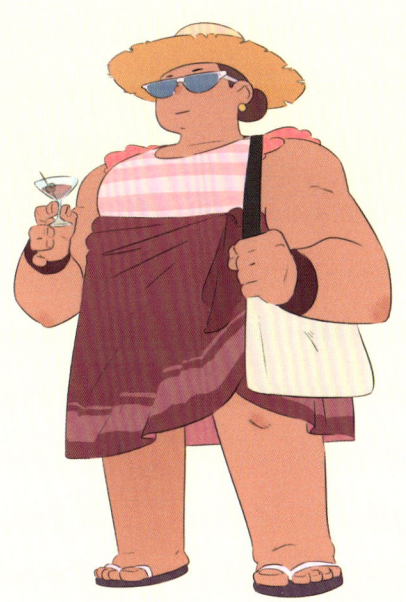
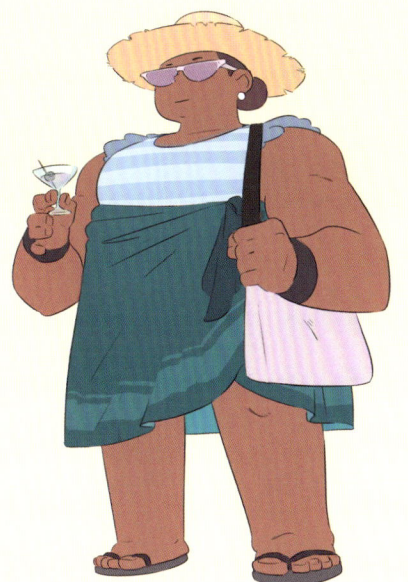
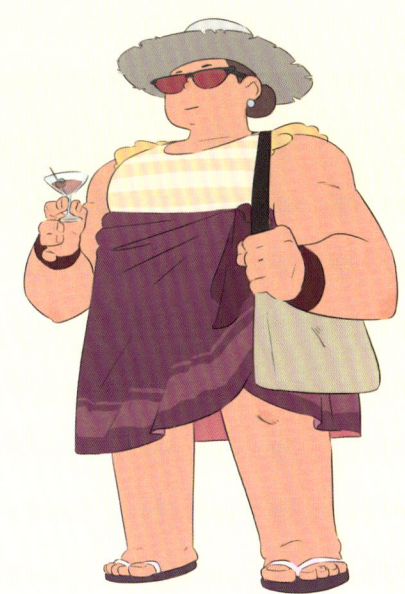

THE STRONGEST COLORS

A bad color decision can ruin all your hard work. Treat color as a tool to help you express more of the character. If the colors are too dark they could create a bad vibe – remember, our family are enjoying a vacation! Colors can show that a person is rude or friendly, happy or sad. Don't rush this step, think carefully about every decision.

OUT FROM THE SHADOWS

To push the coloring further, let's play with the volume by using light and shadow. Add a layer on top of your drawing and play with adding shadow, trying different colors and seeing what mood the results evoke. Ensure that you don't make the character too dark and lose detail. Find the contrast that will guide the audience's eye to the parts of the design you find most important.

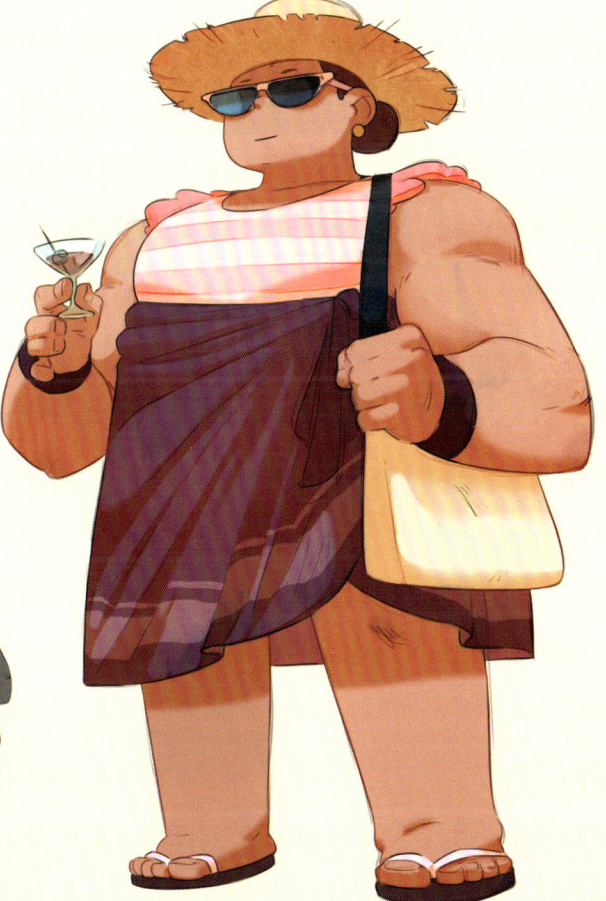

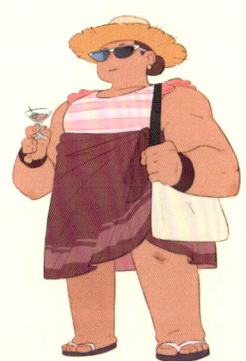
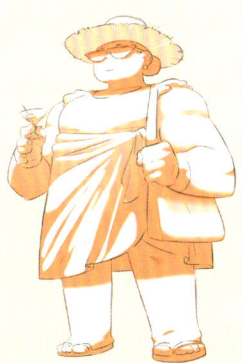
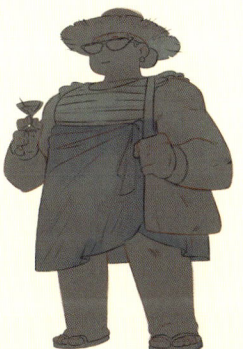

THE KID

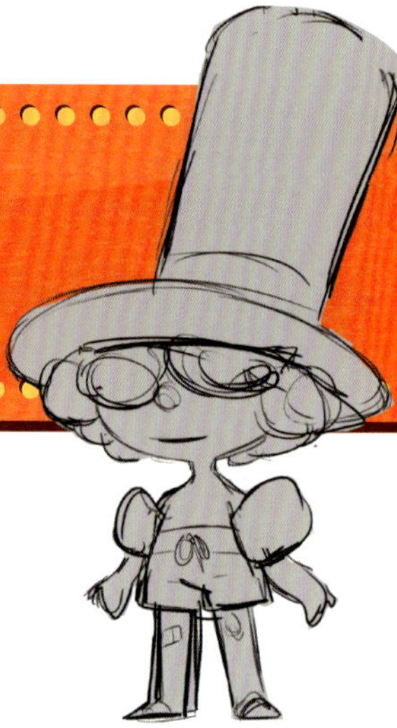

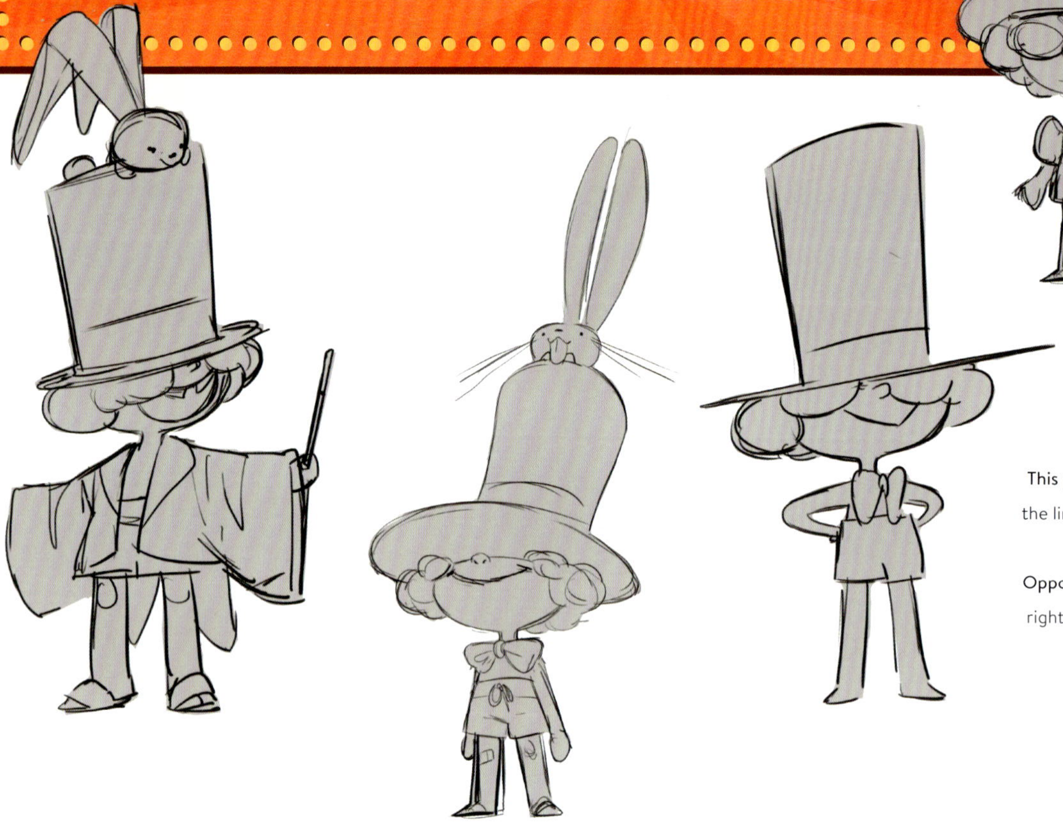

This page (top): Try to find a balance between every aspect of the brief

This page (bottom): First, clean up the line art, and then add the detail

Opposite page (top): Choosing the right color for the hat is important as it dominates the design

Opposite page (bottom): The giant hat comes to life once shadows are added

CHILD'S PLAY!

Our final family member is the kid – he's the circus magician, pulling a bunny rabbit from his hat! With a character idea in mind, stay loose while sketching out different options to bring him to life. If something doesn't work, this is the time to test and find a character and pose that's going to work. Return to looking at references if you need some more ideas.

DISAPPEARING TRICK

Think about the line art. Lines have their own style – you can use a thick line, a thin line, or even a line of variable size. Don't make the design too busy – leave space with less detail to contrast other areas with more detail. This will help to focus attention and create a good contrast in the overall design. Think about breaking up the duller areas of the design, such as teeth or ears. Beware of overdoing it – remember to keep "rest" areas where detail is scarce.

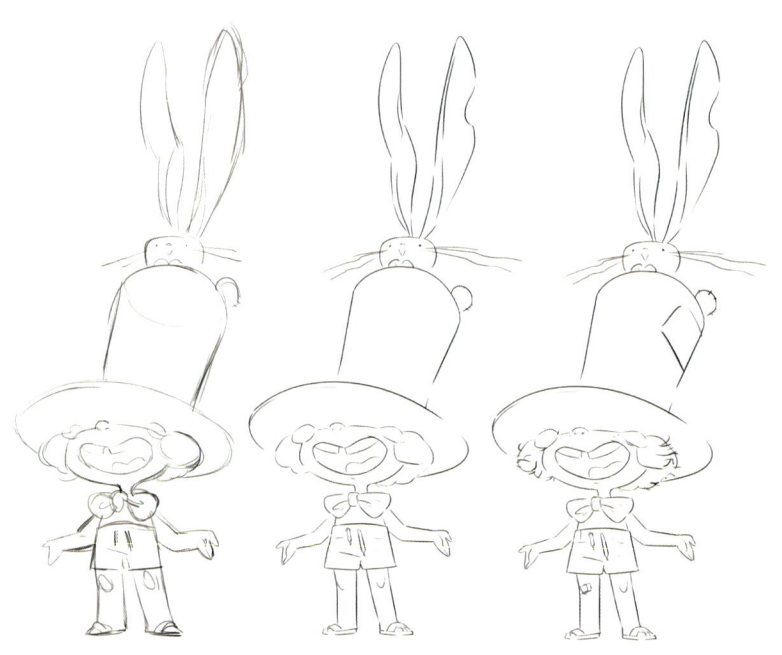

MAKING MAGIC

You can express the psychology of your character though your color choices. Colors can express energy, calm, or even a mystical vibe. Keep in mind the mood of your character while you try out different combinations. Only through trial and error can you really find out what works and what you need to discard.

TRICK OF THE LIGHT

For our magician's final trick, let's give him some volume and texture. Remember, you can create contrast in the design through the use of light and shadows. Changing the saturation of colors will also help to guide the viewer's attention. And with that, our family is complete – let's wish them well on their vacation!

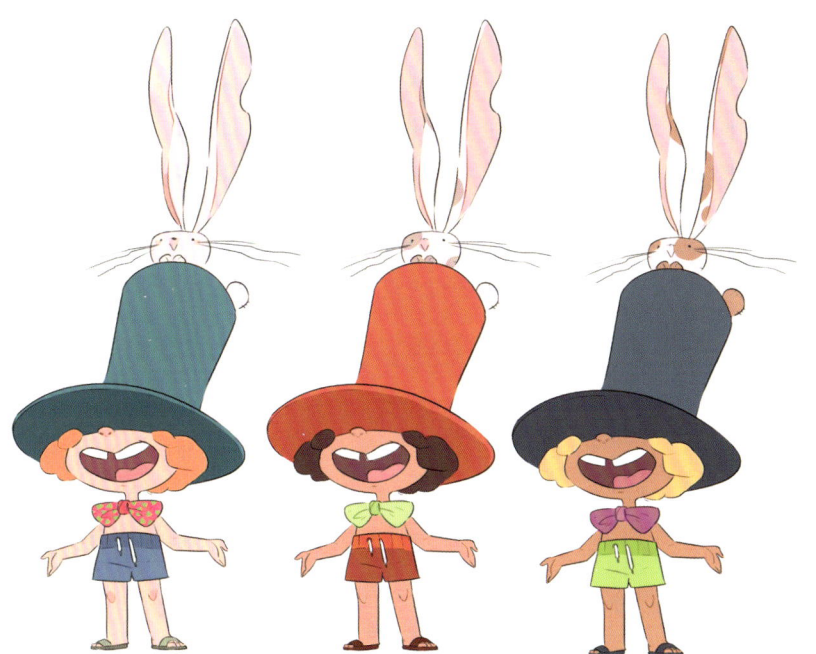

"REMEMBER, YOU CAN CREATE CONTRAST IN THE DESIGN THROUGH THE USE OF LIGHT AND SHADOWS"

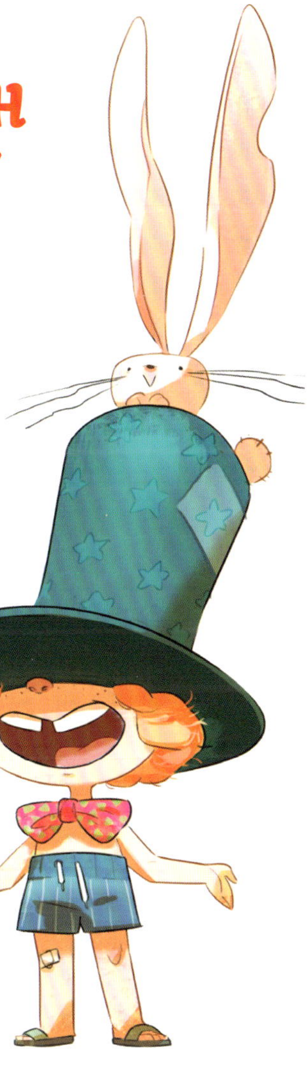

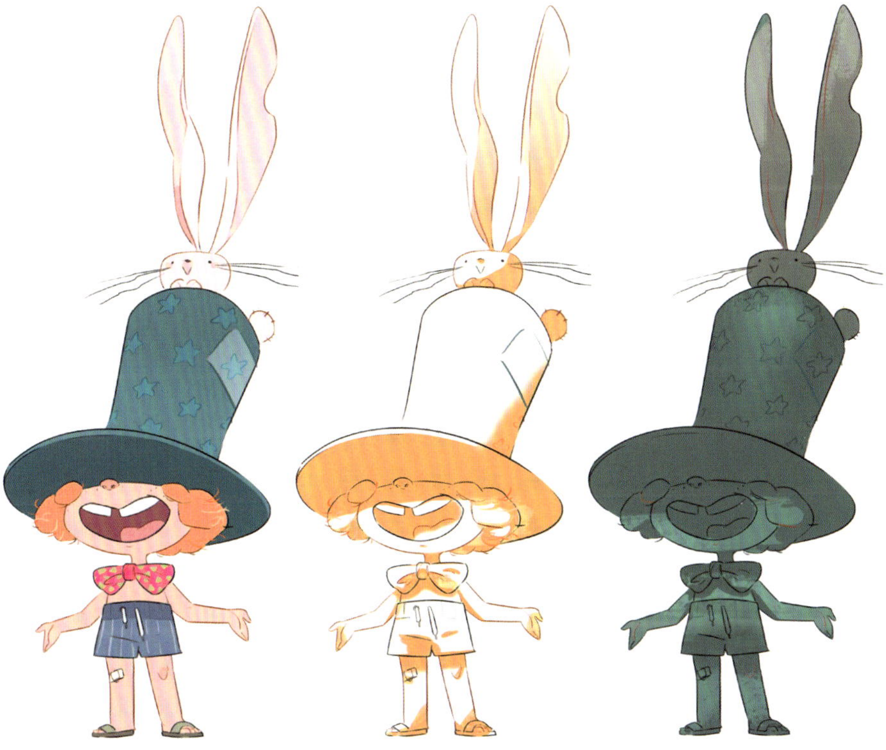

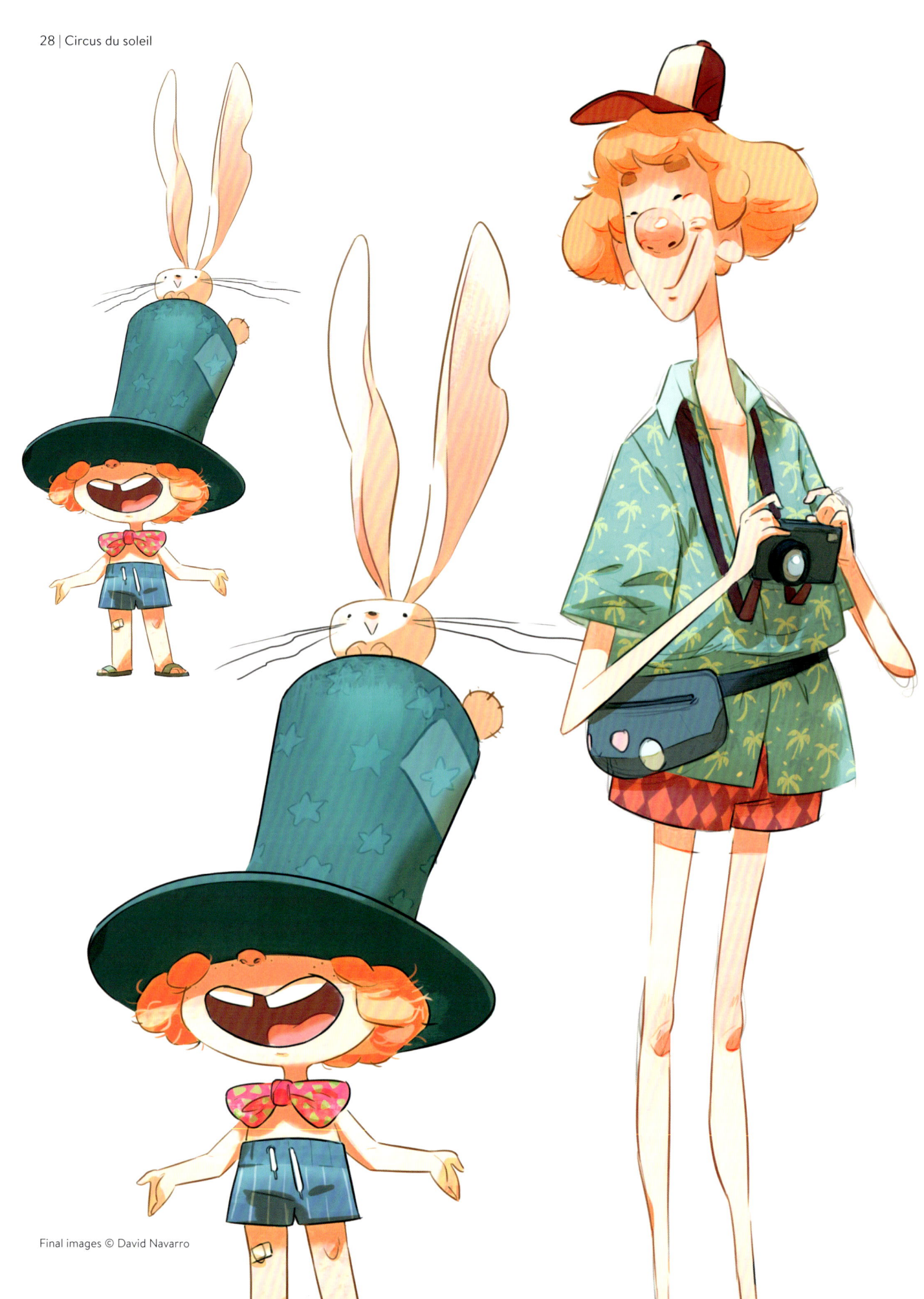

Final images © David Navarro

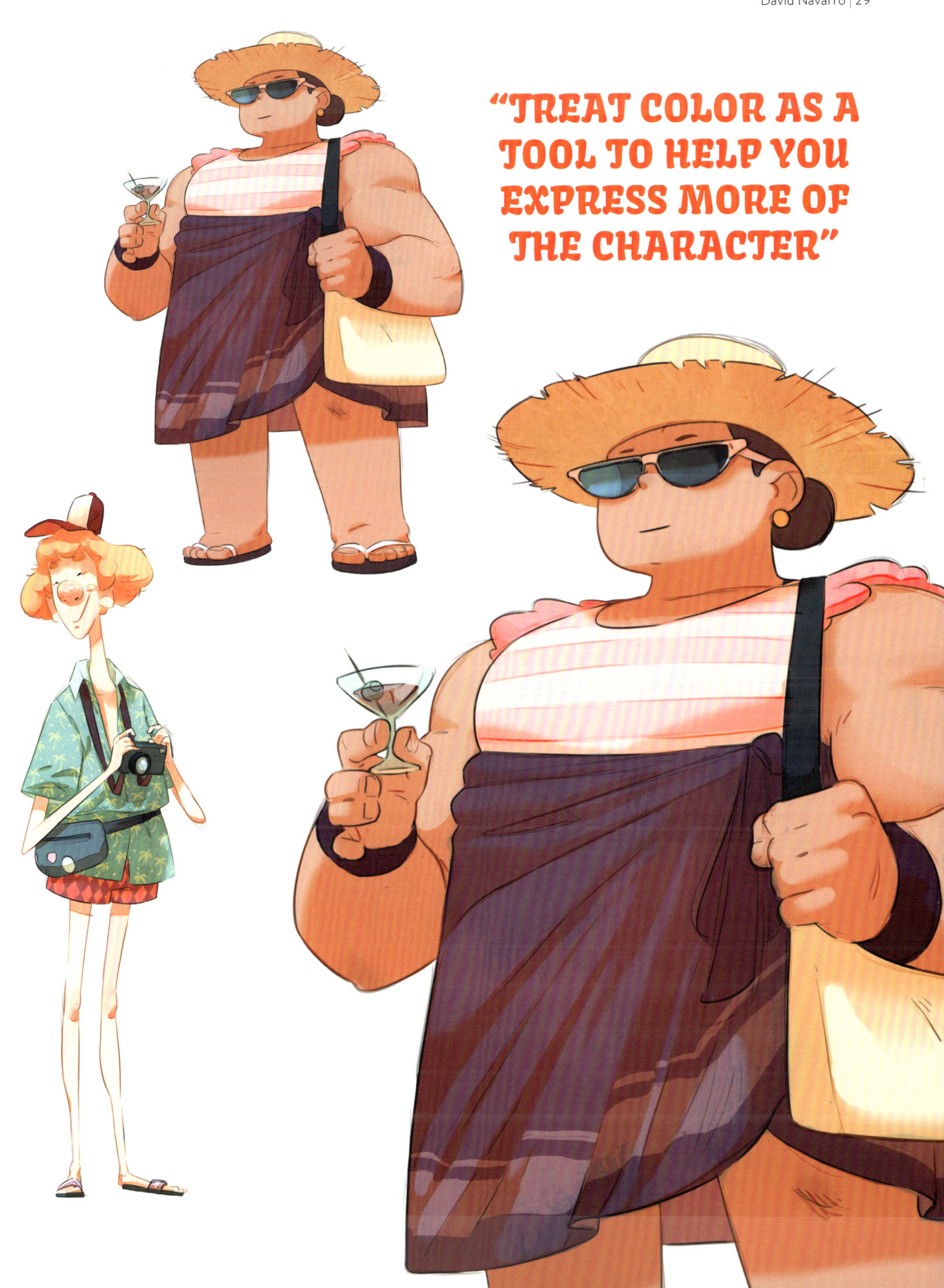

"TREAT COLOR AS A TOOL TO HELP YOU EXPRESS MORE OF THE CHARACTER"

The Know-it-Owl Takes Flight

ROGER PÉREZ

At the start of our drawing career, designing a character can seem a daunting process, in which we tend to focus mainly on the technical aspects of drawing and anatomy. But by far the most important thing to consider is that the appearance and attitude of our design fit the personality and the role they are going to play in our story. Our subject is a "brainy bird," so let's work through some steps to create a character that fits this description.

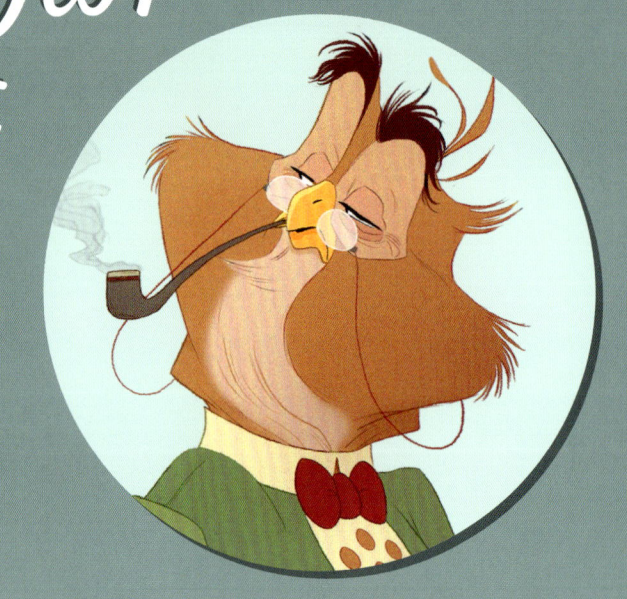

"BE SURE TO ONLY USE STEREOTYPES SPARINGLY"

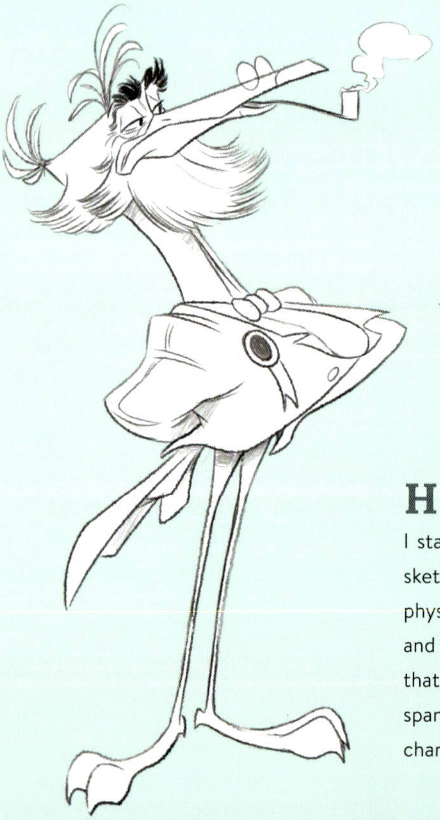

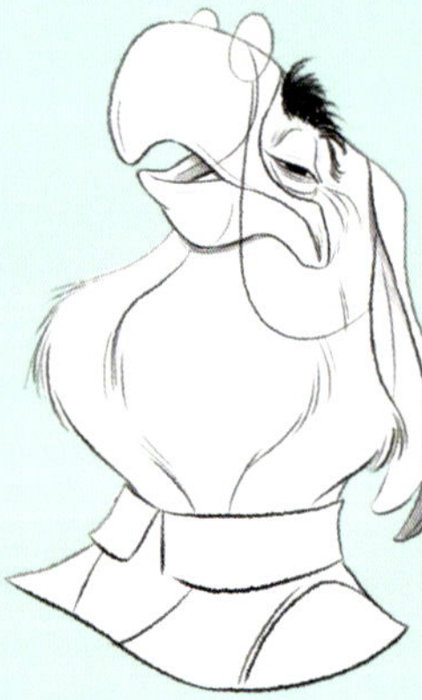

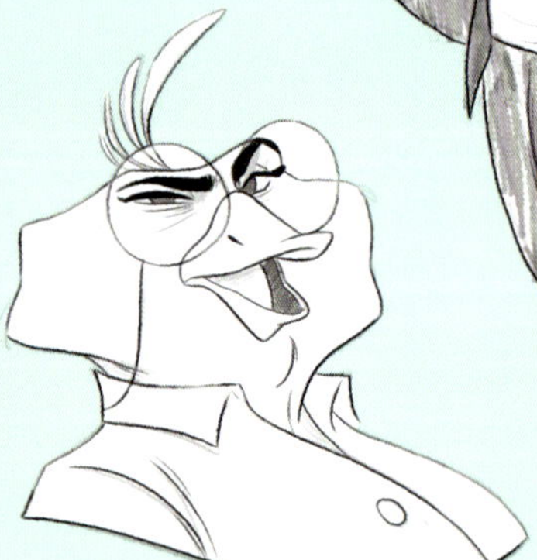

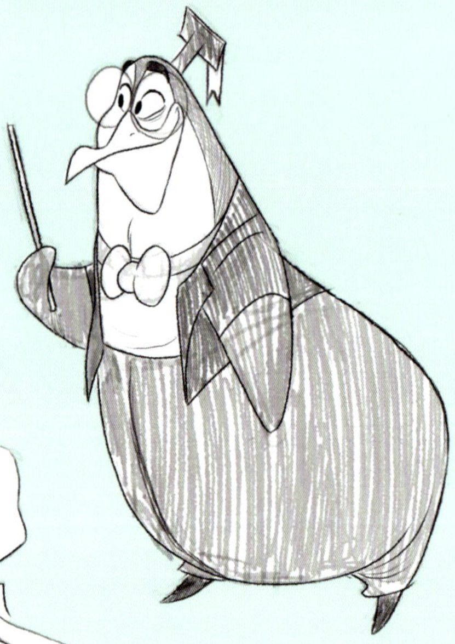

HIT THE BOOKS

I start by looking for references on the subject and drawing a few sketches that will help us understand the character's general physiognomy and the attitude I want them to have. A serious manner and items such as glasses or books can help to relate to the audience that the character is intellectual. Be sure to only use stereotypes sparingly. Remember, a little goes a long way – don't overload your character with too much detail.

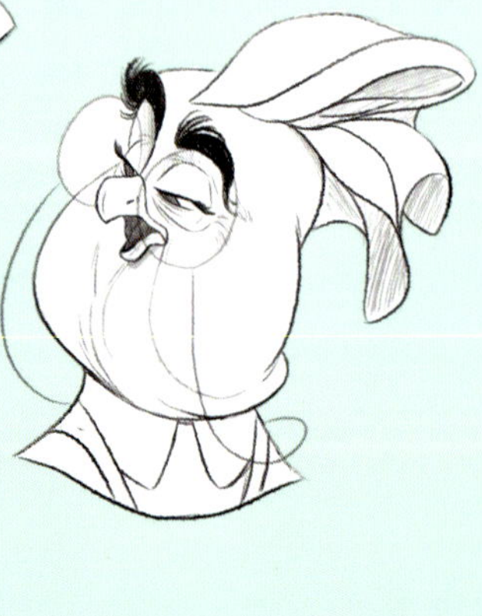

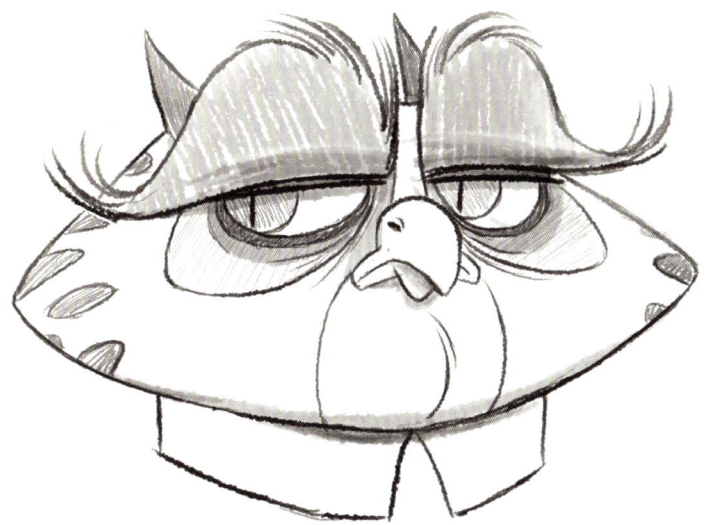

BIRD BRAINS

I choose to make my "brainy bird" an owl, as they have been seen as a symbol of wisdom for thousands of years. Choosing a creature with a recognizable link to the theme will make it easier for the viewers to relate to them.

TAKING FLIGHT

Next, I move on to the owl's figure. We can break the character down into simple geometric shapes to better understand how it works. This step will help us draw the owl in different poses, if necessary. We also want to give more prominence to the important parts of the owl's body. As we want the character to read as wise, the head should occupy more space than usual in the design.

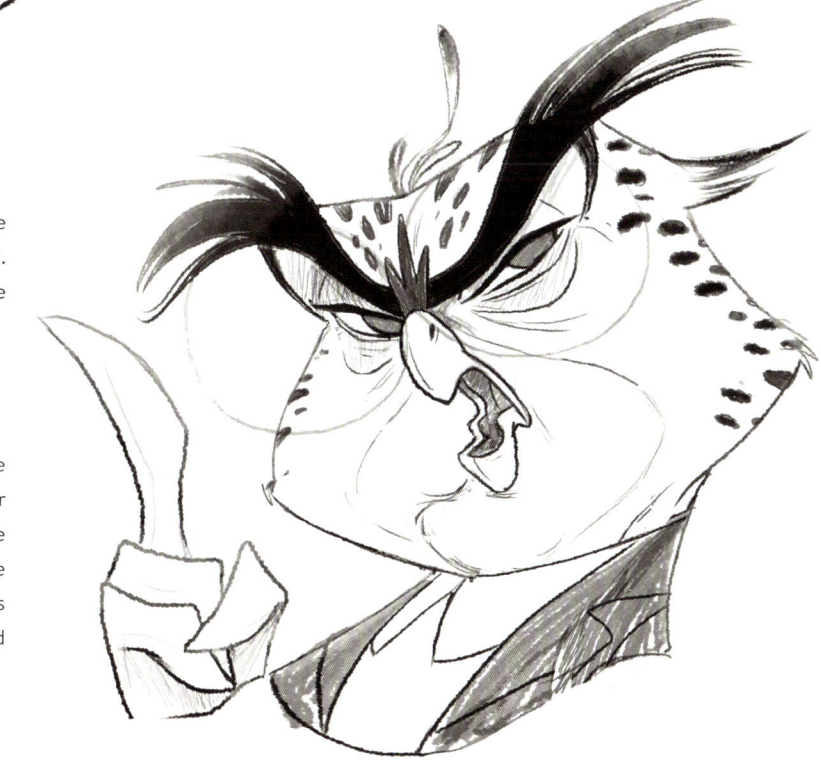

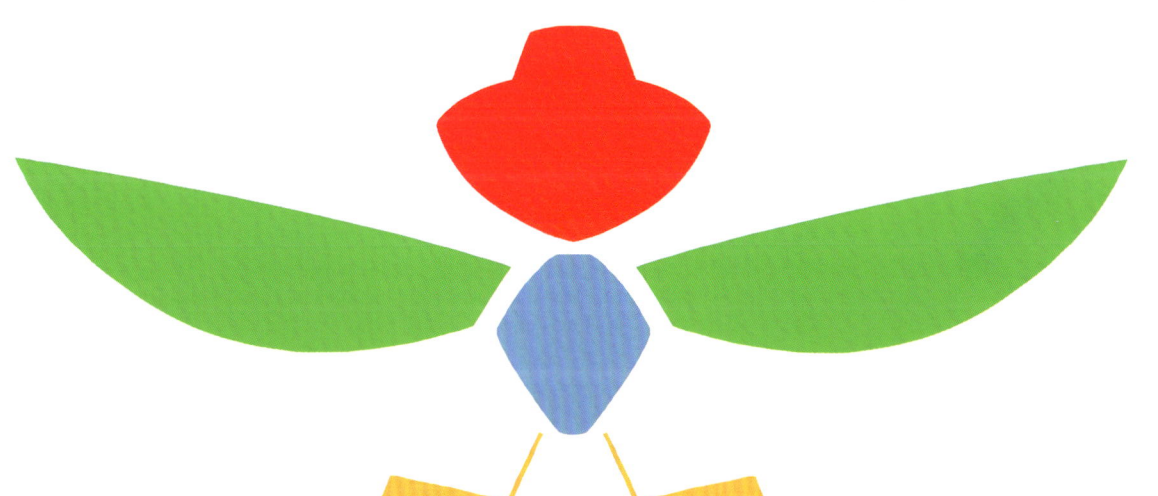

SHAPING THE SILHOUETTE

When creating the silhouette, I push the shapes of the design as far as I can while making sure that the character is still recognizable. If you are no longer able to clearly see who your character is or what they are doing, it's best to start over.

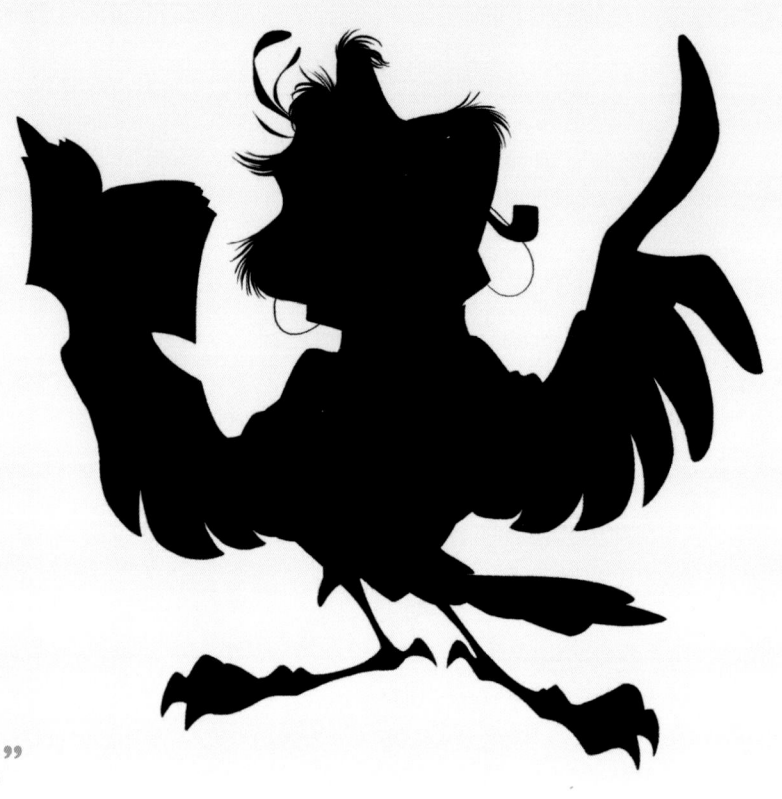

"I PUSH THE SHAPES OF THE DESIGN AS FAR AS I CAN WHILE MAKING SURE THAT THE CHARACTER IS STILL RECOGNIZABLE"

A FEATHER-LIGHT TOUCH

When drawing the line art, I try to keep the expressiveness of the sketch intact, not making the lines look too soft or lacking in energy. Add more detail to those parts on which you want to focus attention, leaving those that are less important empty.

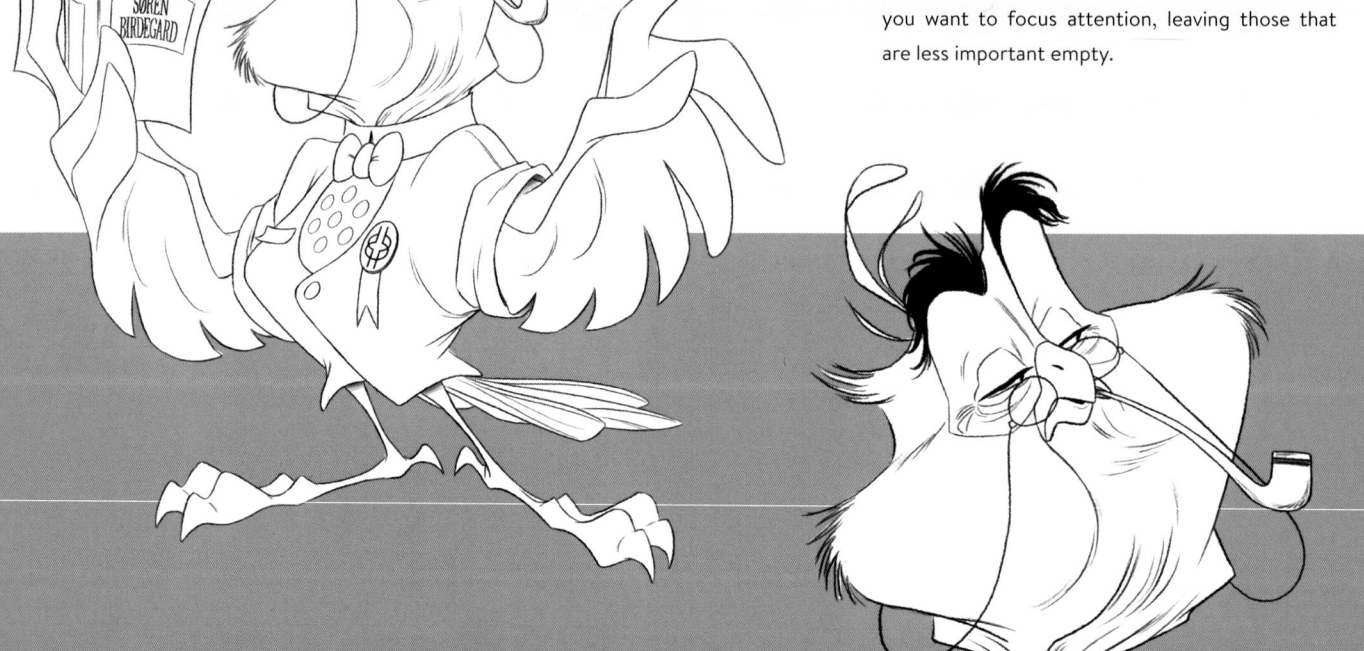

"WE DON'T JUST LOVE CHARACTERS BECAUSE THEY ARE WELL DRAWN – WE LOVE THEM BECAUSE THEY TELL A GOOD STORY"

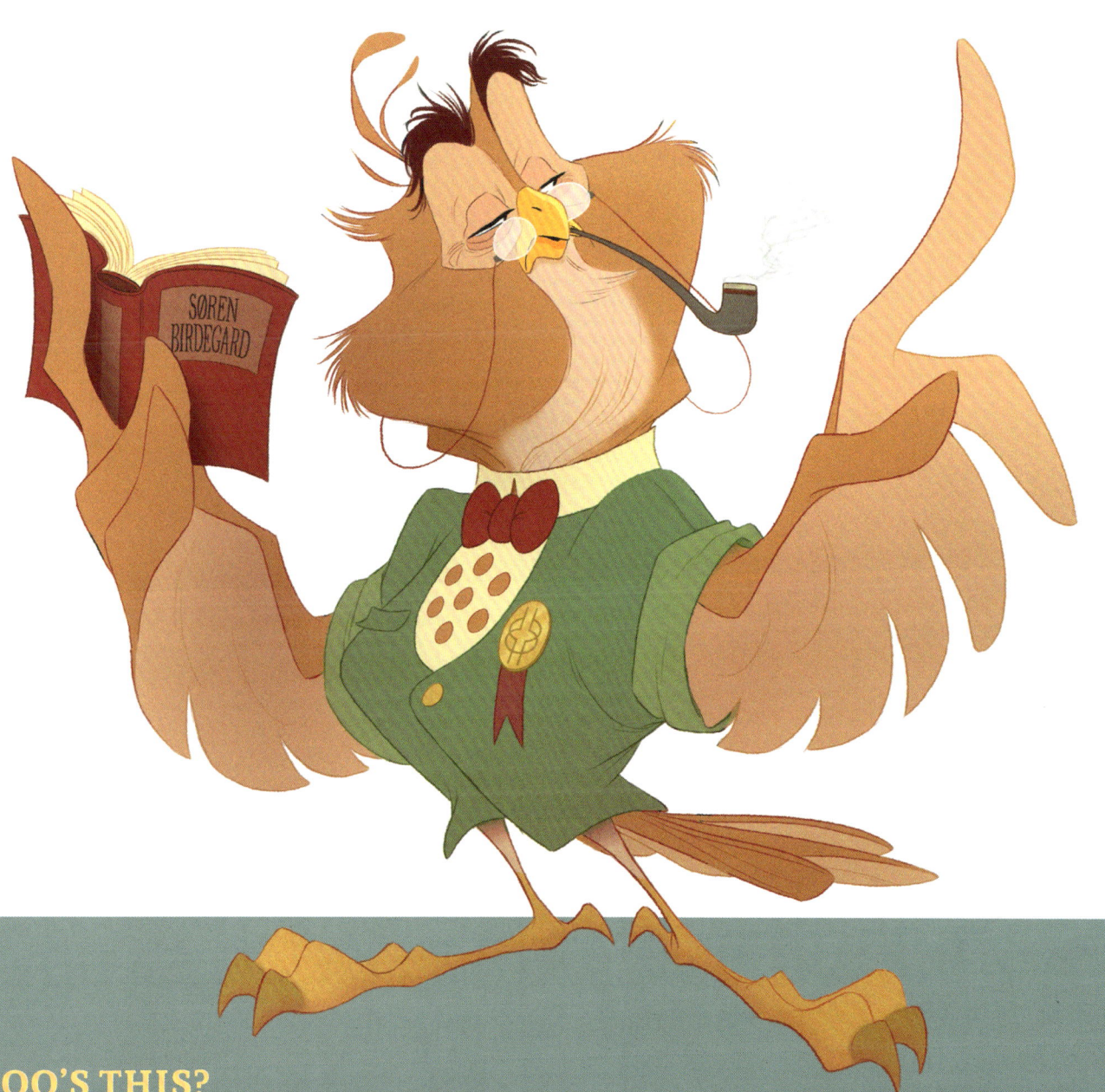

HOO'S THIS?

Our brainy bird is ready to paint! I add some flat color, shadow, lighting, and adjust the values. Try to have fun with this final step, attempting new things and exploring new possibilities. Remember, we don't just love characters because they are well drawn – we love them because they tell a good story.

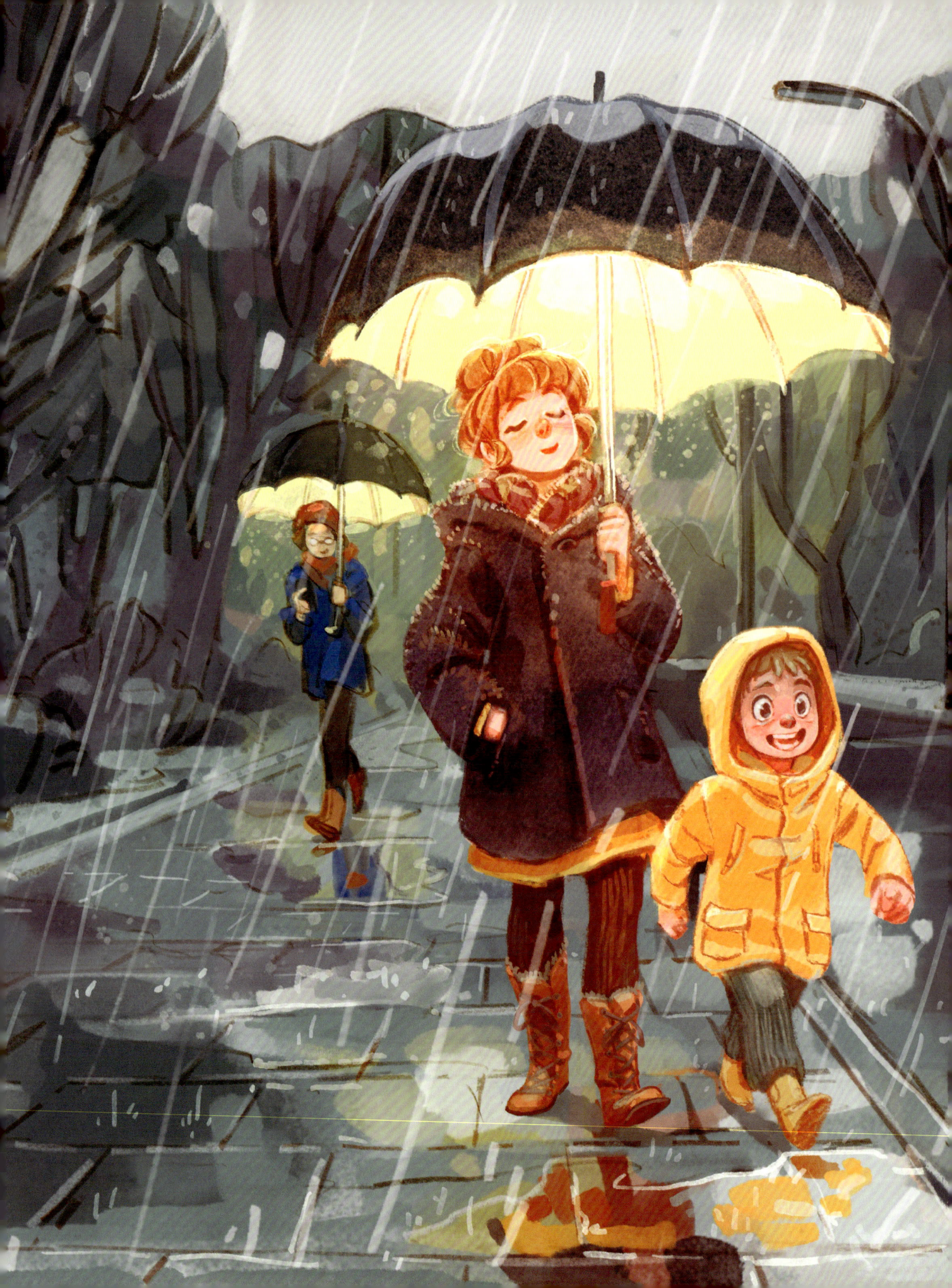

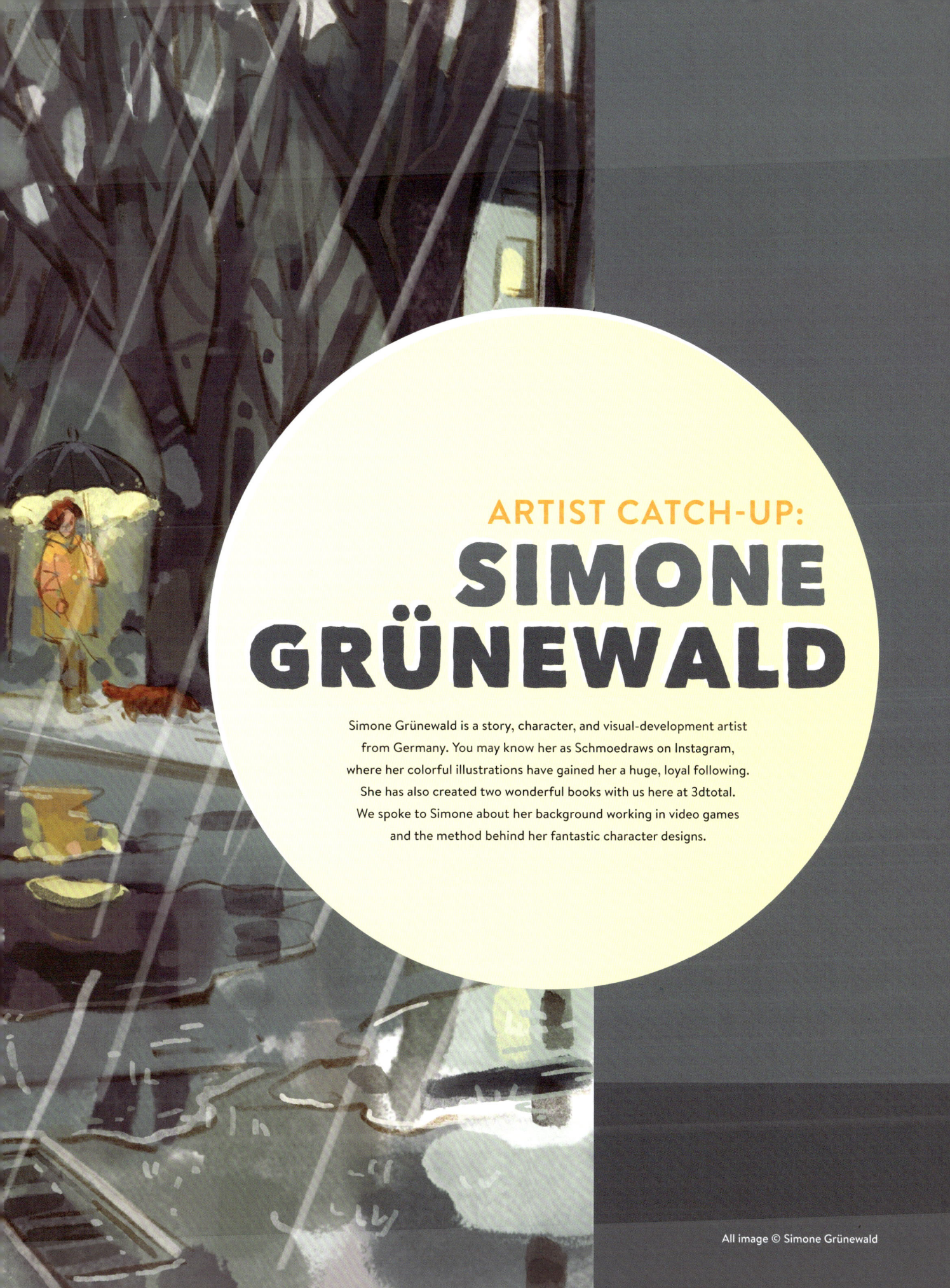

ARTIST CATCH-UP:
SIMONE GRÜNEWALD

Simone Grünewald is a story, character, and visual-development artist
from Germany. You may know her as Schmoedraws on Instagram,
where her colorful illustrations have gained her a huge, loyal following.
She has also created two wonderful books with us here at 3dtotal.
We spoke to Simone about her background working in video games
and the method behind her fantastic character designs.

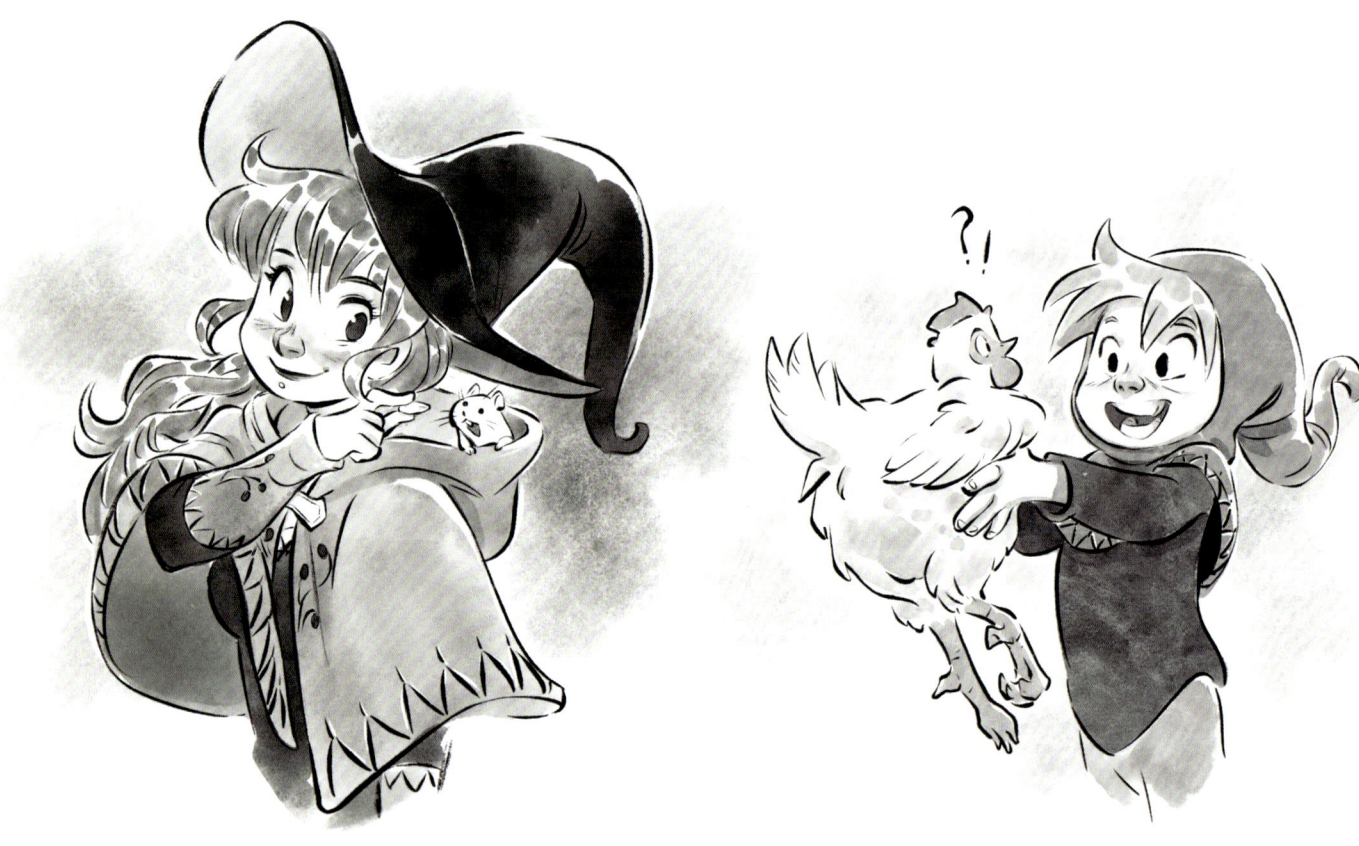

Hi Simone, welcome back to *CDQ*! Can you catch us up on your art journey so far?

I never planned to become an artist, but I always loved to draw and simply followed every path and opportunity that would let me do just that! After completing my studies at the Hamburg Technical School of Art, I started working as a graphic artist at the Hamburg game company Daedalic Entertainment. As Head of Art from 2009 through 2018 I was happy to put my creative stamp on many in-house game releases, like *A New Beginning*, the *Deponia* series, and *The Pillars of the Earth*.

With the birth of my son, six years ago, a lot changed. I started working as a freelancer and also built a Patreon with the idea of sharing what I've learned over the years. This change in my work life is what made my two books with 3dtotal possible! I find immense joy in exploring new topics and have been honing my craft while continuing to freelance ever since.

What did you learn about character design from working in the video-game industry?

When designing characters for games, I had to keep in mind that more detail meant more work for the animator. So, when designing I tried to always keep in mind adding as little detail as possible while still creating appealing characters. I learned this the hard way! The first designs I did for the game *A New Beginning*, when still at animation school, were very detailed. I remember feeling sorry for the poor souls who would have to animate my characters – and I ended up being one of them!

From then on, I tried to make my character designs simpler, especially those that would need lots of animation – background characters who would be mostly static could have more detail. Keeping something simple, readable, and yet appealing is an art in itself. Simple characters also work as a nice contrast to very detailed and painterly backgrounds.

This page (left): I drew a series of illustrations for Witchtober featuring my family in this witchy setting. My familiar would be a hamster. I love these little dudes!

This page (right): My son's familiar would be a chicken or a cat – he loves both!

Opposite page: These small folk find uses for discarded stuff – I thought about this while upcycling milk cartons with my son to make a birdhouse

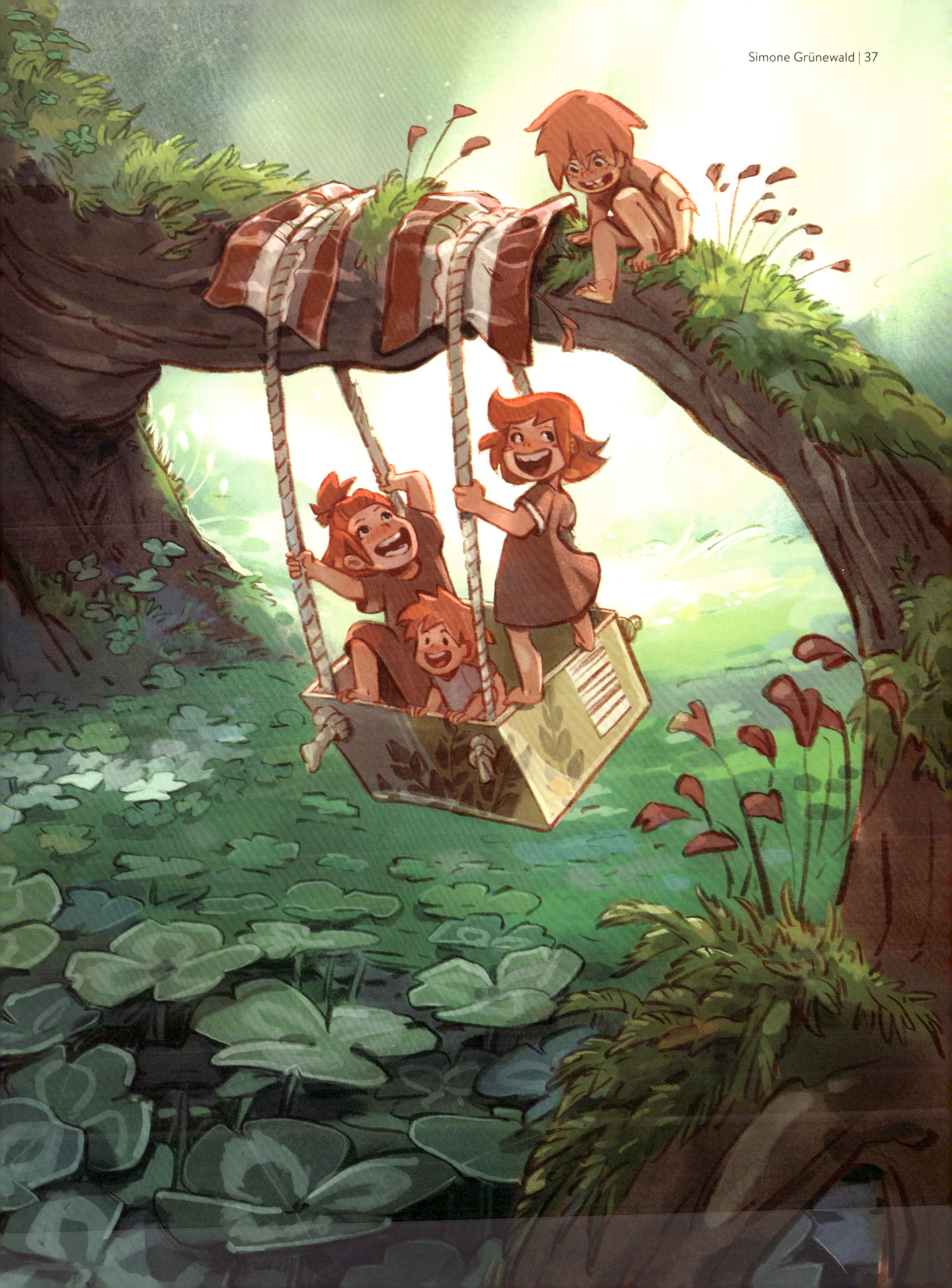

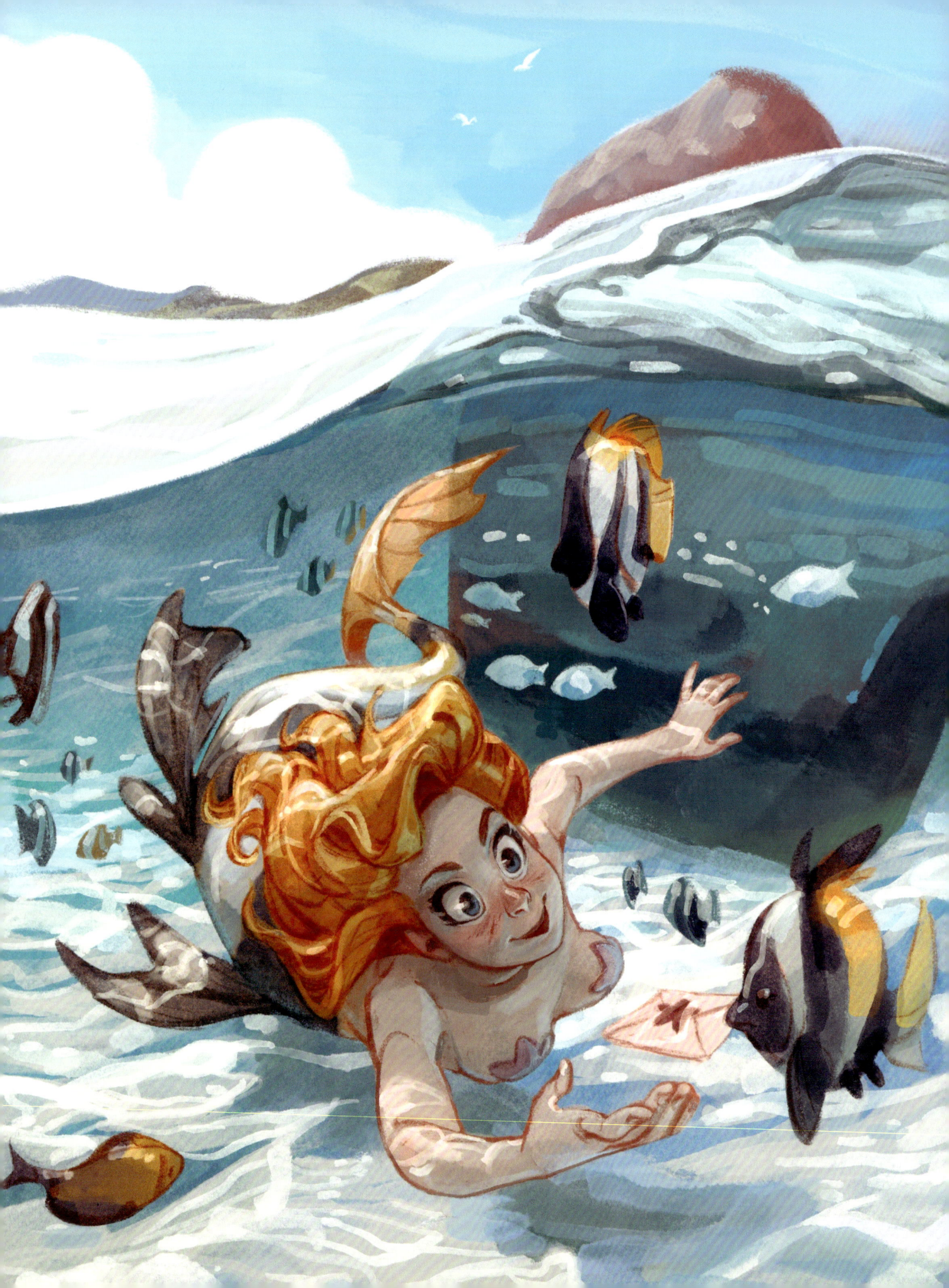

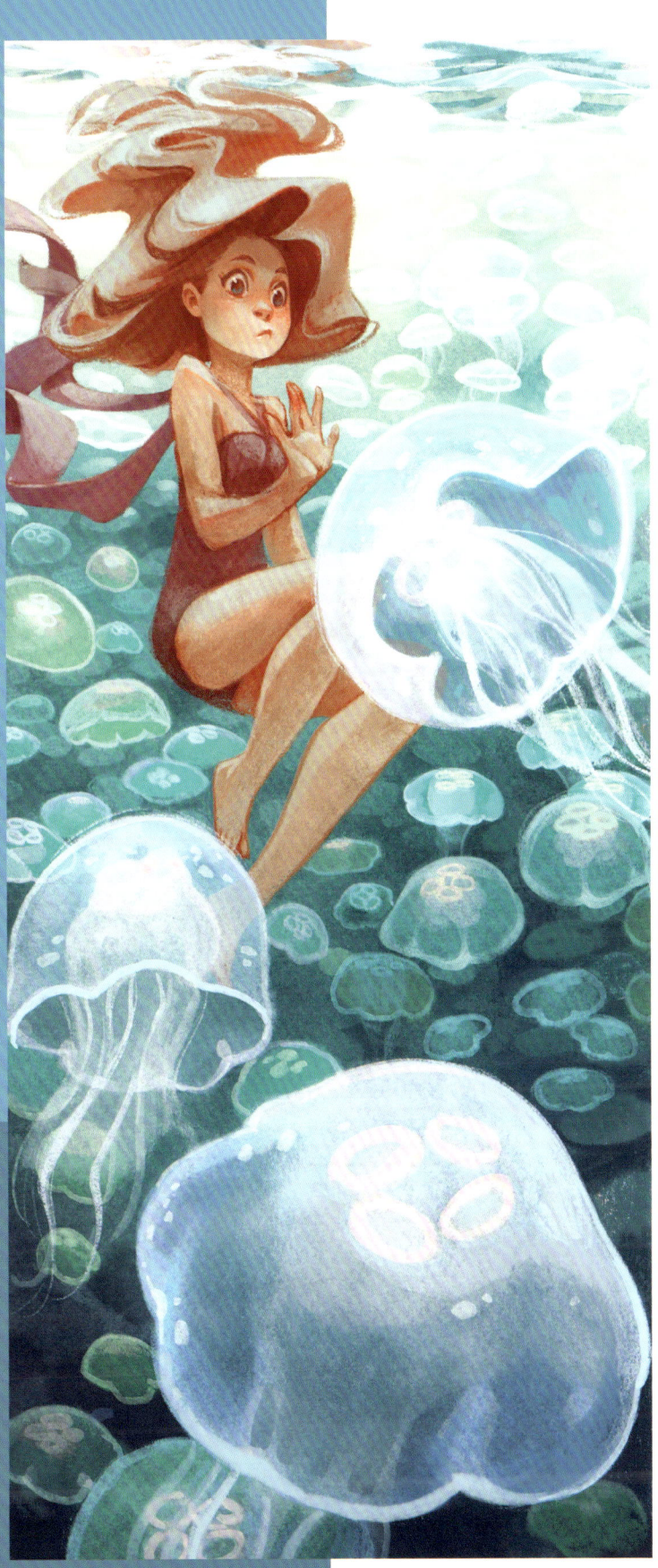

Do you have any advice for artists who want to work in video games?

I ended up in video games more by accident than design, but what brought me there was my passion and commitment to art. I didn't look too far for school or jobs; I simply jumped on whatever opportunity presented itself that seemed to promise art in my future. Some of these opportunities illustrated to me what I didn't really want to do, like work in advertising. In the end, I got my start at Daedalic thanks to recommendations from two of my teachers at college. My advice to any young artist would be to wholeheartedly commit to what you're passionate about and show your art to your teachers – to everybody! Don't be scared to ask for advice and make sure everyone knows what you are passionate about and good at, so if an opportunity arises someone will think to recommend you for the role.

Nowadays, creating video games is much easier than it used to be, so look out for people you work well with during your art studies and consider starting your own thing. You can learn so much stuff online – which is great! – but what actual studies are good for is making connections with like-minded people. The larger the network you form, the more likely you are to succeed.

What do you consider the key elements that add up to good character design?

A good design starts with a good idea, an understanding of a well-defined character to work toward, and finding a shape language that fits the overall design. Characters need composition and balancing as much as any illustration does. Balance also applies to the grouping of details and color choices that guide the eye. Appeal is also terribly important, but probably the most subjective part. I try to design characters that I would find appealing and hope others will like them, too!

Opposite page: I guess the envelope must be waterproof…

This page: This was inspired by a video of jellyfish that I watched

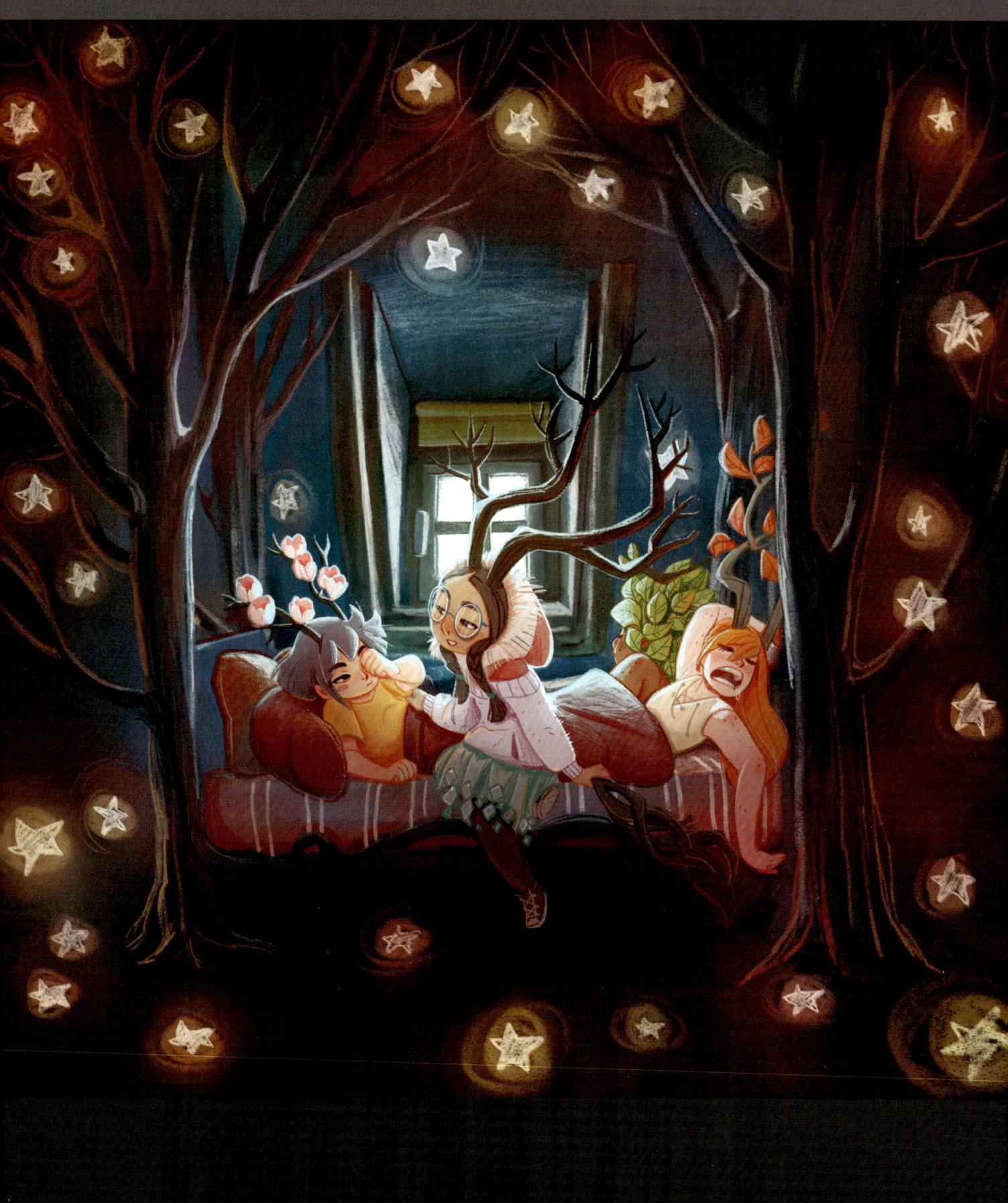

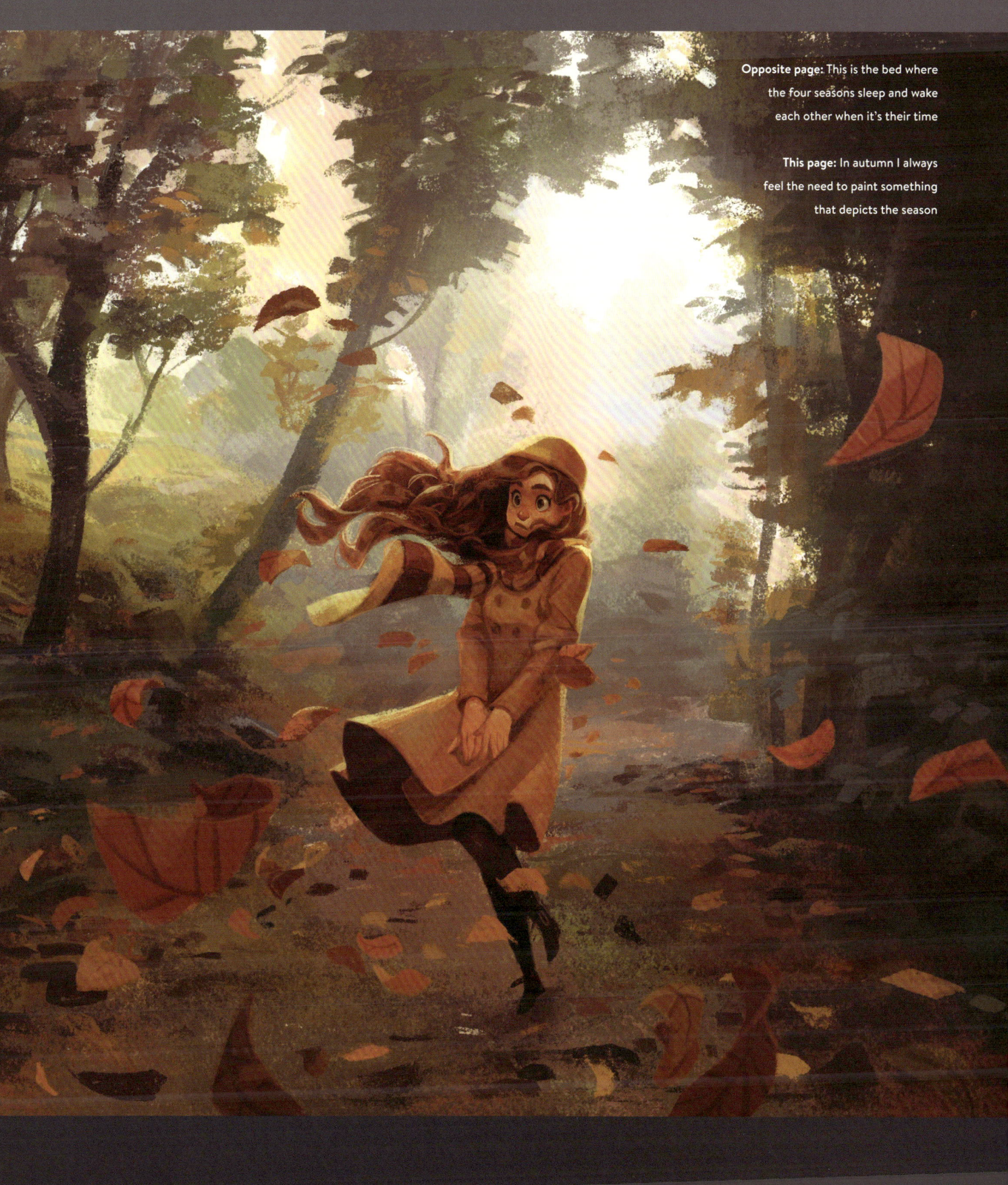

Opposite page: This is the bed where the four seasons sleep and wake each other when it's their time

This page: In autumn I always feel the need to paint something that depicts the season

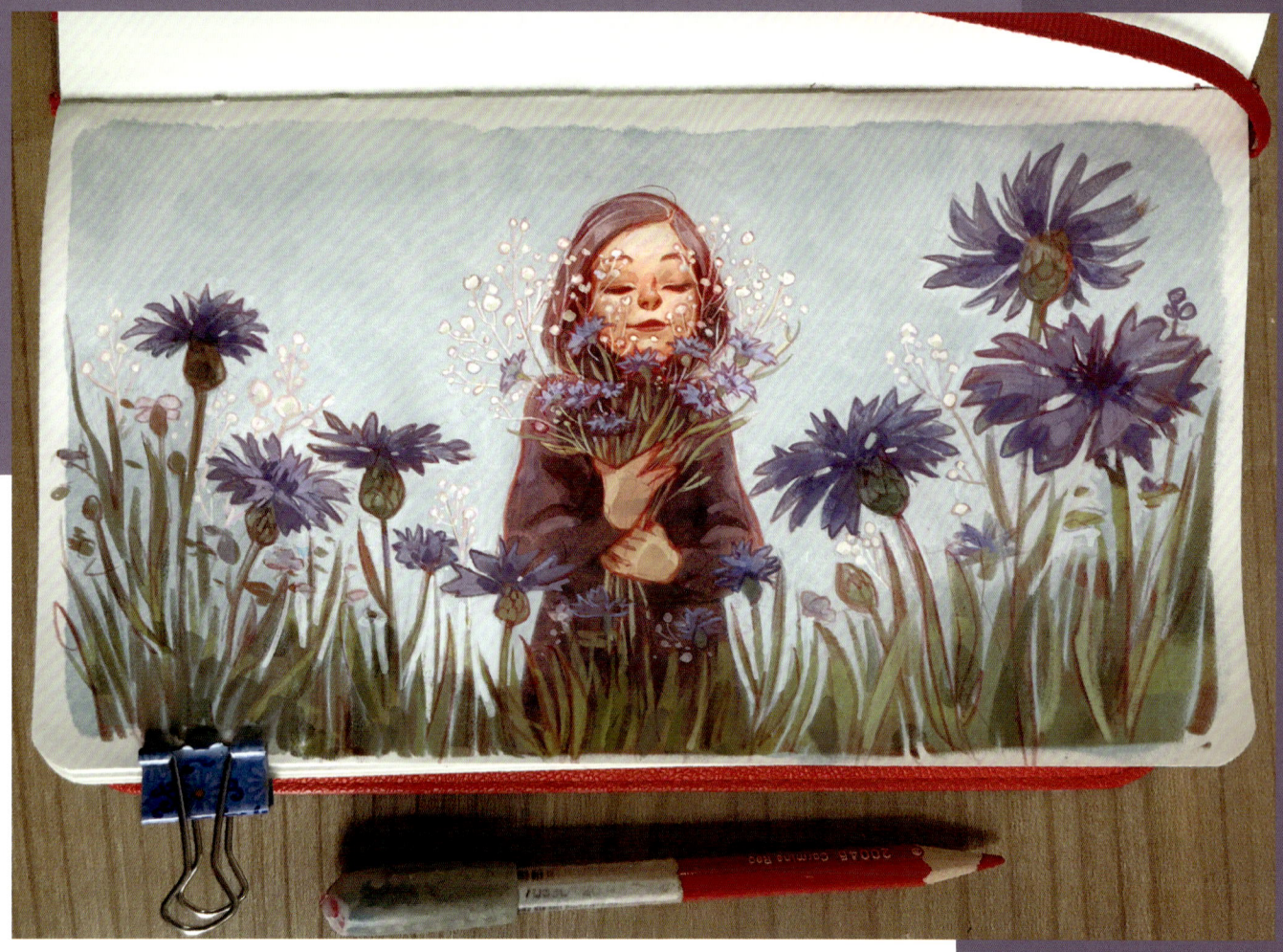

What have been the main inspirations for your art style over the years?

When in art school I almost religiously carried Juanjo Guarnido's *Blacksad* and Alessandro Barbucci and Barbara Canepa's *Sky Doll* around with me. All three artists previously worked at Disney, which shows in their art style, but drawing comics allowed them to create more detailed and refined characters than would have been possible in an animated movie.

I'd also say mangas like *Dragon Ball* and *Ranma ½*, and all the Studio Ghibli films have inspired me over the years. Throw in some *Flower Fairies* by Cicely Mary Barker from my early childhood and that about sums it up!

Thanks for talking to us Simone! Finally, do you have anything coming up we should be looking out for?

Earlier this year, I recorded a course for Domestika, an online community for creative people, where you can learn from expert professionals. Other than that, I also worked on a children's book, *The Magic Tree*, which should be releasing soon. I'm really proud of the Illustrations I did for that book. Look out for updates on all my projects on my social media!

This page: My favorite flowers are cornflowers and wildflowers in general; I love exploring floral illustrations every now and then

Opposite page: Celebrating walking through spring

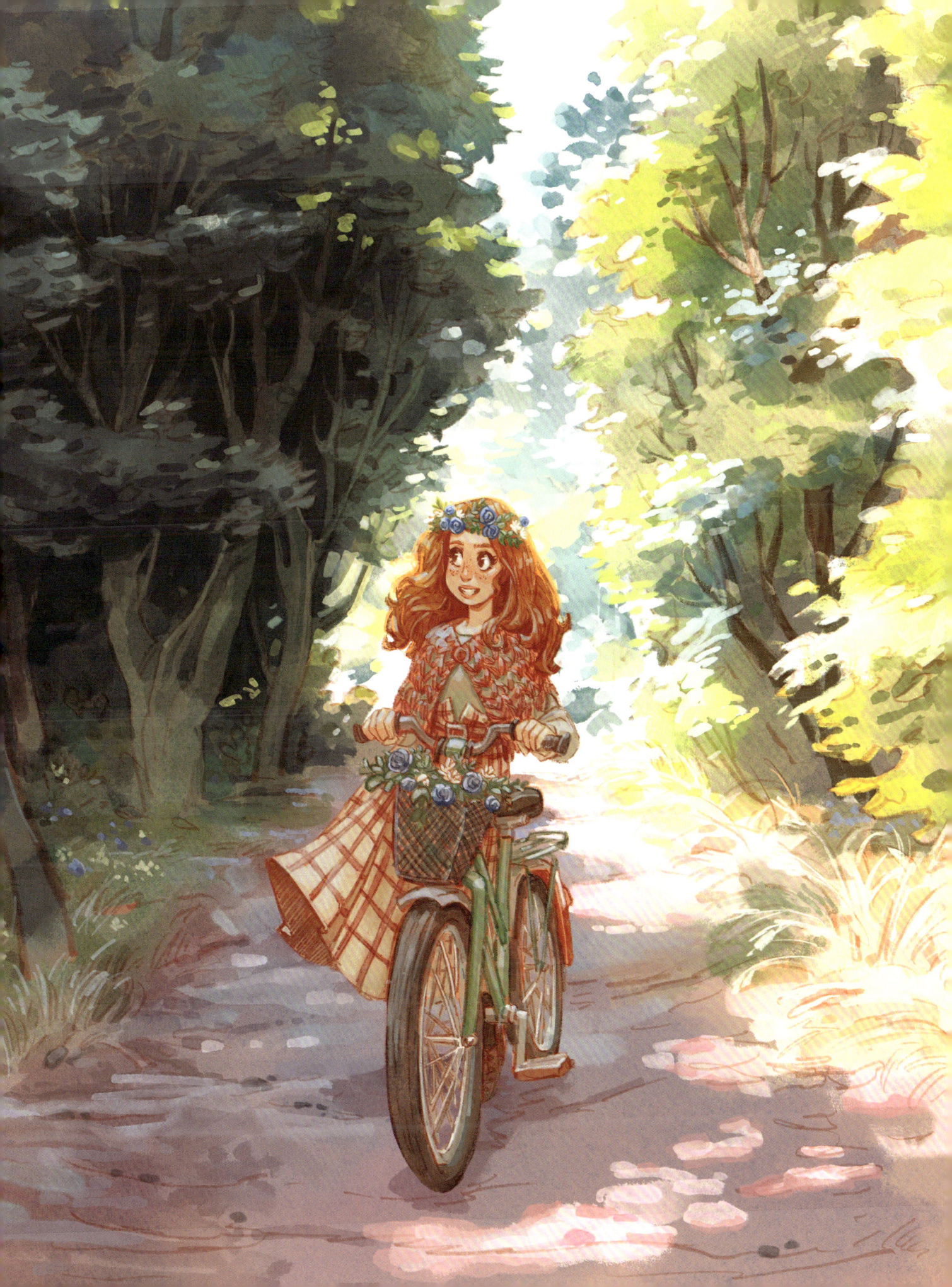

CHARACTERS
WITH A STORY TO TELL

ALEX RELLOSO

Characters are always part of a larger story, intended to be the main ingredients in the plot of movies, books, comics, games, and more. This is why I love approaching character design by thinking of the "story" first - infusing a narrative into my characters so they embody it.

I have worked as both a storyboard artist and character designer. As a storyboard artist, you are often asked to come up with gags and funny situations for a character, or to imagine interesting aspects of their daily life to improve a story. There's no doubt these exercises have helped me to create more complete characters.

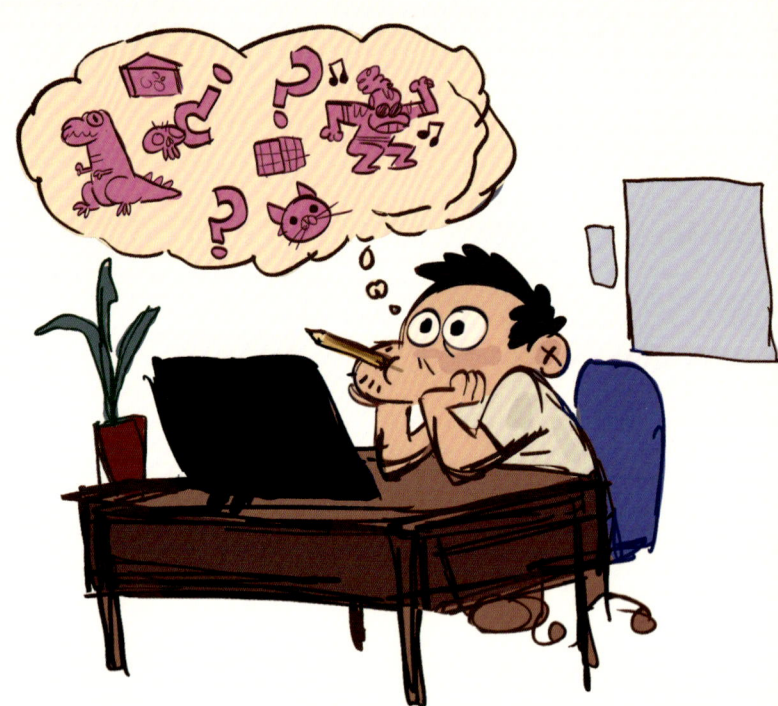

LET'S MAKE A WIZARD!

So, let's say we want to design a wizard. Instead of just doodling him standing up, holding a wand, or in another cliché pose (like throwing a spell) let's go deeper and find out who he really is. What does he eat for breakfast? What kind of music does he listen to? Maybe he's a fan of soap operas! Whatever you decide, go beyond cliché and give your character true personality.

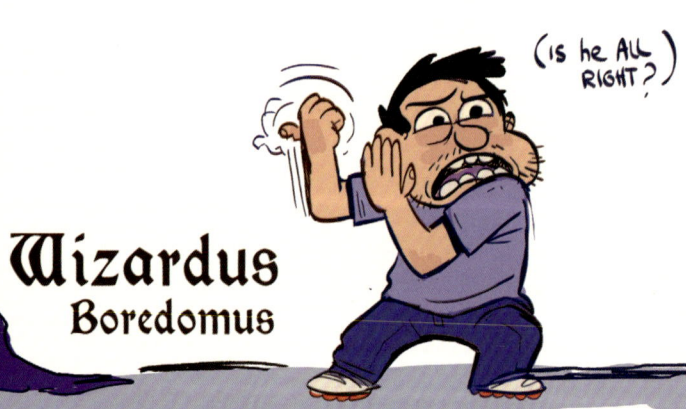

Wizardus Boredomus

(IS he ALL RIGHT?)

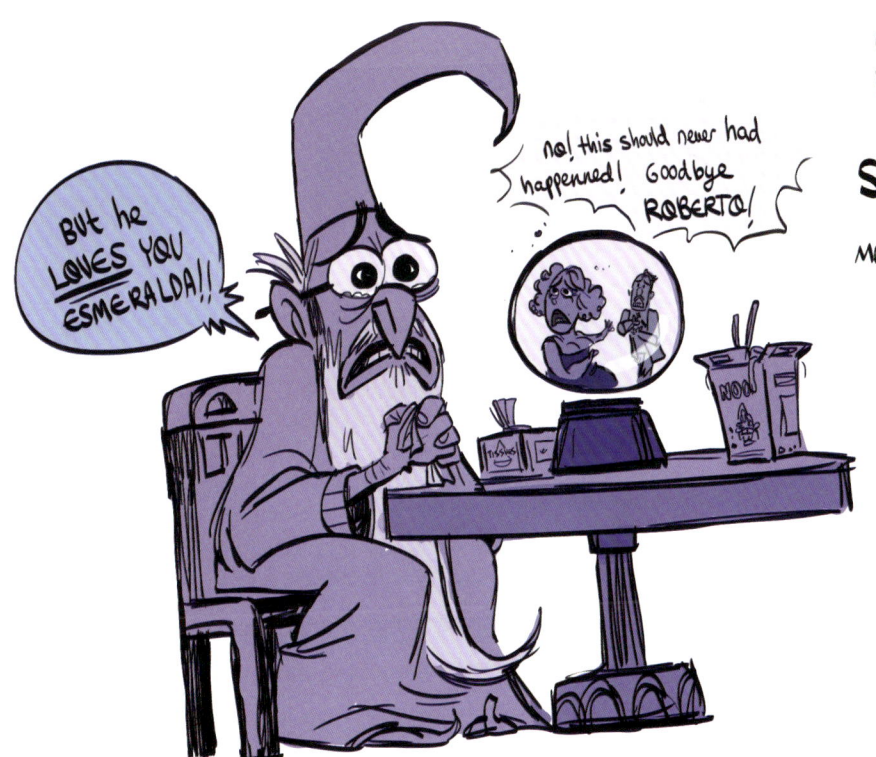

GET INSIDE THEIR HEAD

Ask yourself questions about your character, such as: what is their secret hobby? What do they do at the weekend? Do they have any pets? If you are developing a character from scratch, this method can be super fun and you'll learn a lot about who you are trying to create. I've also seen this process work well with projects in which characters have already been defined, in terms of psychology and personality.

"RESEARCH YOUR SUBJECT EVERYWHERE YOU CAN, DIGGING INTO BOOKS AND MINING THE INTERNET"

HIT THE BOOKS

Research your subject everywhere you can, digging into books and mining the internet. You'll find many amazing stories and anecdotes that will spark original ideas for your design. Go outside and look around. Maybe you'll bump into people or situations that will inspire you – maybe the guy waiting at the bus stop looks exactly like the sorceror you're trying to design?

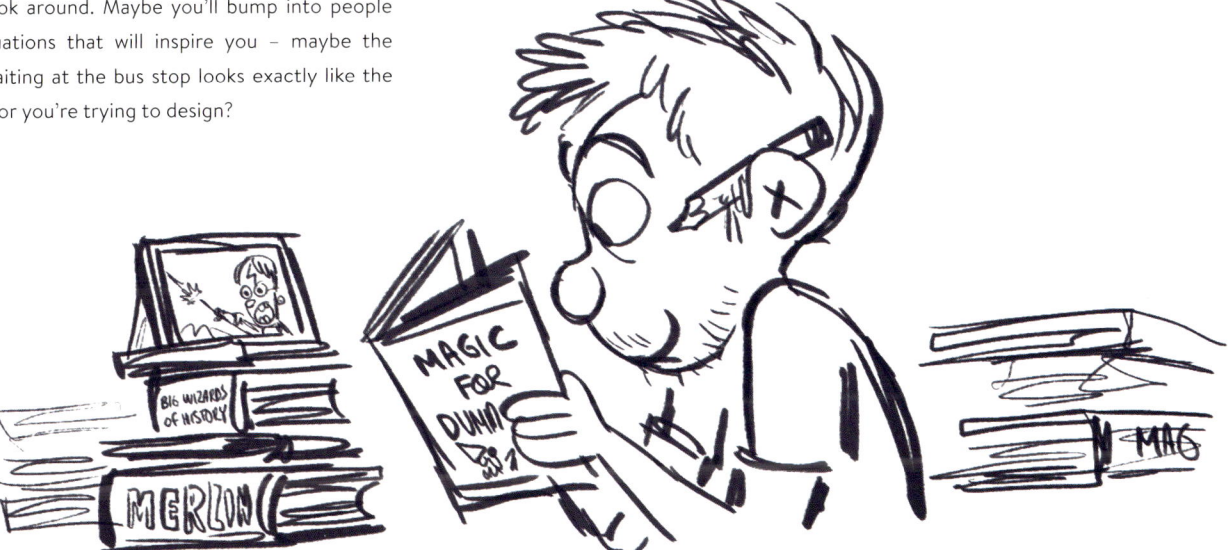

RETHINK
THE CLICHÉ

Use clichés as a base to come up with original ideas. Let's think about "wizard" clichés. Traditionally, they brew potions, can travel on a broom, and wear tall hats. How can we innovate within each of these ideas to get to know more about our character?

The more we question how our characters behave and challenge our traditional idea of who they are, the more we can push their attitude in original and exciting directions. There are no incorrect questions to ask – everything helps us get closer to the ideal version of the character we are building.

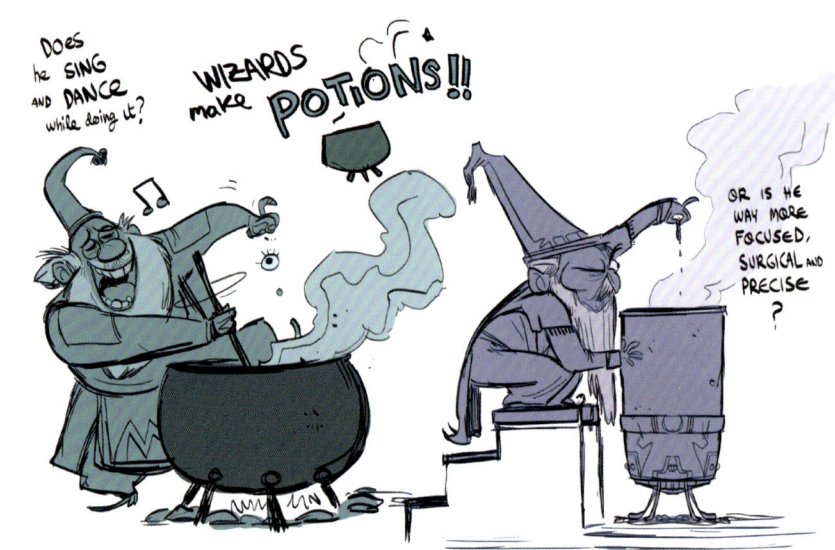

DOES he SING AND DANCE while doing it?

WIZARDS make POTIONS!!

OR IS HE WAY MORE FOCUSED, SURGICAL AND PRECISE ?

ASKING these QUESTIONS LEADS US TO A BETTER UNDERSTANDING AND COMPREHENSION of our CHARACTER!

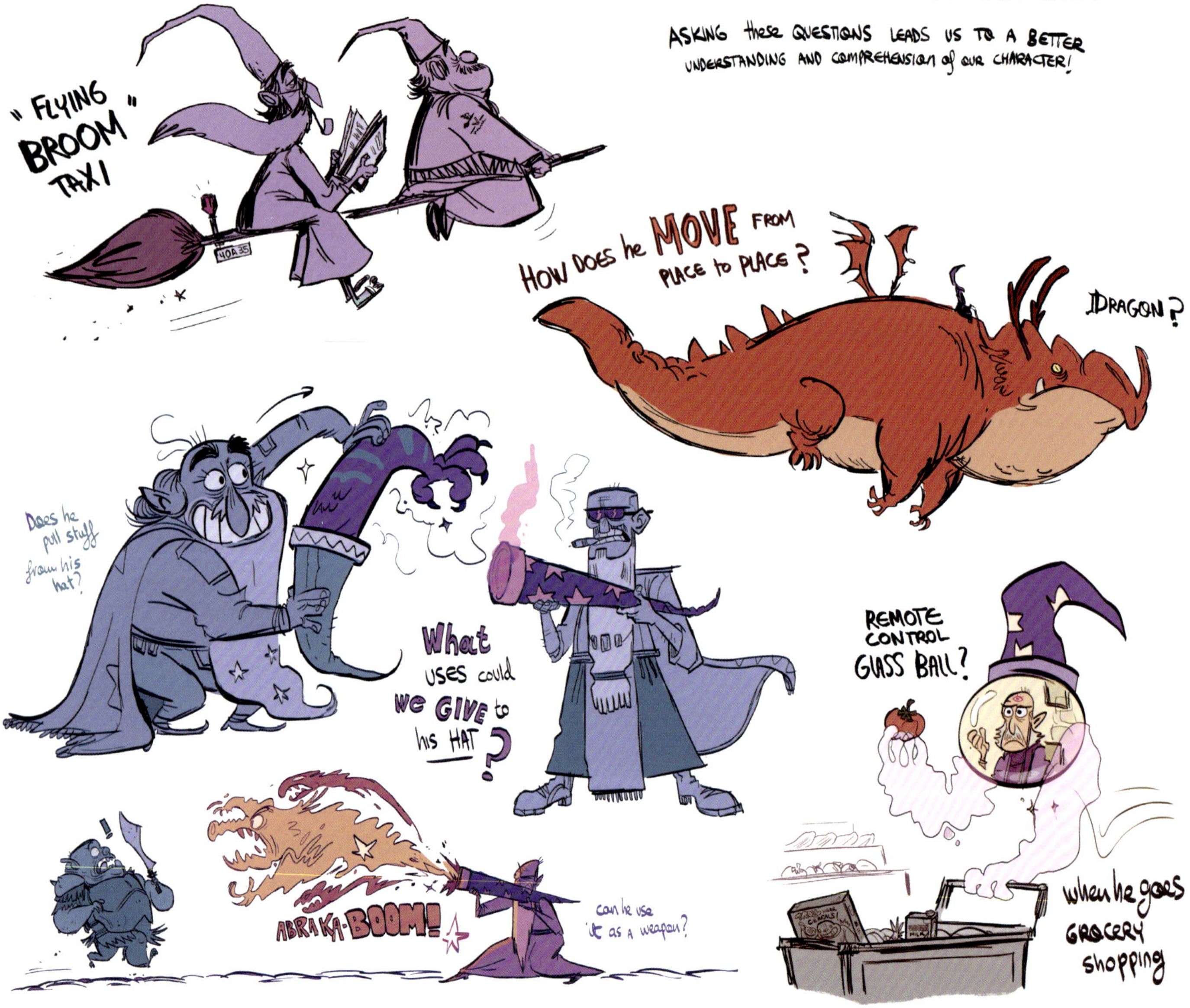

"FLYING" BROOM TAXI

NOA 35

HOW DOES he MOVE FROM PLACE to PLACE?

DRAGON?

Does he pull stuff from his hat?

What USES could WE GIVE to his HAT ?

REMOTE CONTROL GLASS BALL?

ABRAKA-BOOM!

can he use it as a weapon?

when he goes GROCERY shopping

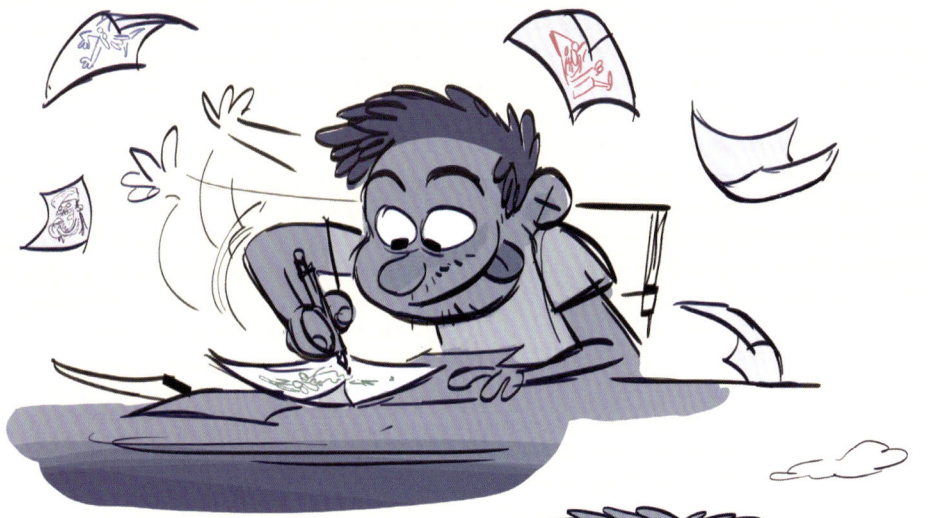

ALWAYS BE SKETCHING

Always carry a sketchbook with you, in order to quickly put down any random thoughts and ideas you might find. Don't worry about your sketches being too "clean" either. I fill the pages of my notebook with scribbled doodles, random thoughts, annotations, and variations. There will be time to clean up later – the important part is to find cool ideas wherever you can!

NARRATIVE MOMENTS

Building a specific story moment will lead you to new discoveries. For example, what if the wizard sets up a poker game? Drawing a narrative scene will spark other ideas, which in turn will lead to even *more* ideas! Be careful, this process can become overwhelming if you let it, stuck in a never-ending loop of finding new things to draw. At some point, it's good to stop, breathe, and evaluate what you've created. With time, you'll get better at asking more interesting and on-point questions which will help you come up with a wide range of funny ideas and moments for your character that reinforce the perception of them as "alive."

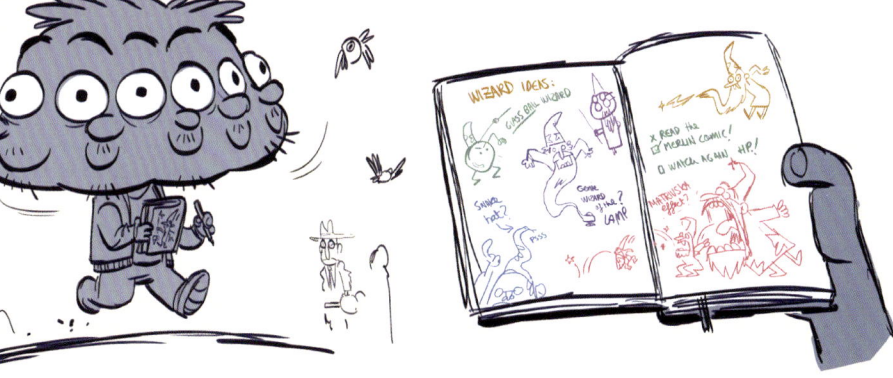

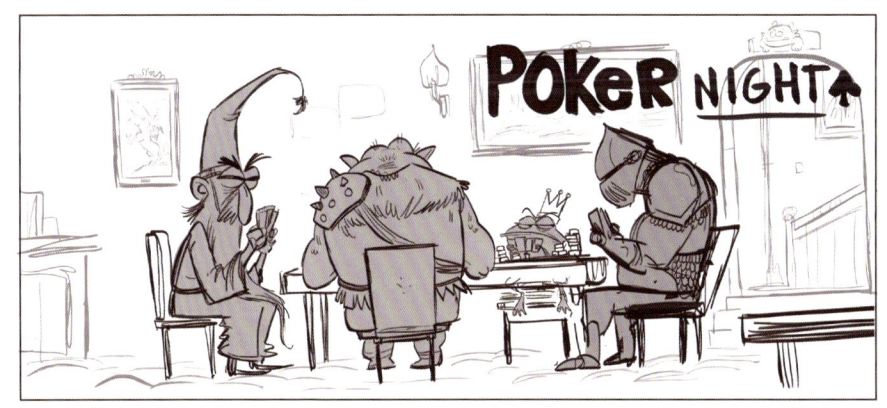

THAT'S WHAT FRIENDS ARE FOR

Many of the best ideas come from chatting about different iterations and, "oooh that's cool, and what if...?" from your friends. Overall, try to have fun in the creation of your characters. I recommend this approach because I enjoy it myself. I hope you have fun too, and find some cool stories and characters along the way!

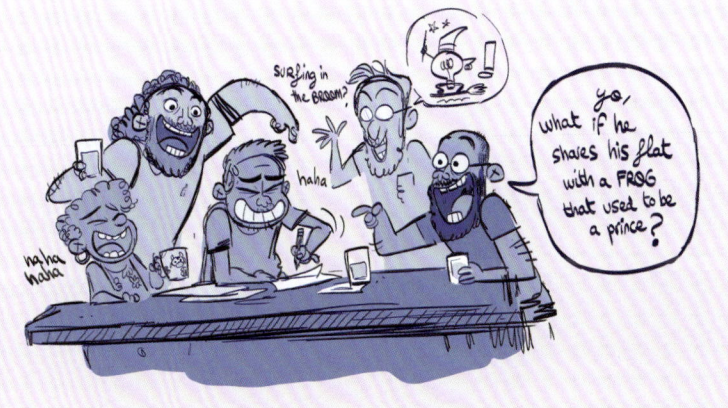

HOW I STYLIZE
JENNIFER VOIGT

My usual workflow starts with creating a messy scribble, which I then gradually shape into a character. I always want to keep as much of the initial energy as possible, but still create a readable and appealing design. Let me show you the techniques I use, based on some general principles of design and storytelling, to achieve this balance of expression and readability. I will also share some tips on how to get the most out of your sketches. Grab a pencil and let's start drawing!

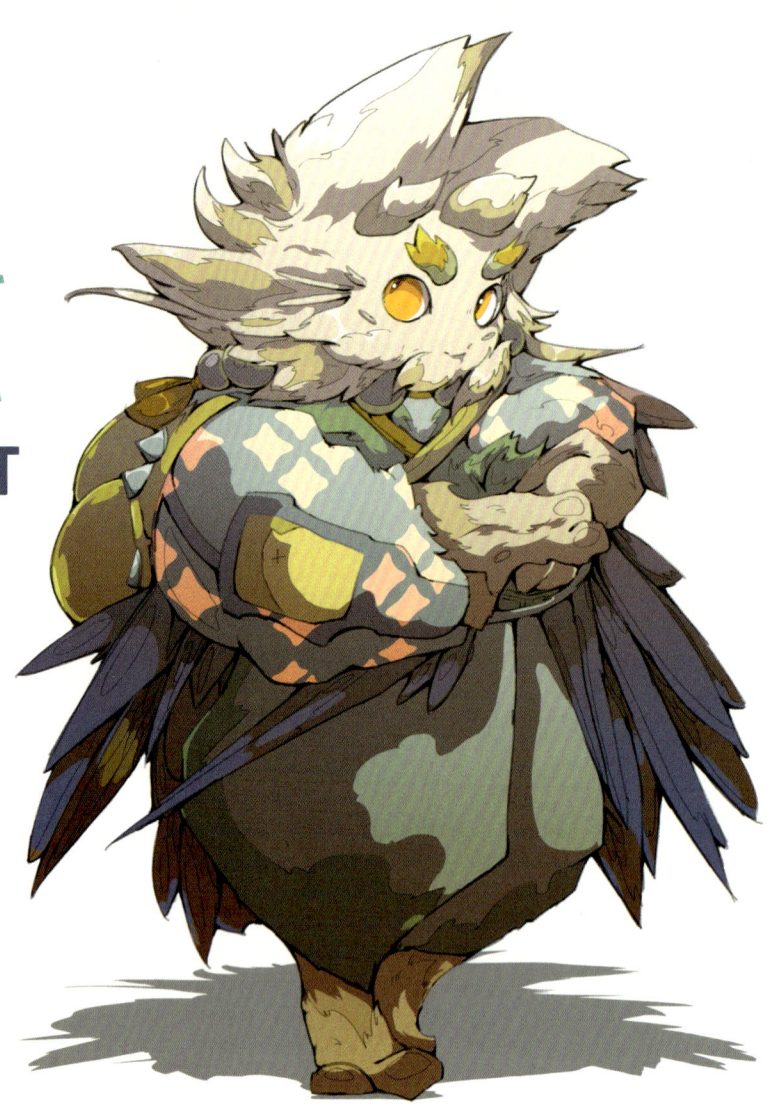

KEEPING IT ORGANIC

By identifying the main shapes of your sketch, you can easily enhance their dynamics. In this example, I use round shapes in different sizes to create an organic design. The placement and contrast in sizes leads to an organic flow throughout the character.

KEEP MOVING

When drawing characters in motion, it's always helpful to stay close to their line of action. You can use any part of their design to support this motion and stylize specific elements in your favor. My initial sketch for this drawing was similar to the final image – I wanted to build the design around the diagonal line, so I kept her arms straight and stylized her feet into small triangular shapes.

CREATING STYLIZED MOTION

When drawing static poses, you can use specific parts of the design to introduce some motion through stylization. Even though this character is standing still, I decide to draw the hair in a dynamic way. This not only creates a more interesting silhouette, it also sneakily leads the eye back to the character's upper body.

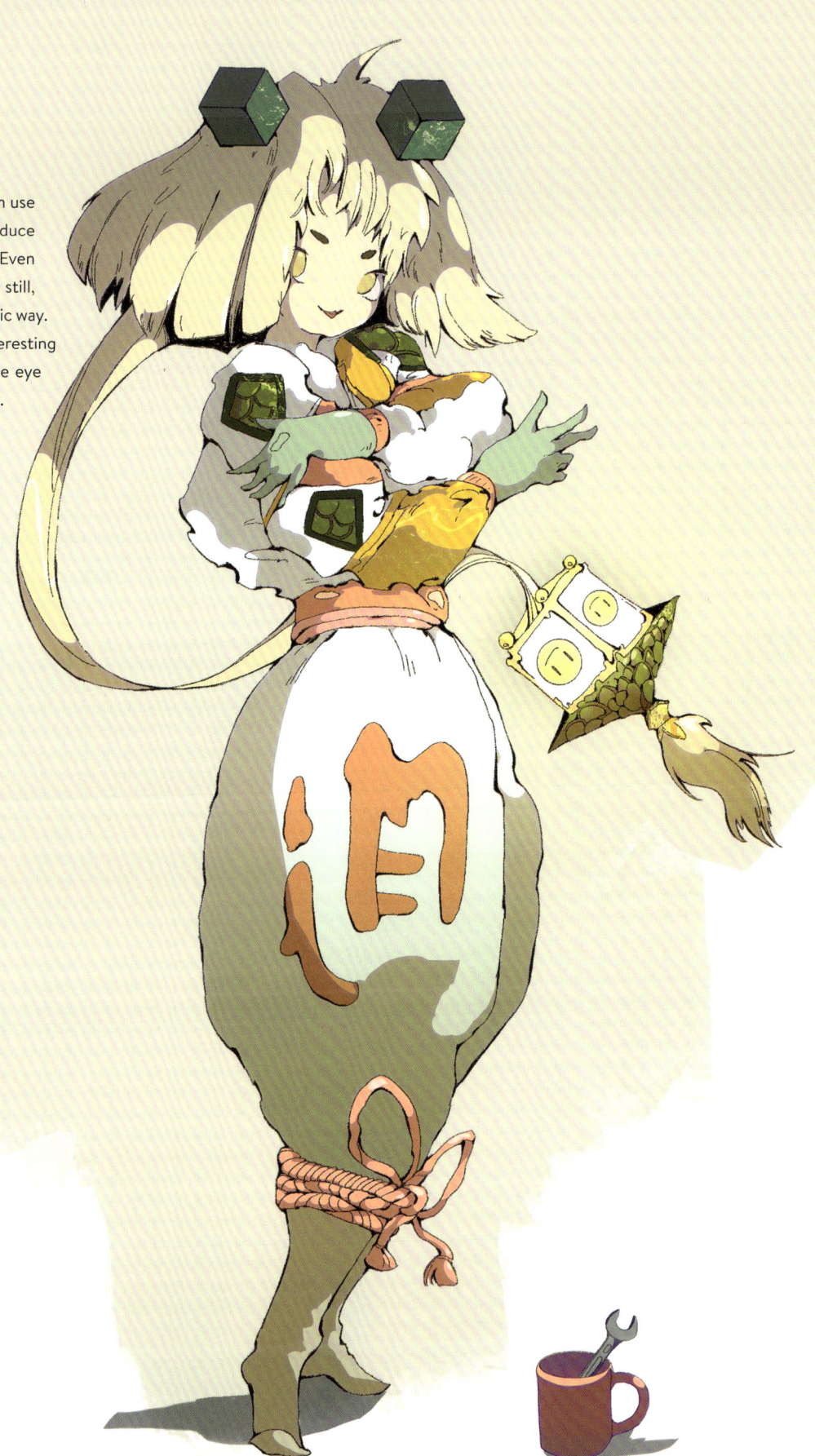

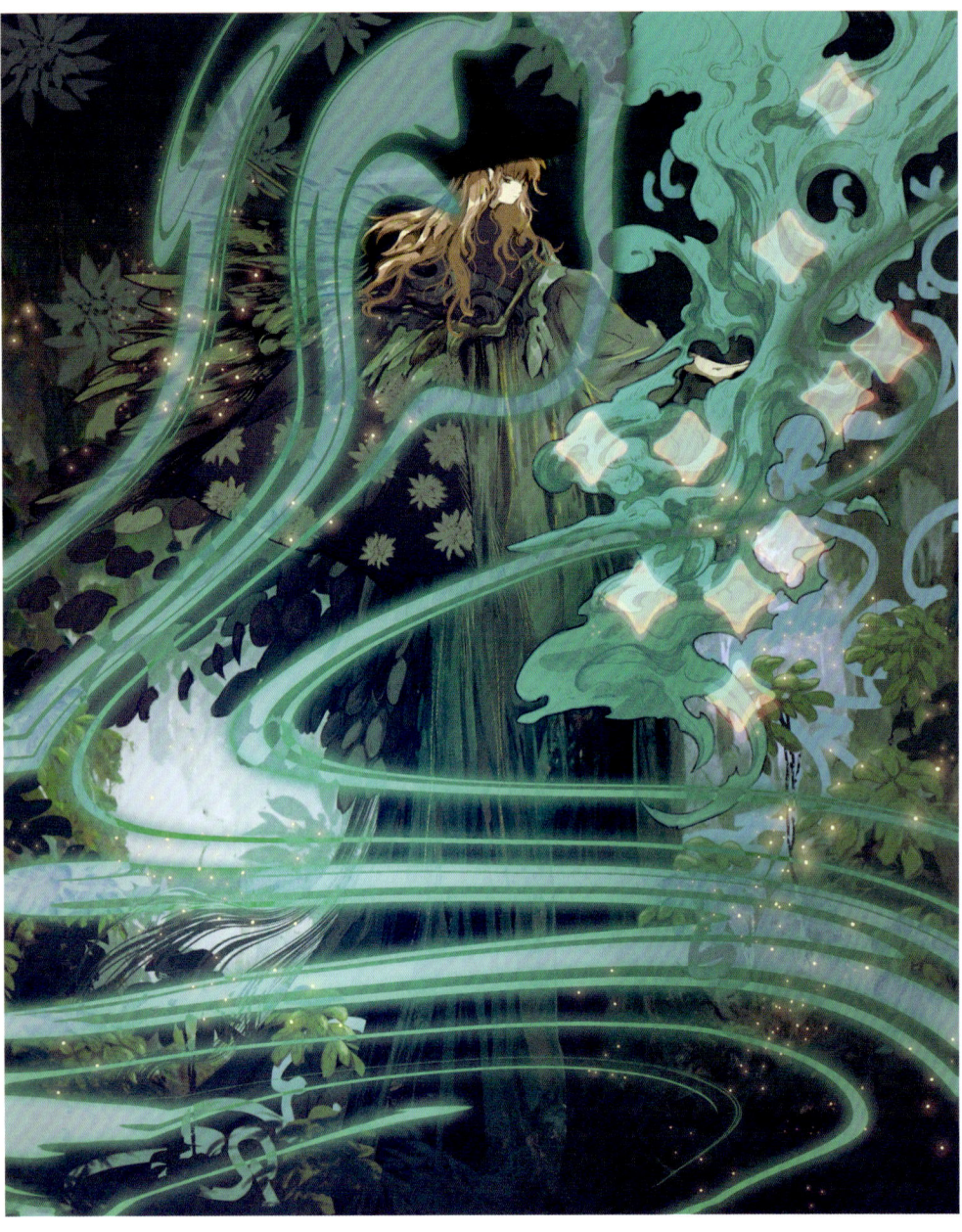

GROUP THINK

You can easily guide the viewer's eye by grouping details and increasing their density around certain parts of your character. The main shape of this design is a triangle. By placing several smaller similar shapes in the upper area, this part becomes the focal point. I then follow this lead by having a lot of small and detailed elements in this area. The other areas only have rough folds and no particular patterns on them to keep them less busy.

USE LAYERS TO YOUR ADVANTAGE

If you're stuck during the process of designing a character, it can help to just make a new layer and draw bold and freely on top. It's easy to get attached to a certain design and lose sight of its key points. If that happens, a new layer to capture only the most essential parts can make the difference.

BE OPEN TO EXPLORE

There's never only one right way to do things. Allow yourself to be open and explorative during the process – even an accidentally placed detail or texture can bring an interesting perspective to your design. I often place random things purposely just to see where they might lead.

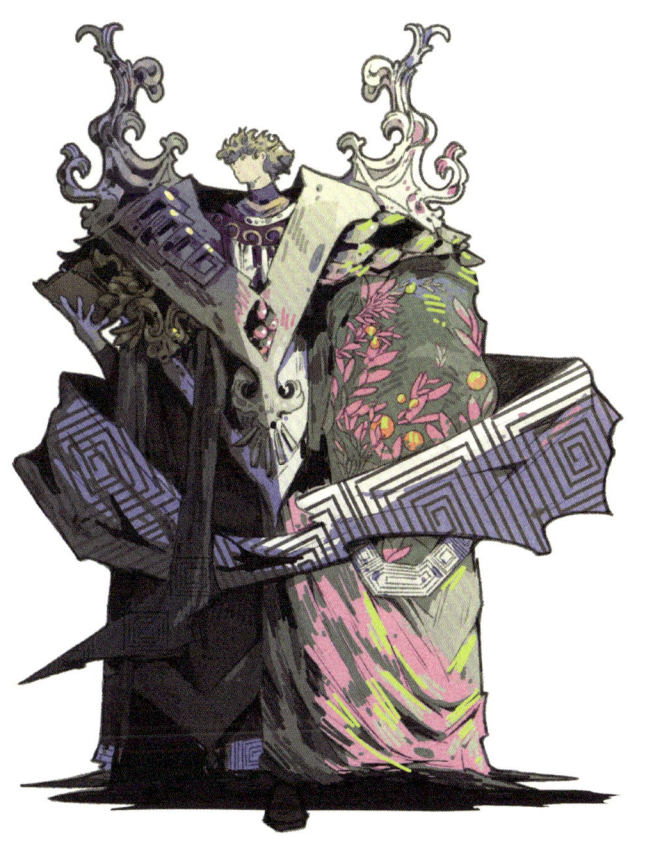

BENDING THE RULES

While there are obvious benefits from following the natural physics of certain materials, ignoring them can also lead to great things. Remember, you're always allowed to bend the rules if it helps to tell a story. For this design, the character is supposed to appear dignified, carrying a huge burden and responsibility. So, why not draw his robe solid like stone? The geometrical shapes and partial lack of folds in the pattern are further design elements that support this decision.

A DELICATE BALANCE

If you find yourself with a scene that is overloaded with detail, it can be helpful to place a calm anchor. Once again, you can use contrasts to balance your design. This character is the focal point of a really busy illustration – the surroundings are full of organic lines. I use the design of the character to anchor the scene by giving her a very geometrical, almost triangular silhouette. The design draws the eye toward the character and keeps the scene together.

"IF YOU FIND YOURSELF WITH A SCENE THAT IS OVERLOADED WITH DETAIL, IT CAN BE HELPFUL TO PLACE A CALM ANCHOR"

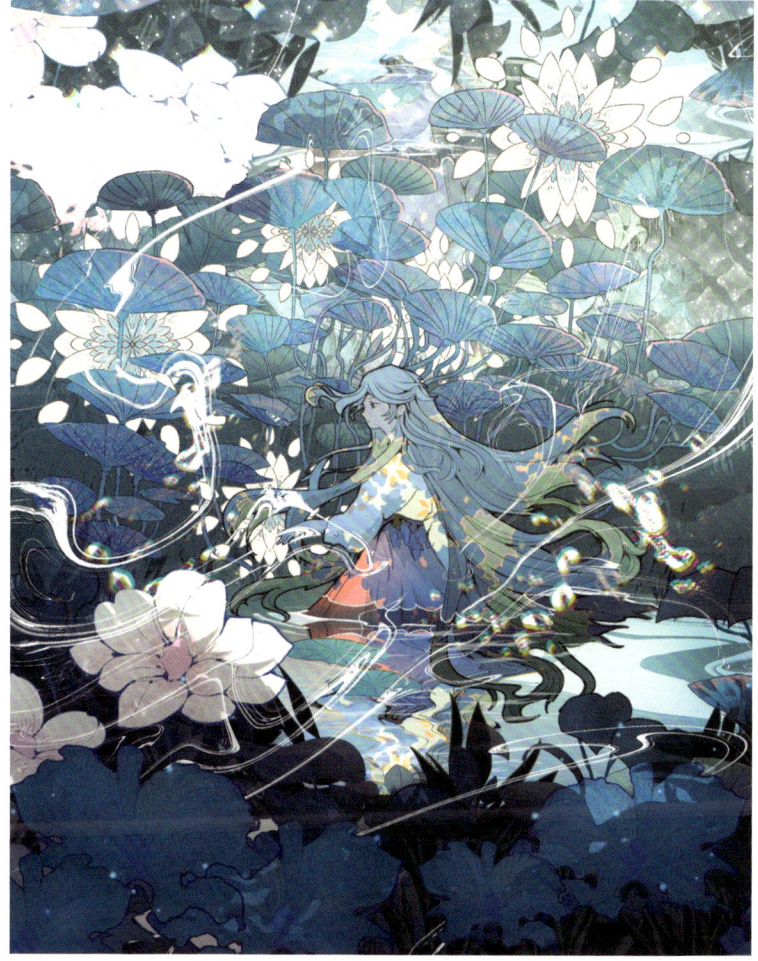

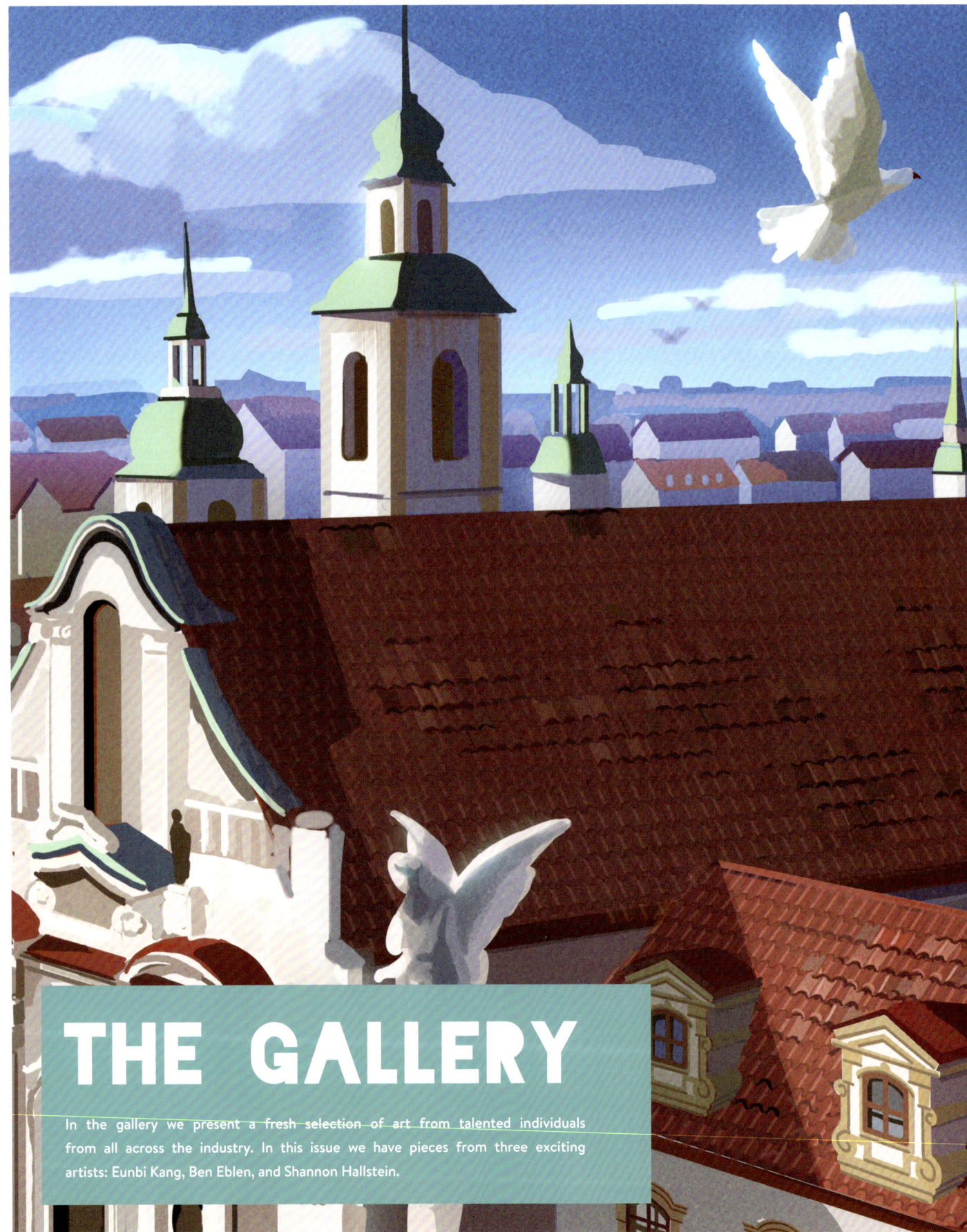

THE GALLERY

In the gallery we present a fresh selection of art from talented individuals from all across the industry. In this issue we have pieces from three exciting artists: Eunbi Kang, Ben Eblen, and Shannon Hallstein.

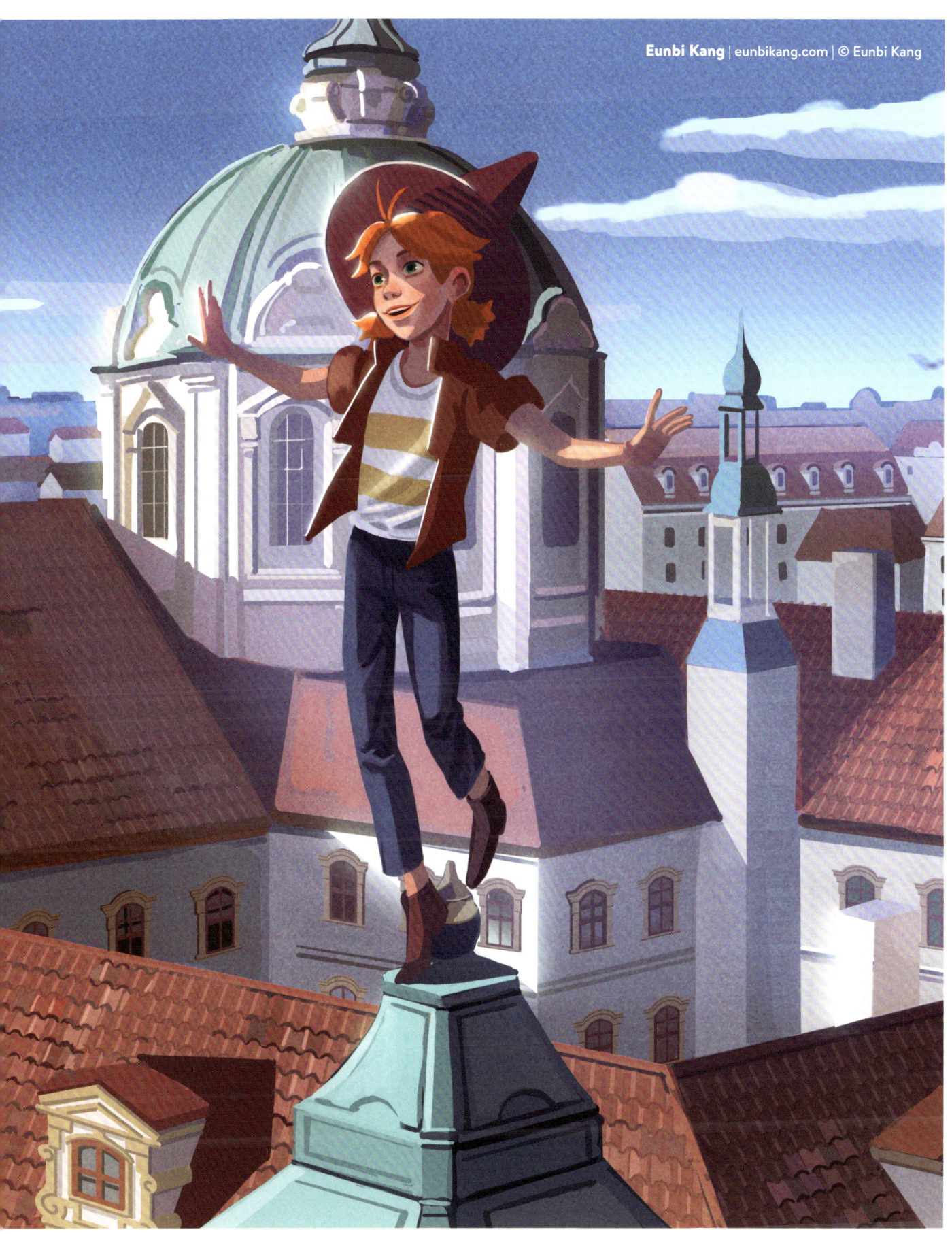

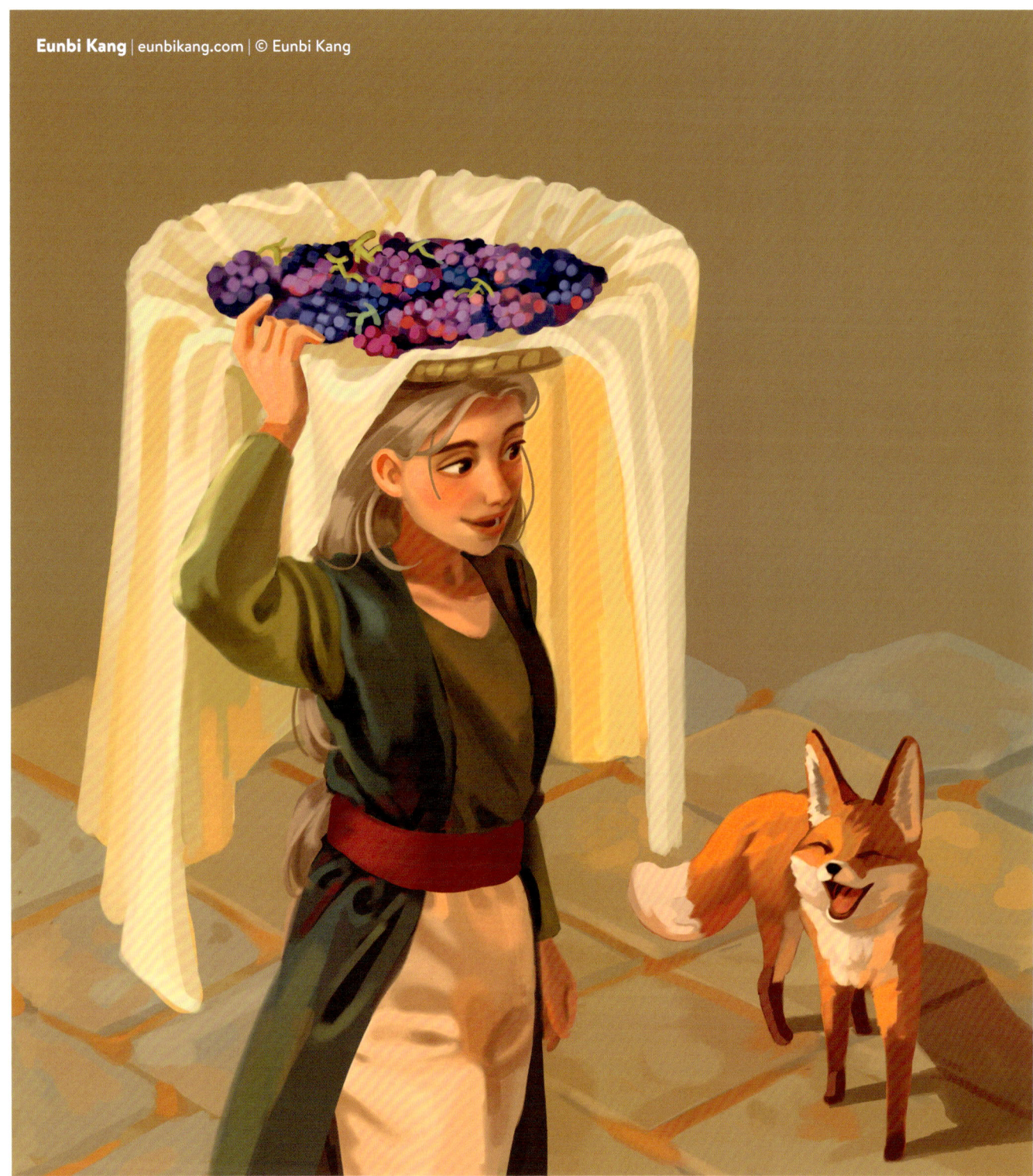

Eunbi Kang | eunbikang.com | © Eunbi Kang

EUNBI KANG IS A KOREAN VISUAL-DEVELOPMENT ARTIST AND ILLUSTRATOR WHO WON THE CONCEPT-ART AWARD IN 2022 FOR INDEPENDENT ENVIRONMENT. HER WORK IS INFLUENCED BY 3D ANIMATION STYLES, WITH A FASCINATION FOR VIBRANT COLOR PALETTES AND FANTASY THEMES.

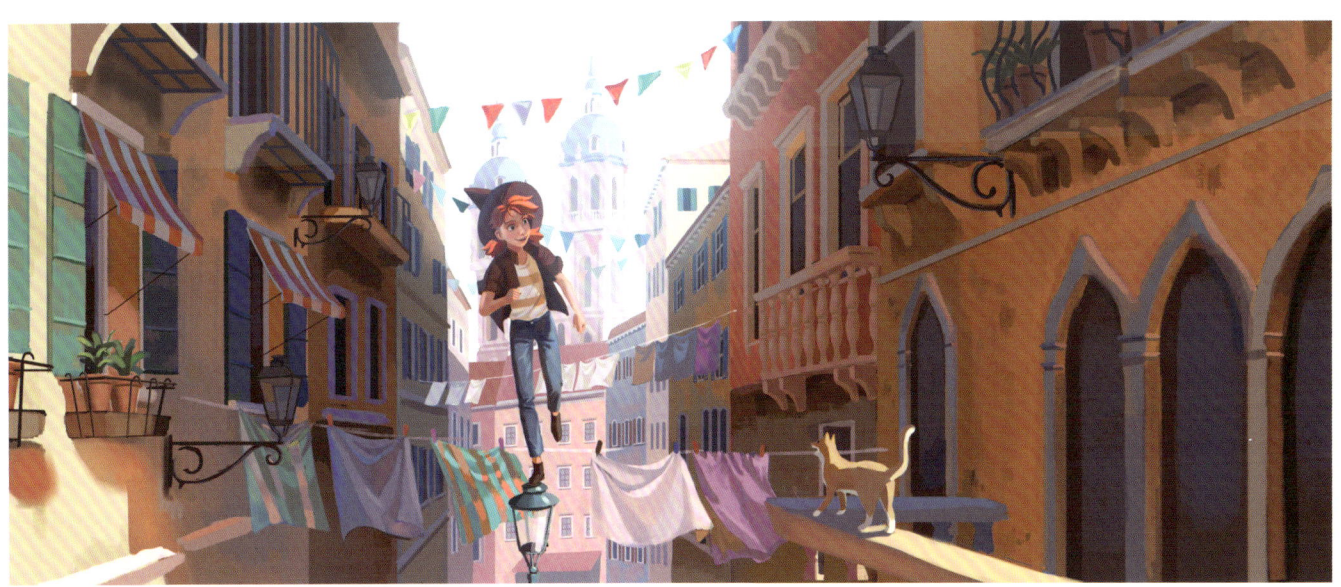

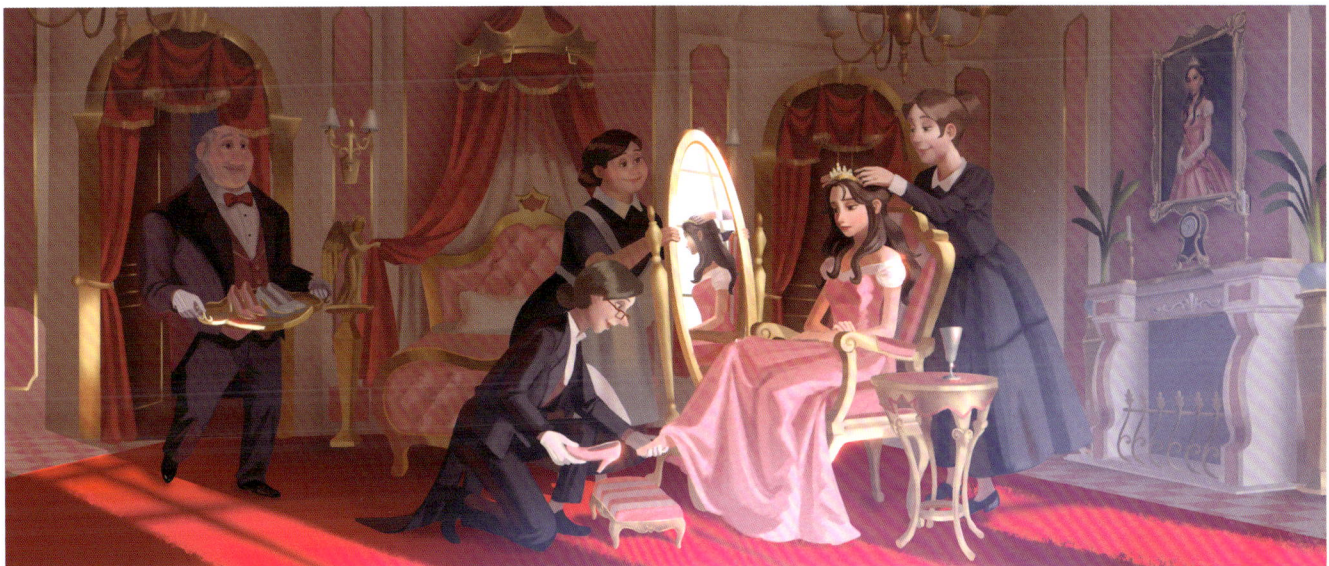

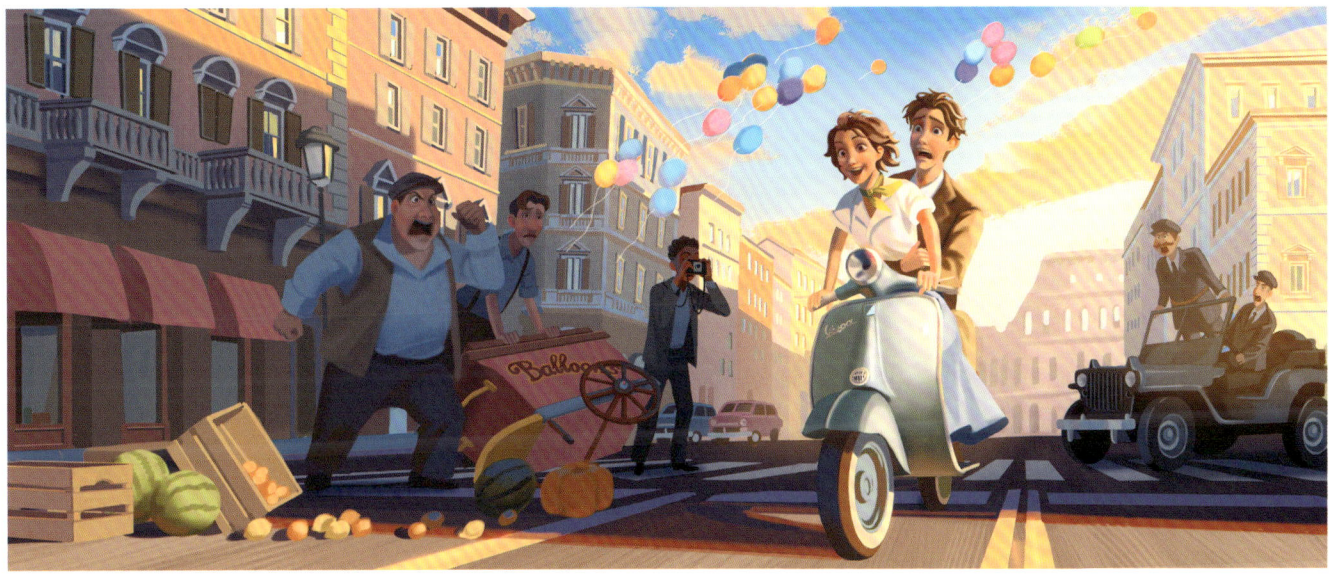

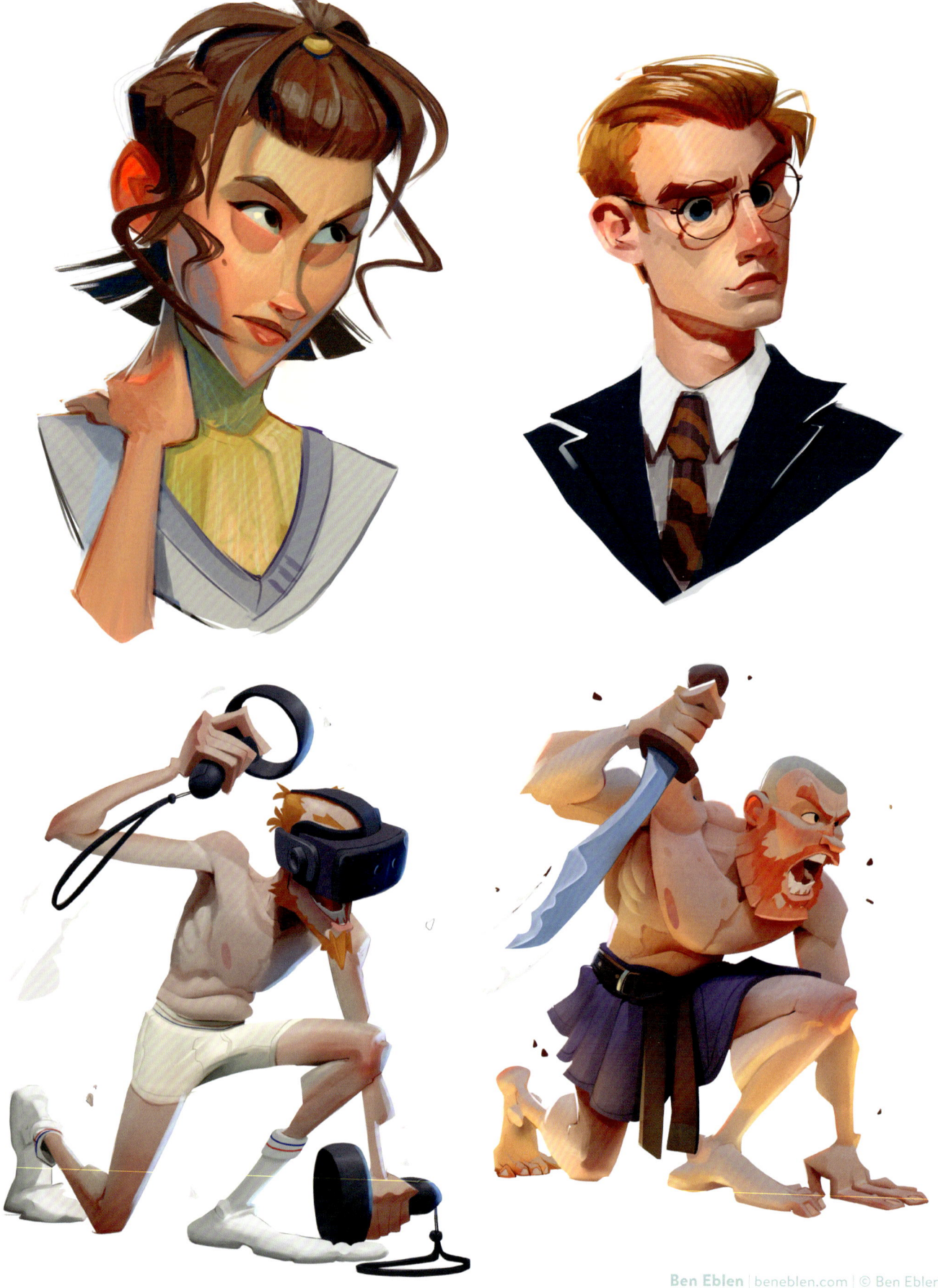

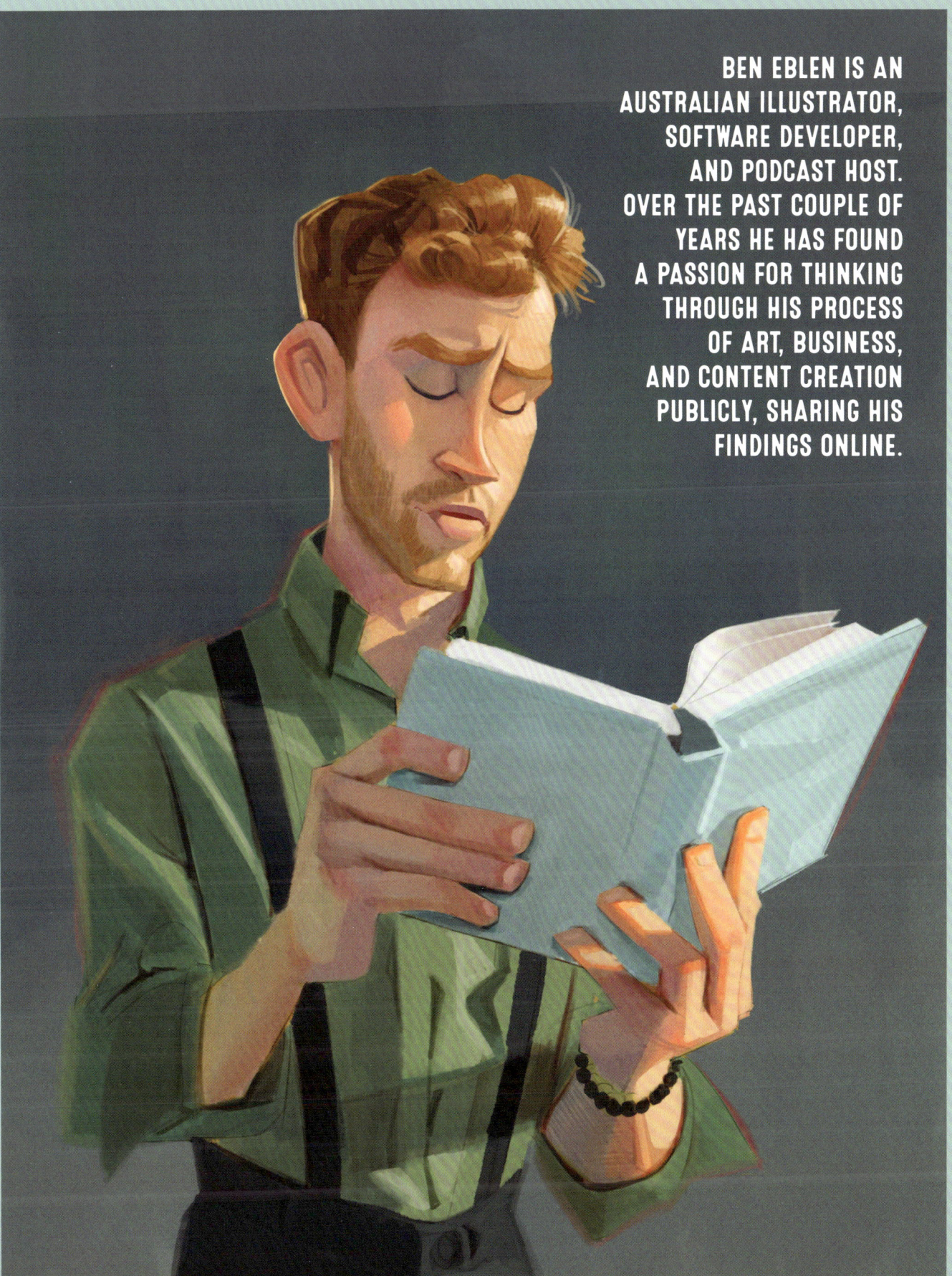

BEN EBLEN IS AN AUSTRALIAN ILLUSTRATOR, SOFTWARE DEVELOPER, AND PODCAST HOST. OVER THE PAST COUPLE OF YEARS HE HAS FOUND A PASSION FOR THINKING THROUGH HIS PROCESS OF ART, BUSINESS, AND CONTENT CREATION PUBLICLY, SHARING HIS FINDINGS ONLINE.

Shannon Hallstein | shannonhallstein.com | © Shannon Hallstein

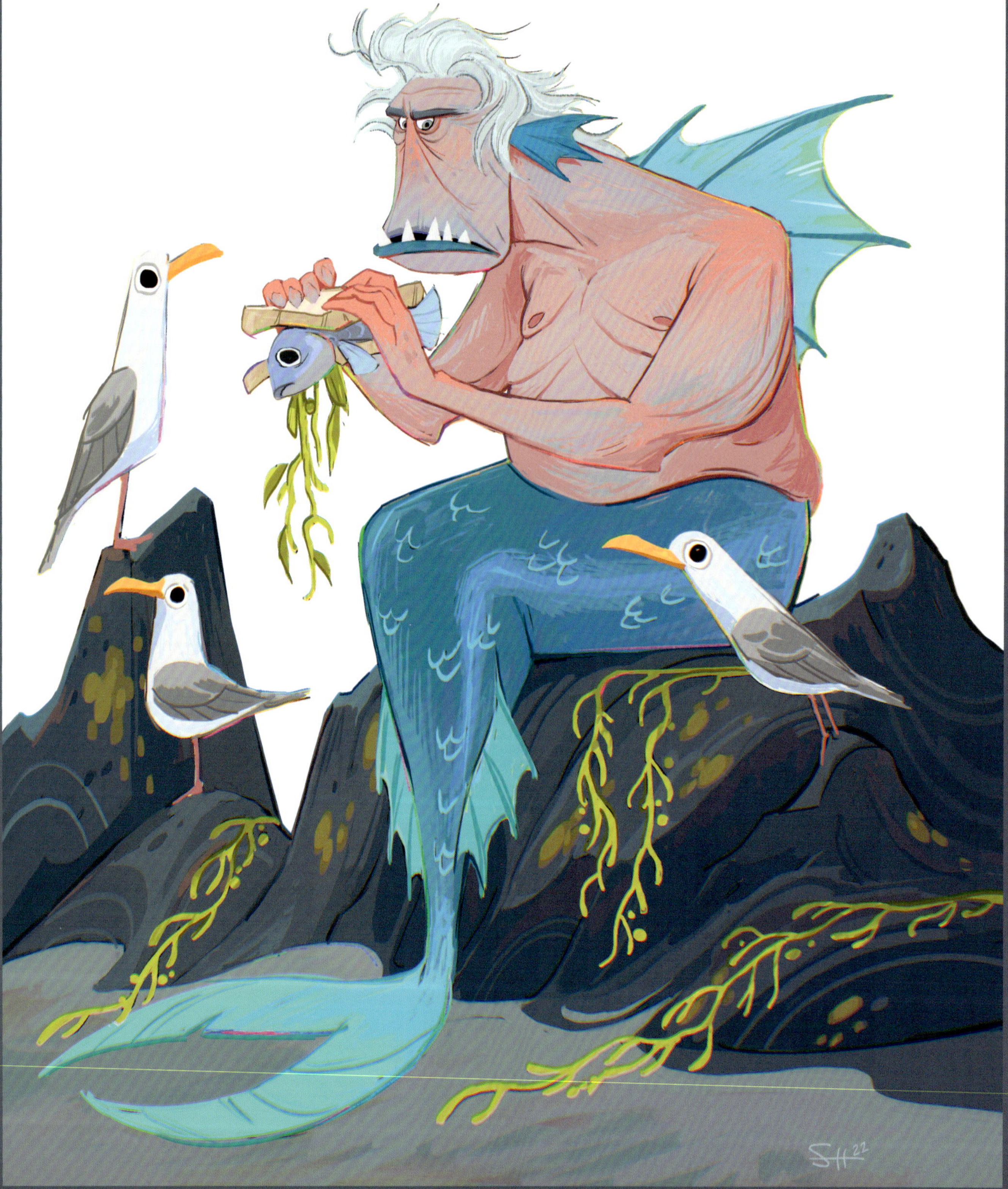

SHANNON HAS BEEN A VISUAL-DEVELOPMENT ARTIST WORKING PROFESSIONALLY IN THE INDUSTRY FOR FIVE YEARS AT MULTIPLE STUDIOS, SUCH AS DREAMWORKS, WARNER BROTHERS, AND WALT DISNEY ANIMATION STUDIOS.
SHE LOVES THE COLLABORATIVE PROCESS OF WORKING ALONGSIDE OTHER TALENTED ARTISTS TO BE NOT ONLY INSPIRED, BUT TO CREATE SOMETHING TRULY SPECIAL.
IN BETWEEN PROJECTS, SHE LIKES TO PAINT HER OWN STORIES, PLAY GUITAR, AND BAKE DELECTABLE TREATS.

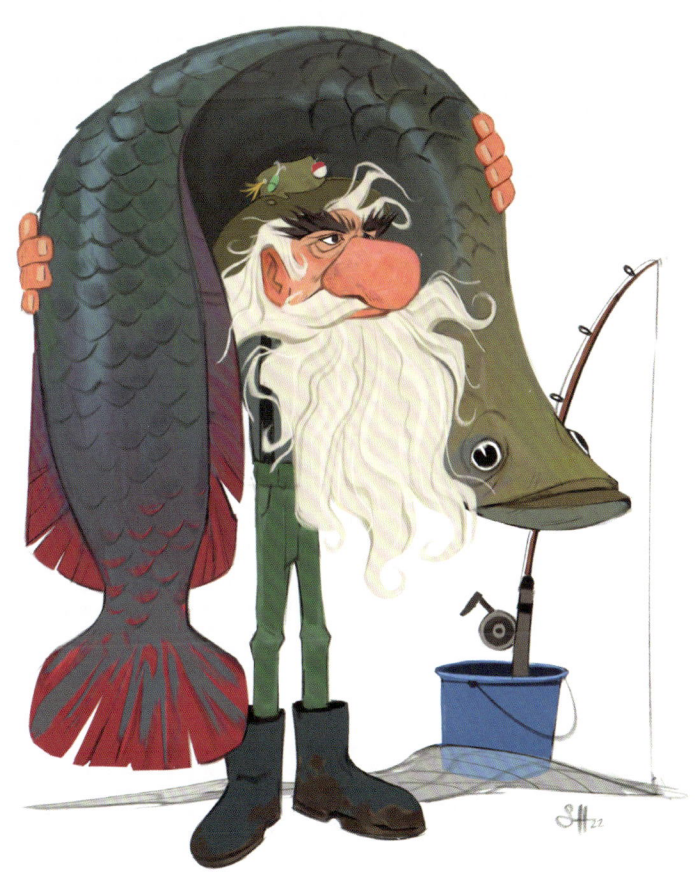

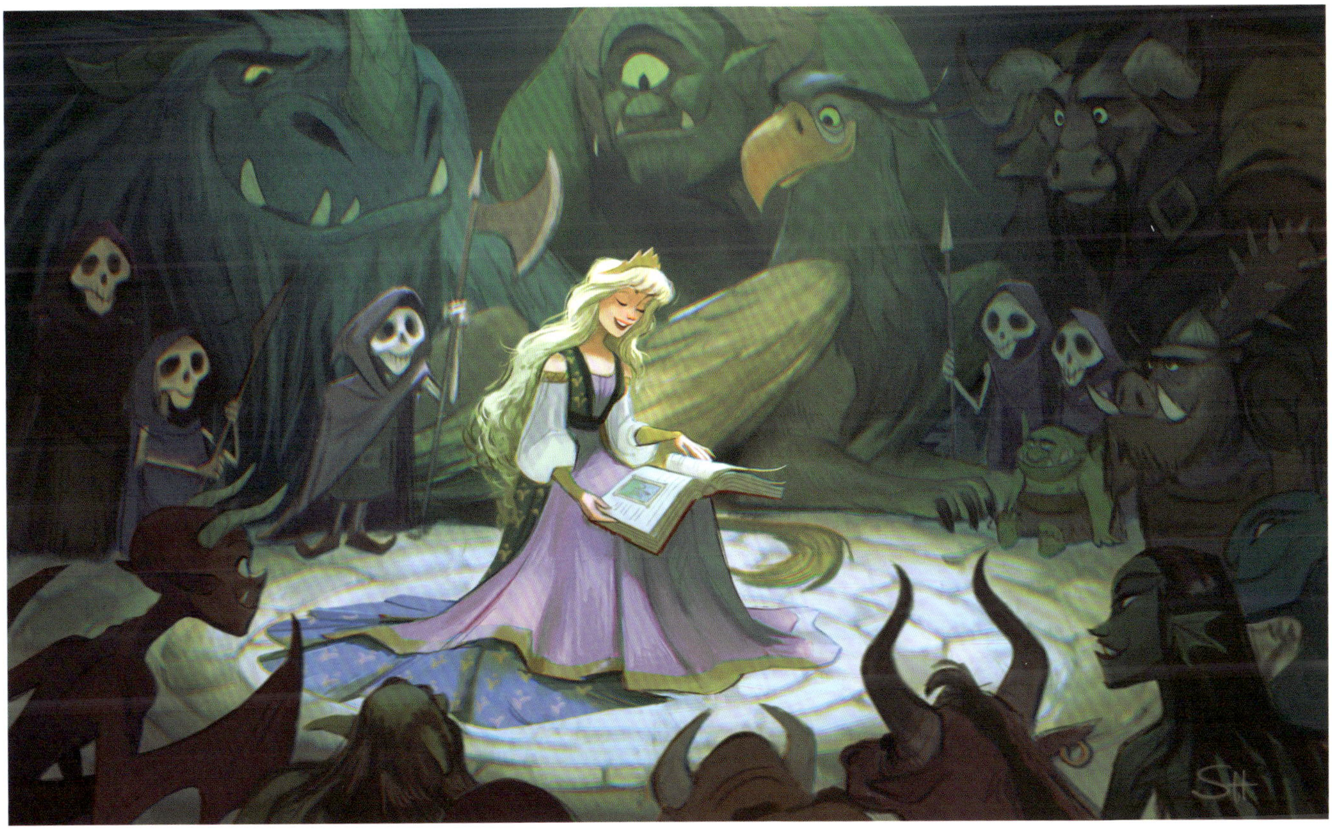

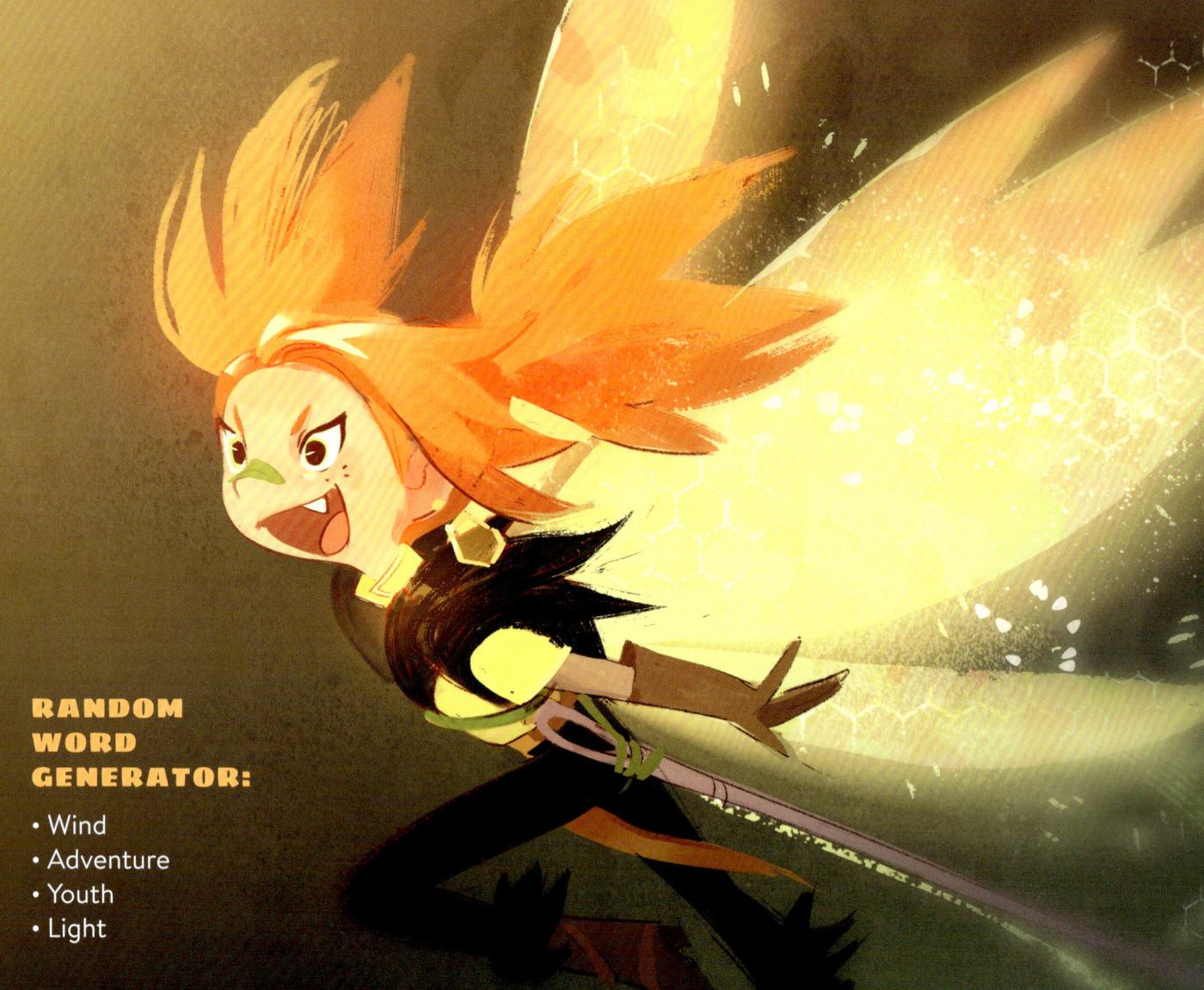

RANDOM WORD GENERATOR:

- Wind
- Adventure
- Youth
- Light

STING LIKE A BEE

ANASTASIIA PLATOSHYNA

In this tutorial I will cover my approach to creating a character design based on a four-word prompt. The keywords that I am working with are "Wind, Adventure, Youth, Light." I will demonstrate how to come up with initial ideas based on this prompt and how to transform them into a finalized character design. I hope you enjoy this creative journey as much as I enjoyed working on my character! Feel free to use your preferred medium to create your own version – my personal setup is a Wacom Cintiq 24, Adobe Photoshop, and an MSI laptop.

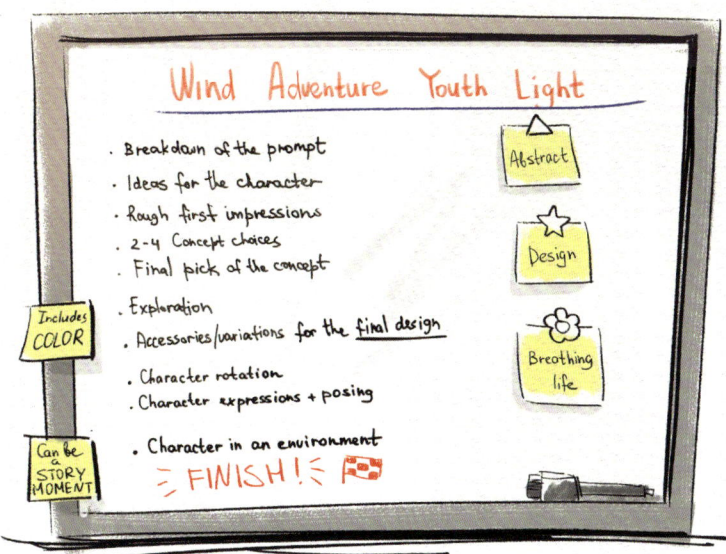

This page (top):
I use my trusty white board to plan

This page (bottom):
Using sticky notes is a great way to generate ideas

HOW TO BEGIN?

Staying organized will help you be efficient with your work, especially when you have tight deadlines! Even if you are creating your own project, planning your work ahead of time makes it easier to stay on track and focused. Breaking down the task into smaller manageable pieces will lighten your load as well as provide a more defined structure. Get a notepad or a white board to jot down your plan of action. You can even estimate how long each step will take you to complete. The more you practice organizing yourself this way, the more accurate your estimates will become.

BRAINSTORMING

Once you have a clear map of action, write down the prompt. I use sticky notes because they make it very easy to quickly cycle through my ideas. I write down any associations that come to mind when looking at each of the four words. There are no wrong answers or bad choices – it can be anything that pops into your head. Once you put your associations and abstract thoughts onto paper, you will start noticing some interesting combinations.

Next, narrow these ideas down to those that appeal the most. There are so many variations now – where to start?

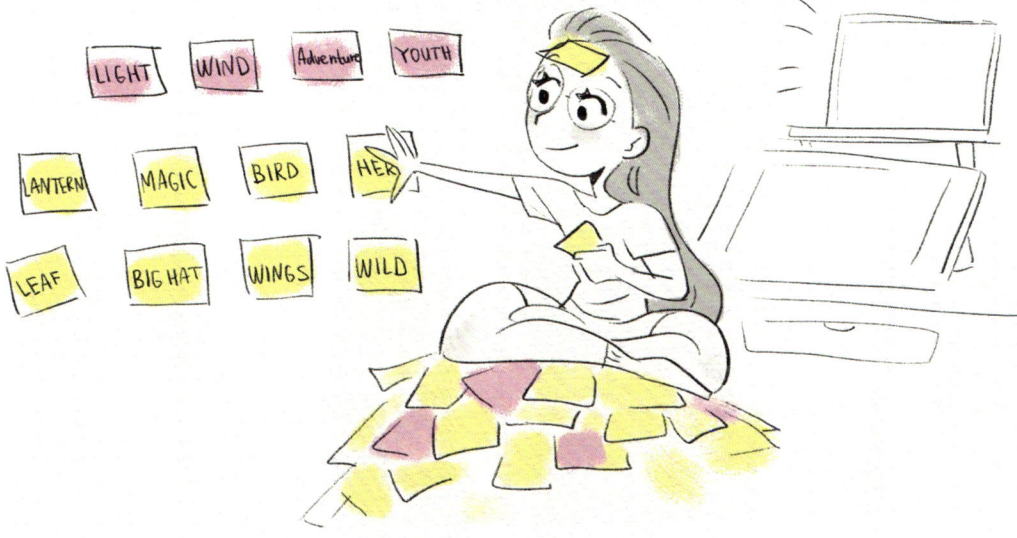

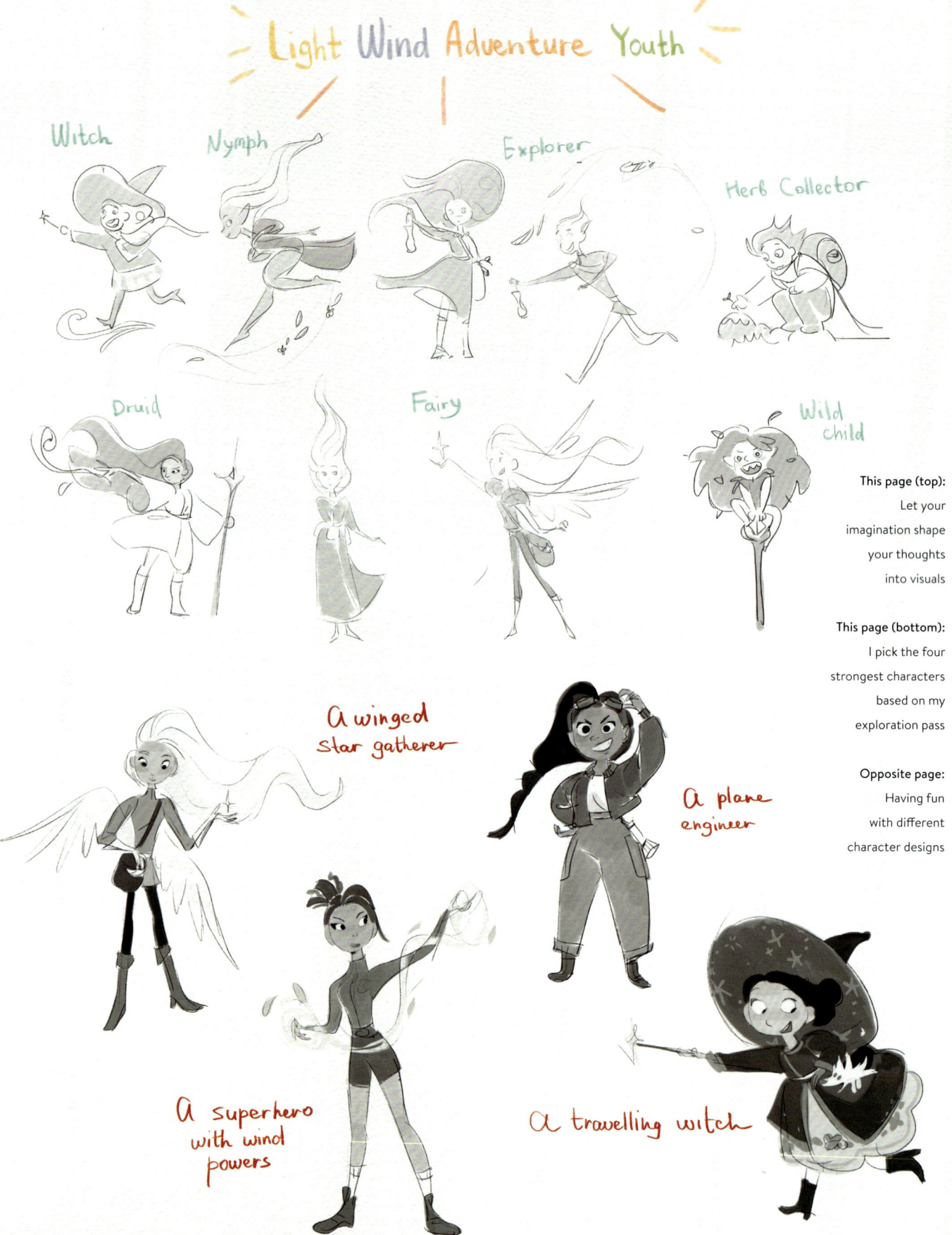

Light Wind Adventure Youth

Witch

Nymph

Explorer

Herb Collector

Druid

Fairy

Wild child

This page (top):
Let your imagination shape your thoughts into visuals

This page (bottom):
I pick the four strongest characters based on my exploration pass

Opposite page:
Having fun with different character designs

A winged star gatherer

A plane engineer

A superhero with wind powers

A travelling witch

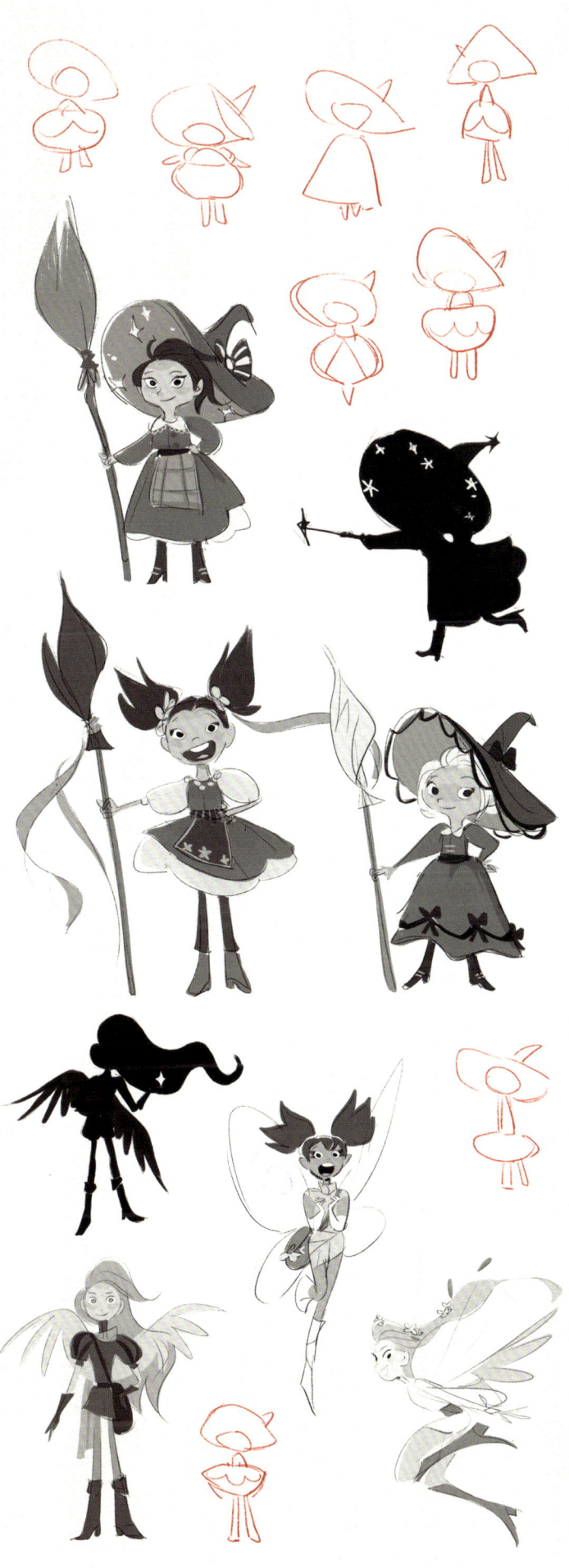

VISUALIZATION

It's time to start turning ideas into drawings. Your first explorations should evoke an immediate association with the prompt. I start sketching out the ideas that I came up with during the brainstorm session. The key is to keep in mind the prompt and stay true to the spirit of the assignment. All four elements should be present, even if you want to make one or two the focus and have the rest be supporting elements or items. Keep your sketches quick and loose and don't get too attached to any of the gestures just yet.

UNIQUENESS AND APPEAL

Now that you have a nice variety of raw concepts, pick out any that could lead to interesting characters with intriguing backstories. While visual appeal is very important, don't forget the traits your character needs to have. I try to keep a strong focus on at least two of the prompts and treat the other two as more complementary – this way I can balance the design a little better. For example, my first design has "wind" and "adventure" as the primary words, and "youth" and "light" secondary. Any of these sketches could be developed into a character, but only one will be your best personal interpretation of the prompts.

TAKING A CLOSER LOOK

To make it easier to pick one idea, sketch out your options in an exploratory way. By dabbling in each concept you can get a clearer idea of which direction you want to take.

I pick two concepts to develop further based on how much potential I think they have. I choose the winged star-gatherer and the witch because those two feel the most fun to me. Both explorations perfectly combined all four prompt words really well. I develop each further and find an interpretation of the winged character that draws me in, so I decide to proceed with a fairy concept.

RESEARCH AND REFERENCE

With a direction decided upon, it's time to do some research to make your character feel more believable and authentic. What species is your character? How old are they? Where do they live? Is it a real place? What's their lifestyle? Asking yourself these questions (and more) will help you choose your reference material and inform your design decisions later on. Researching your design will help make the character feel more grounded, even if they are fantastical. Consider putting all your reference material on a board or have a digital space that can display them.

SILHOUETTE AND SHAPE LANGUAGE

Next, we need to think of a strong silhouette and how to visually balance all of the character's elements and features. You do not have to start with complex shapes right away – you can use simple circles, squares, or triangles as the basic building blocks.

Readability is essential for a successful design, so the silhouette of your character needs to be clear. It should tell you something about their personality. Think about who your character might be – if they are friendly, use rounder shapes, if they are more edgy or even villainous, sharp shapes like triangles will help communicate that type of personality.

Rough Thumbnails

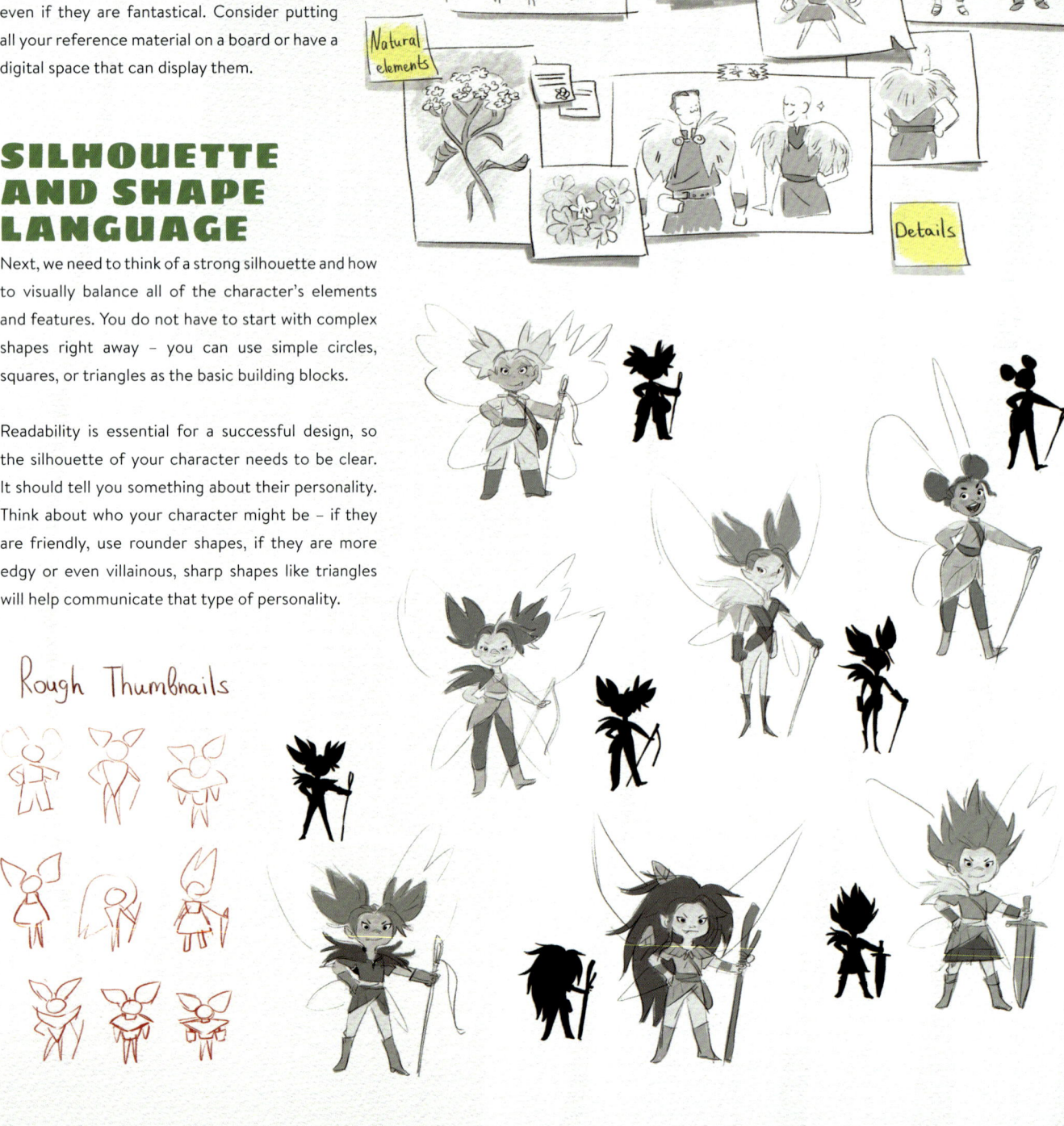

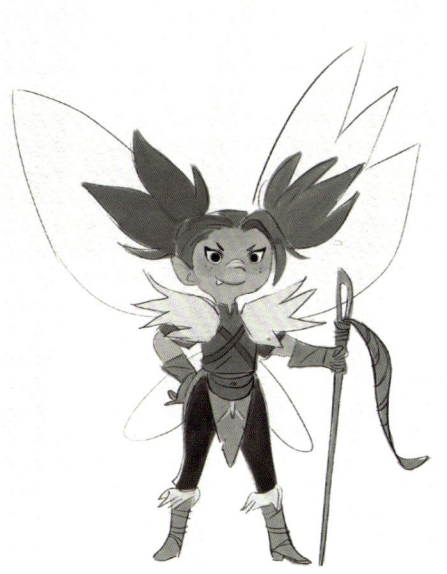

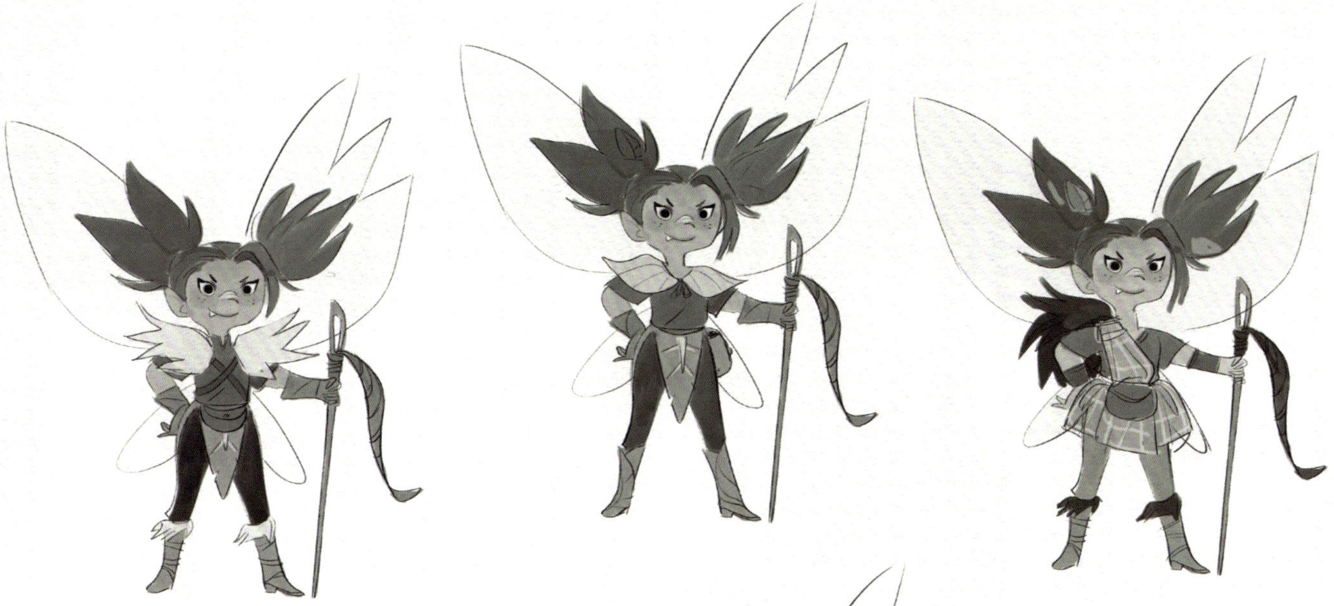

DESIGN WITHIN DESIGN

After establishing the overall silhouette, it's a good idea to explore various materials, textures, and accessories. The objective here is to give your character more depth. Do not forget about the character specific items that can help to flesh out their personality and backstory. I choose a needle for my fairy which resembles a bee's stinger. Make sure to refer back to your references or even add some new ones.

MEDIUM MATTERS!

When you work on a design you should keep in mind which medium you are illustrating for. The way you present the final look will be quite different depending on if the project is 2D, stop-motion, or CGI. 2D usually requires a very precise and clean final result, whether it is for a hand-drawn or rigged animation. Rigged animation has other limitations, because the design is further broken down into separate elements; all the parts of the character must be organized into a seamless structure that can be used to animate the design later. Stop-motion puppets are limited by real-world materials and physics. Design for CGI generally needs to have a lot of information on how all the shapes look in 3D space. Materials and textures should be considered when working on the design as well.

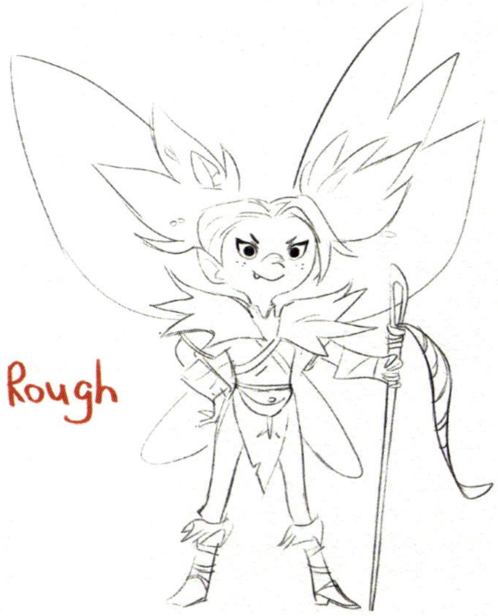

Rough

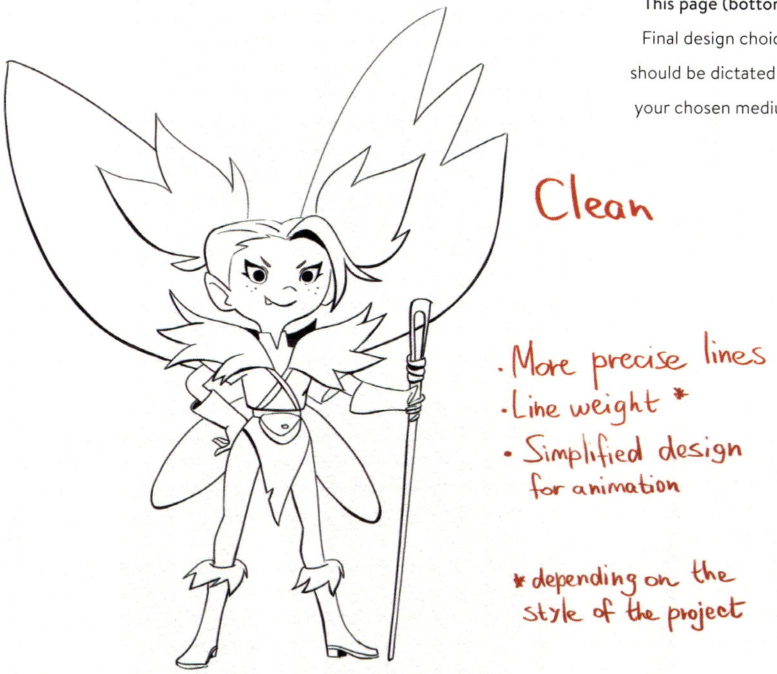

Clean

. More precise lines
. Line weight *
. Simplified design for animation

* depending on the style of the project

Opposite page (top):
Collecting reference material helps make your character feel more authentic

Opposite page (bottom):
Silhouette variations

This page (top):
Variations of looks, materials, and textures

This page (bottom):
Final design choices should be dictated by your chosen medium

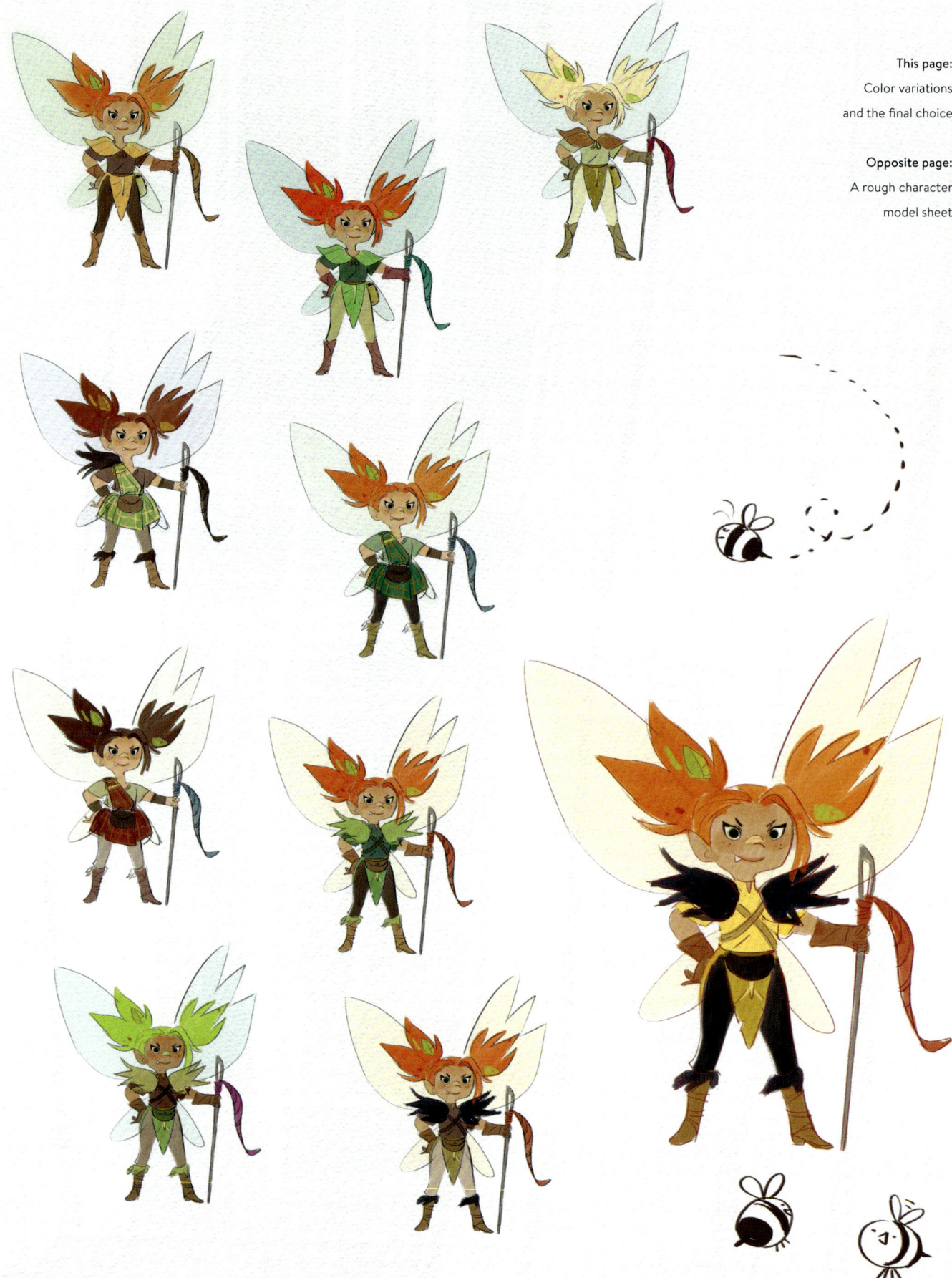

This page:
Color variations
and the final choice

Opposite page:
A rough character
model sheet

COMBINING COLORS

Color communicates as much as the design itself – it's a very powerful visual storytelling tool. Different palettes have different effects on how the character is perceived by the audience. I explore lots of greens, bright yellows, and oranges to convey the idea of youthfulness and the energetic nature of the character. I pick a yellow and black combination to evoke the feeling of a troublemaker and an association with bees. This fairy flies like a butterfly and stings like a bee, for sure! When you work on your color combinations, do not forget to check if the values have a good synergy. To do this, put a black-and-white filter on top of your variations to check the values and adjust them accordingly.

SPINNING AROUND

Rotation (or the model sheet) is a stepping stone toward the final stages of your design. In the industry, more often than not, you need to have a character rotation to inform modeling artists, animators, or pose artists how to interpret your illustration. The design needs to not only be appealing, but also functional. When you work on turning your character, think of the mechanics of their structure, and keep the shapes and volumes consistent throughout. The decisions you make here will carry over to the expressions and posing of your character. You want to show each angle that will provide new information about the design.

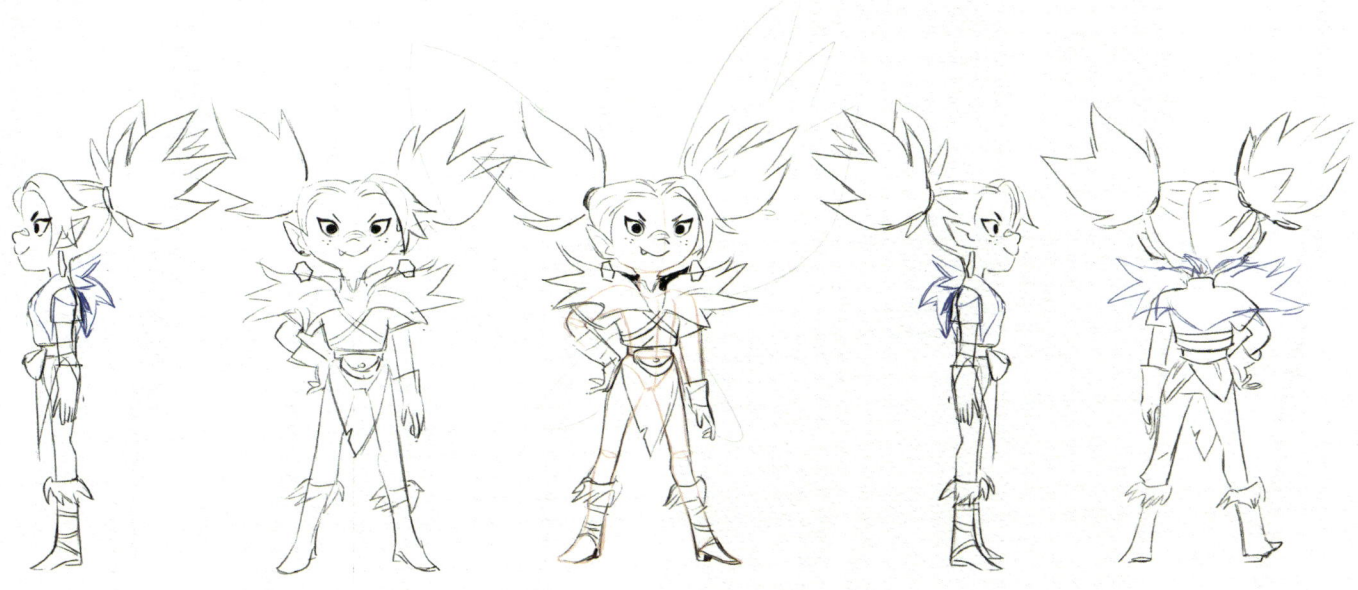

"WHEN YOU WORK ON TURNING YOUR CHARACTER, THINK OF THE MECHANICS OF THEIR STRUCTURE, AND KEEP THE SHAPES AND VOLUMES CONSISTENT THROUGHOUT"

FEEDBACK

Don't be scared to share your progress with others! Sometimes, a fresh set of eyes will pick up on what could be improved. Ask a friend, colleague, or even an artist you look up to for their impressions of your work. Honest feedback gives you a better perspective on your design.

THUMBNAILS

- Trouble maker
- Thick-skulled but fearless
- Takes on tough tasks
- Bashful
- Picks on opponents who are much bigger

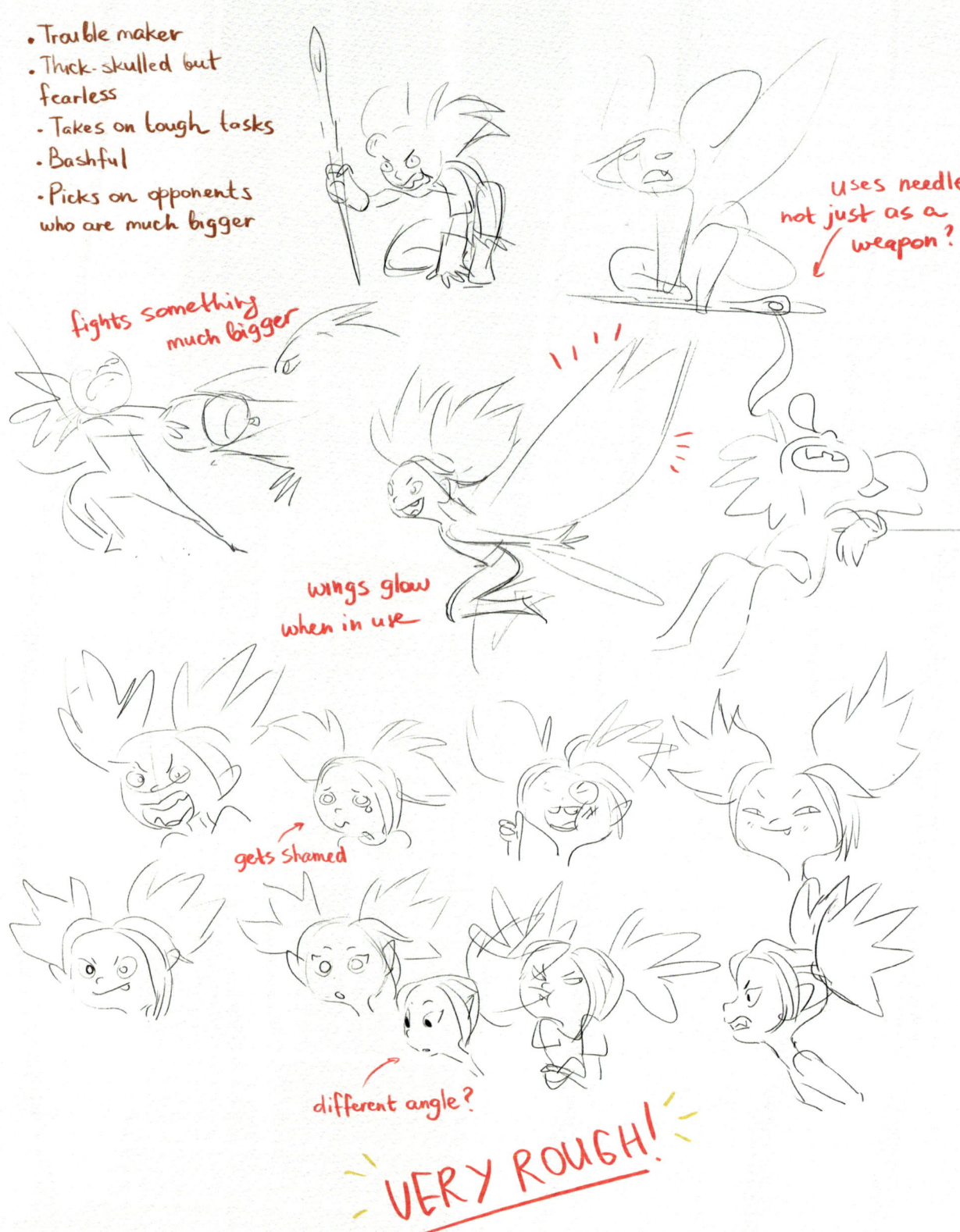

uses needle not just as a weapon?

fights something much bigger

wings glow when in use

gets shamed

different angle?

VERY ROUGH!

GESTURES AND THUMBNAILS

When working on posing and expressions, your ultimate objective is to showcase what your character is all about – you are deciding how best to introduce them to your audience. Make some quick notes and draw some simple gestures to work out which poses and expressions describe your character the best. I draw some loose thumbnails of how my character might act and situations they might end up in. These sketches don't need to be clean or even on model! Just try and channel pure energy and intent. Have fun with them, too – the mechanics can be figured out later.

EXPRESSIONS

Your character has a unique personality that should shine through in how they express their emotions. Humans can be happy in many different ways and the way we show our emotions is also different from everyone else – the same goes for your character. While it's important to showcase the mechanics of the face, tailoring each expression to their personality will give the expressions more depth and sincerity. I choose emotions that communicate my character's stubbornness and her adventurous spirit.

Opposite page:
Very loose sketches and notes help bring the character to life

This page:
A variety of angles and range of emotions

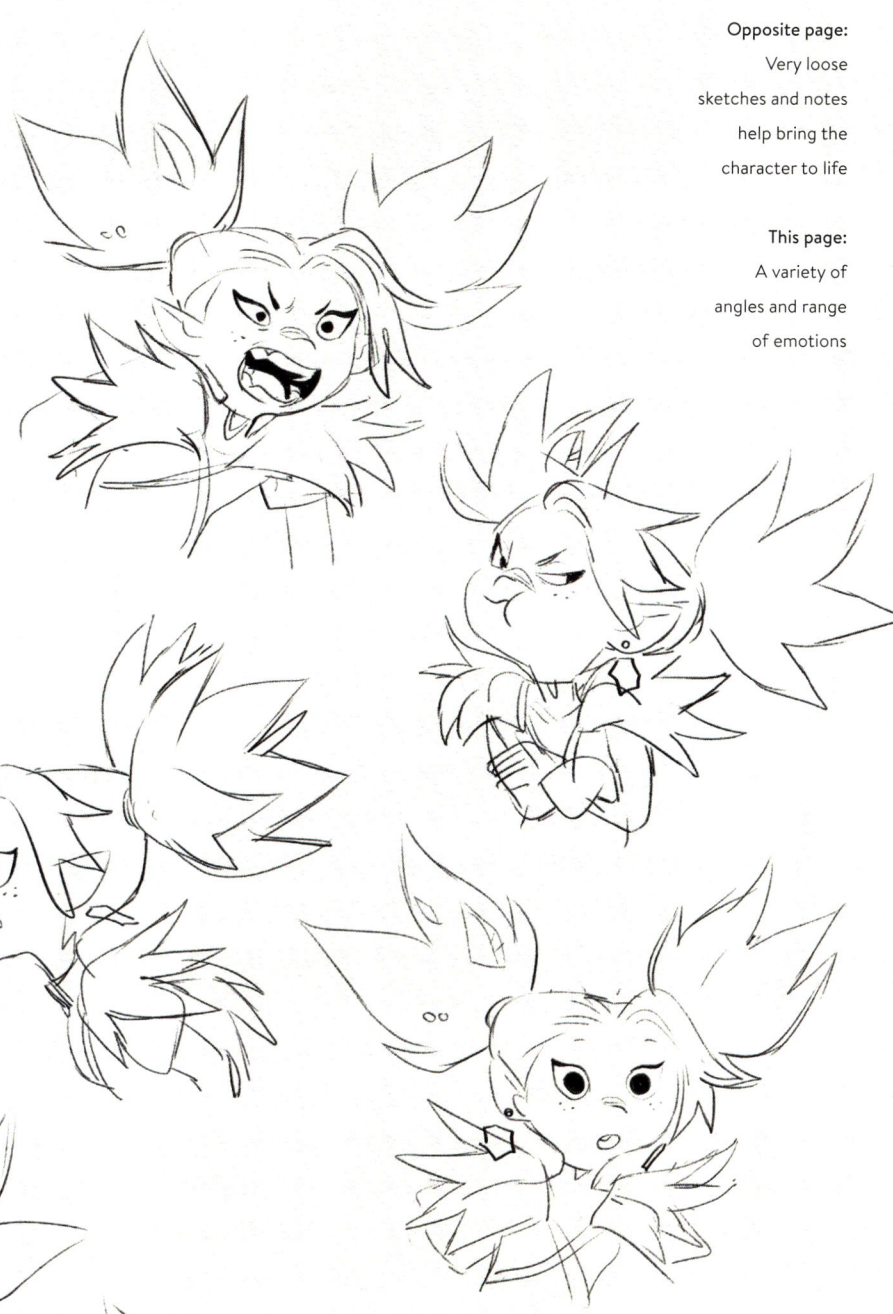

POSING

Posing is an extension of expressions, using body language to emote, rather than the face. Think of the sort of situations your character could end up in – how would they behave? What would their reaction be? Refer back to your thumbnails and notes for inspiration. Posing also helps us understand how the character moves. The goal here is to keep the character consistent while channeling the energy from your thumbnails. You want to keep the shapes interesting and push the poses. Exaggeration helps to make a better silhouette, which in turn makes the intent of the pose clear.

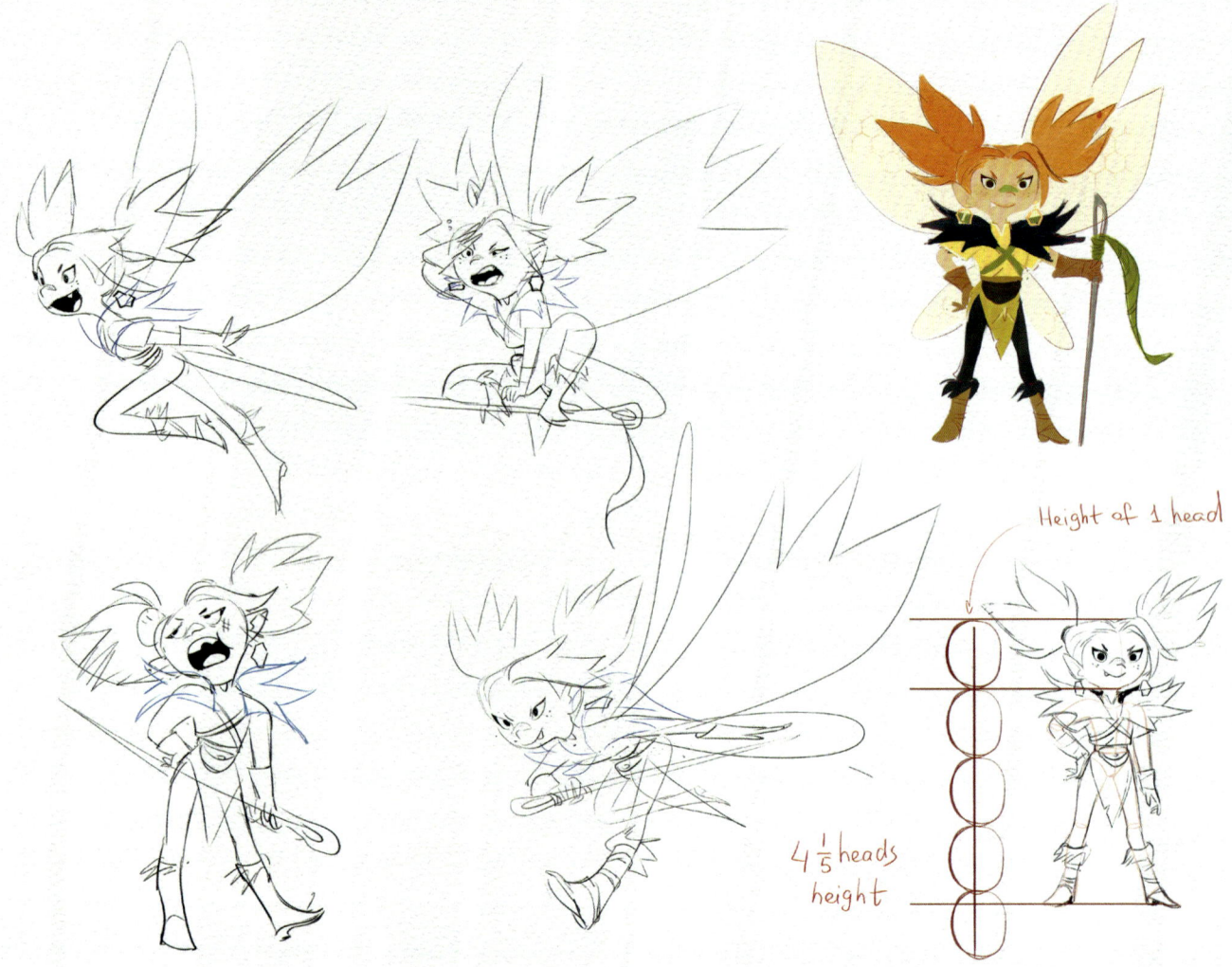

Height of 1 head

4 1/5 heads height

DEVELOPING YOUR SHORTHAND

Life-drawing and café sketching is a great way to improve drawing gestures and anatomy. Doing short photo studies is a good way to be a better draughtsman, too. The way people interact with each other and move can also inspire you with unique ideas for story moments.

This page:
My bee fairy is adventurous, determined, and hot-headed

Opposite page:
My character is placed into an environment

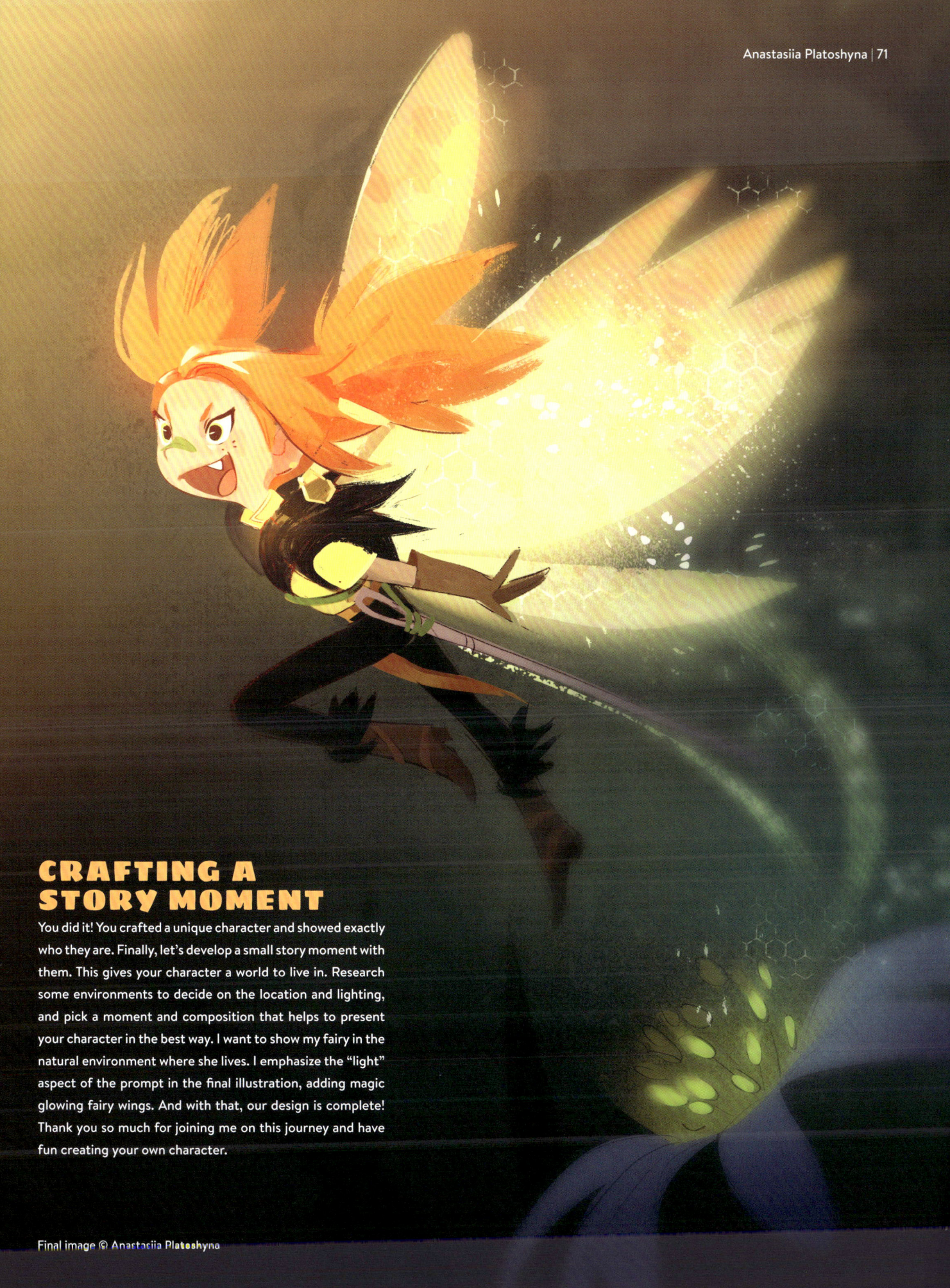

CRAFTING A STORY MOMENT

You did it! You crafted a unique character and showed exactly who they are. Finally, let's develop a small story moment with them. This gives your character a world to live in. Research some environments to decide on the location and lighting, and pick a moment and composition that helps to present your character in the best way. I want to show my fairy in the natural environment where she lives. I emphasize the "light" aspect of the prompt in the final illustration, adding magic glowing fairy wings. And with that, our design is complete! Thank you so much for joining me on this journey and have fun creating your own character.

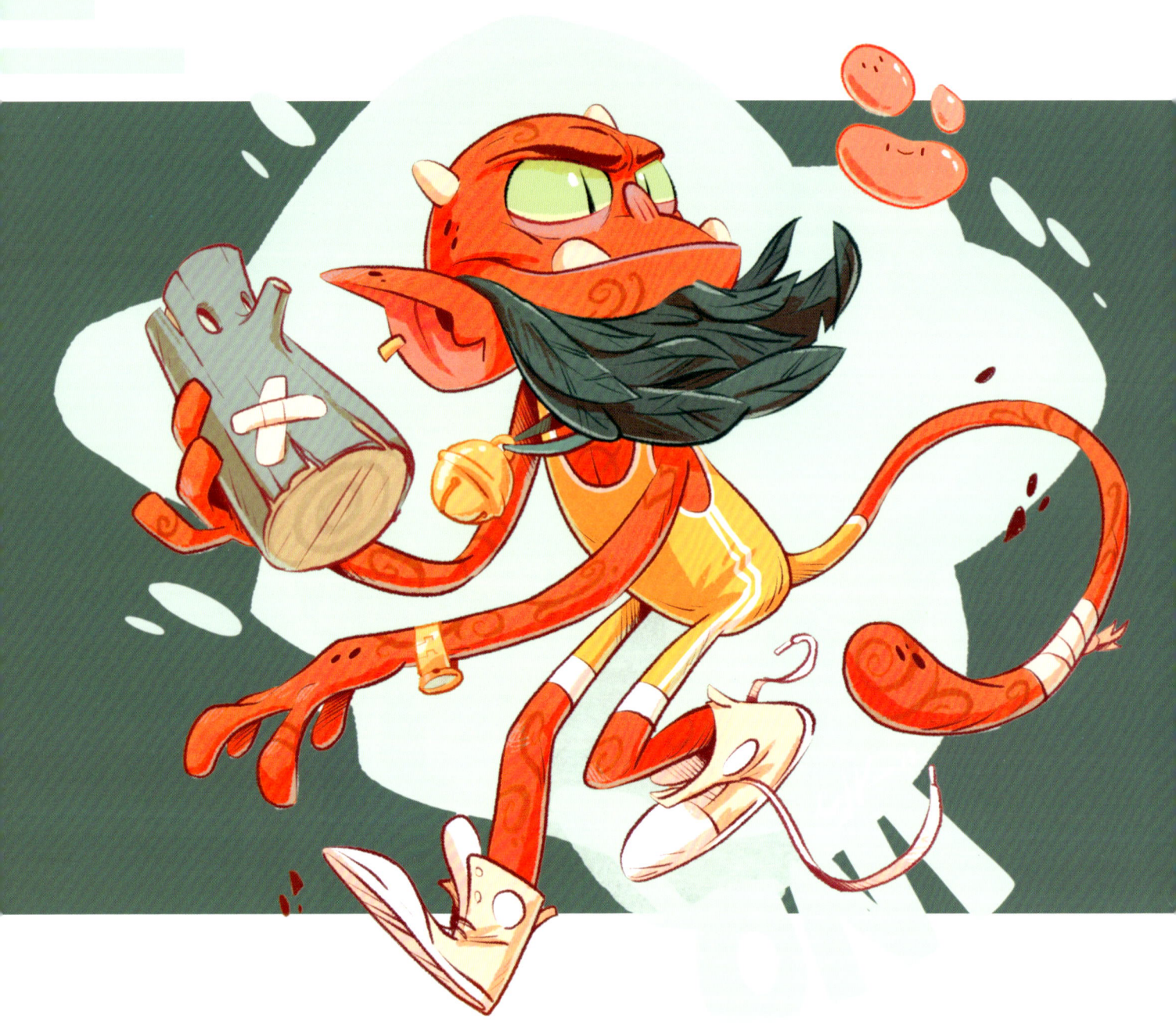

MEET THE ARTIST:
CAM KENDELL

Cam Kendell is a prolific freelance illustrator who has worked with some of the biggest names in publishing and more recently created art for a wide variety of board games. We spoke to Cam about the challenges of working within that particular medium, his tips for working as a freelance artist, and the secrets behind his "gritty-cute" character designs.

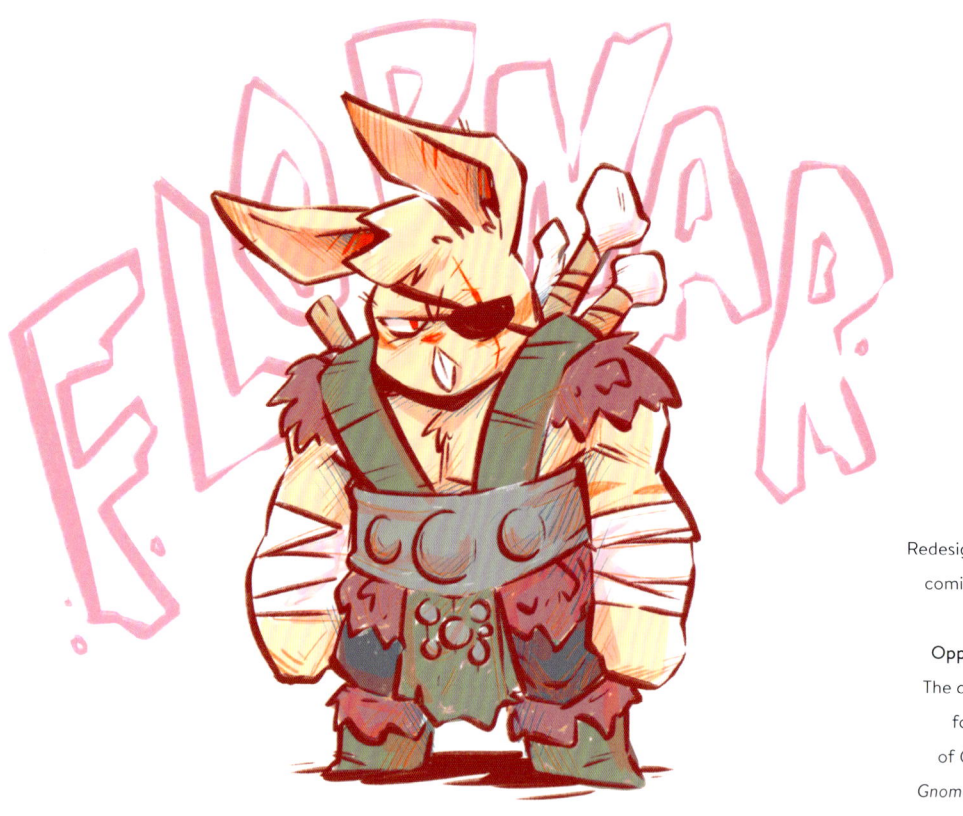

This page:
Redesign of an old
comic character

Opposite page:
The cover image
for issue two
of *Choose Your
Gnome Adventure*

Hi Cam, it's great to speak to you! Could you start by letting our readers know a little about what you do and your career so far?

Thanks so much for chatting with me! It's an honor. Basically, this is what I do: I spend anywhere from four to nine hours a day, five days a week, huddled over a glowing screen pushing pixels around, until a tiny visual world is brought forth before my eyes. I'm a freelance artist!

2022 marked ten years working in the industry as a self-employed illustrator for hire. The early years saw me working with a smorgasbord of companies and clients on an incredibly diverse range of projects – everything from indie comics and character design, to local youth projects, and an absolutely endless number of dental whiteboard videos! More recently, I've largely worked on projects in the board-game and publishing industries.

What would you say are the hallmarks of a Cam Kendell character design?

Gritty-cute? I think (or at least hope) that's what would best describe my designs. My characters are very cartoony and filled to the brim with cuteness. When others comment on my art they often say "how cute," which, honestly, used to really bug me when I was first starting out. I wanted to be taken seriously as an artist and the image of a serious artist didn't mesh with things being "cute." I can now accept that my art is cute *and* I'm a serious artist – the two go together just fine.

I love incorporating a bit of grittiness into my characters – little details that give them a sense of having lived through things. Maybe not terribly horrible things, but things all the same. Most of my characters aren't prancing around in perfectly tailored outfits – unless, of course, that's the story that needs to be told!

Lastly, shapes and emotions play a large role in my designs. I strive to have strong shapes for every character. Ideally, they should be recognizable as a silhouette just as quickly as when rendered out fully. Character design is about telling a story, and stories are about portraying emotion. When I'm designing a character, I'm trying to ensure they can also show emotion clearly.

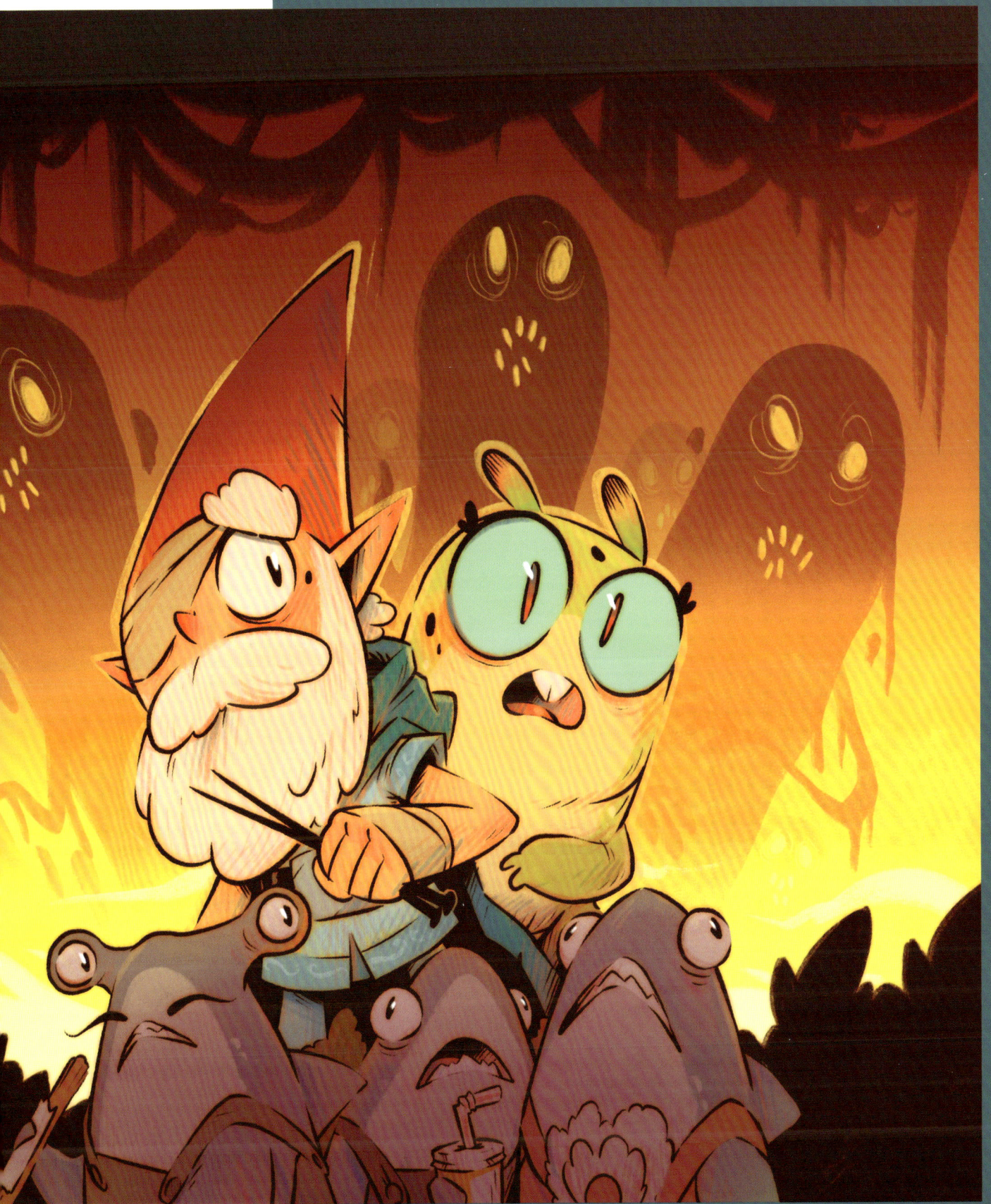

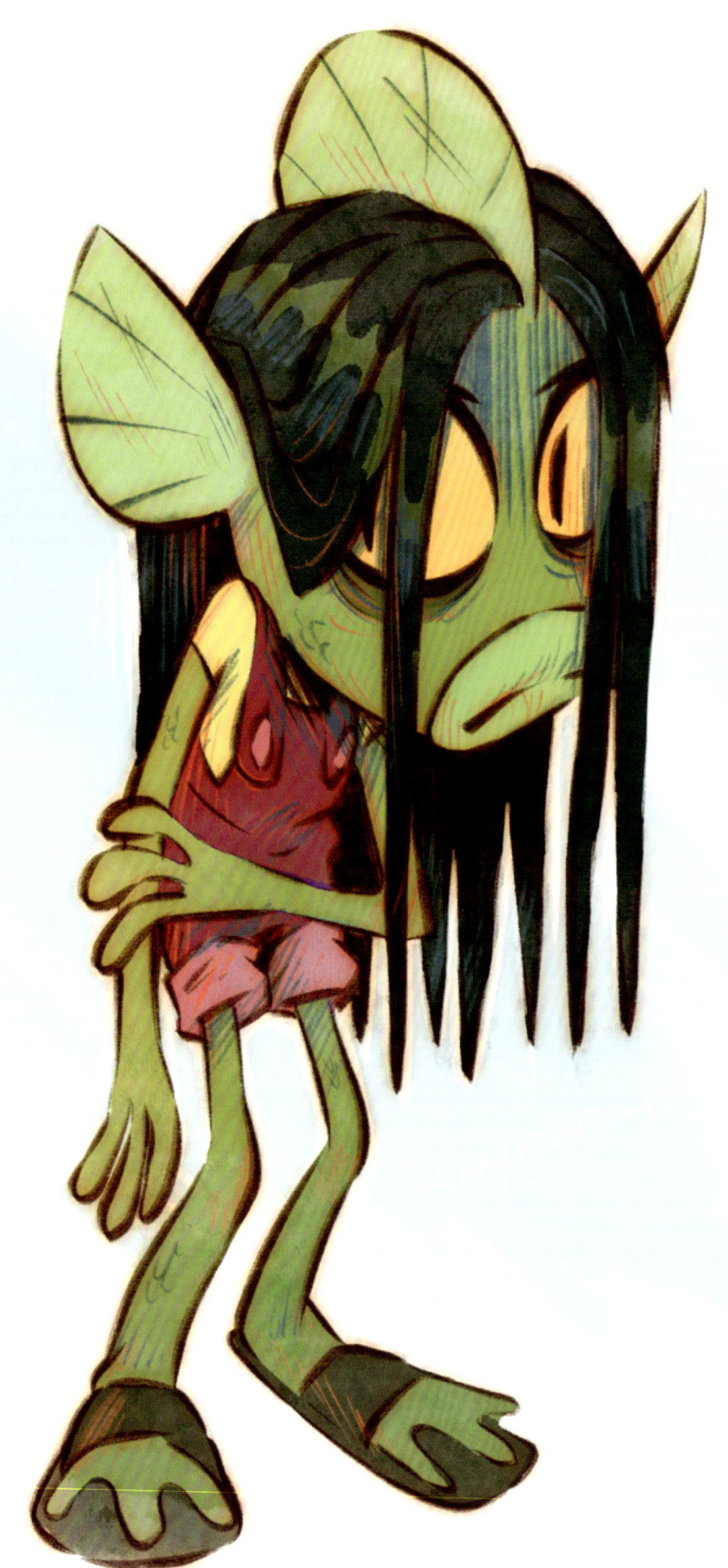

This page: Gill, the
swamp creature –
the new kid in school

Opposite page (top):
Character redesign of
the main character from
a personal project

Opposite page (bottom):
Exploring expressions for
the character Mortimer

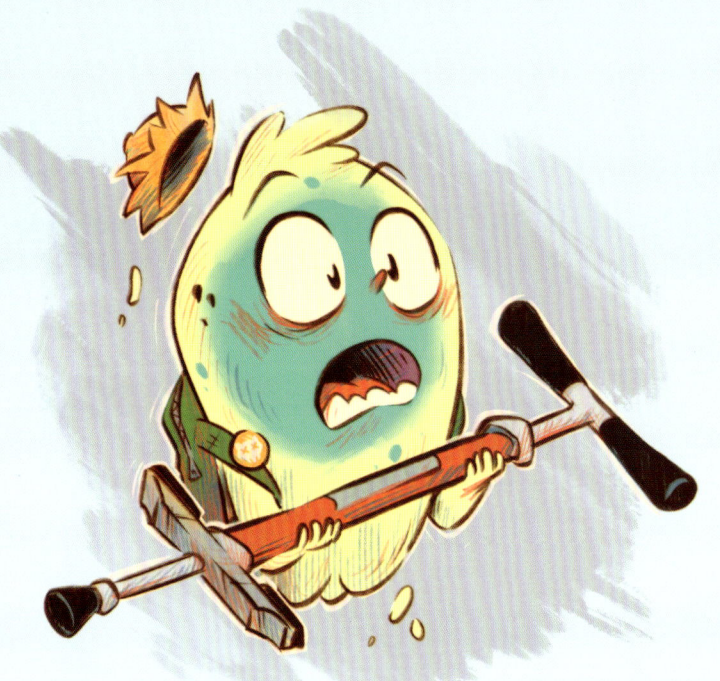

Is there anything specific you have to consider when designing characters for board games?

When I'm designing characters for board games a lot of things are the same as when I'm designing for books or comics. Ultimately, I'm trying to tell a story and attempting to use everything about their design to tell that story: clothing, shapes, expressions, accessories, and more.

One unique element of board games is that I'm typically not going to be drawing the character as many times as I would be for a publishing project (especially comics), so I can afford the time and effort to put a little more story and detail into their designs. I can add extra points of interest to their clothing or accessories that would otherwise be a nightmare if I had to draw them 100 times or more. The best part of doing this is that it gives players little nuggets of detail to find as they're looking at the pieces, waiting for their turn. I love hearing "Oh, look! I just noticed the little..."

At the same time, I have to make sure I don't go overboard. The first priority is to create characters that help the game be playable and to ensure the art serves, not detracts, from the game play. So, all the cool extra details have to be secondary or tertiary reads and not visually distracting.

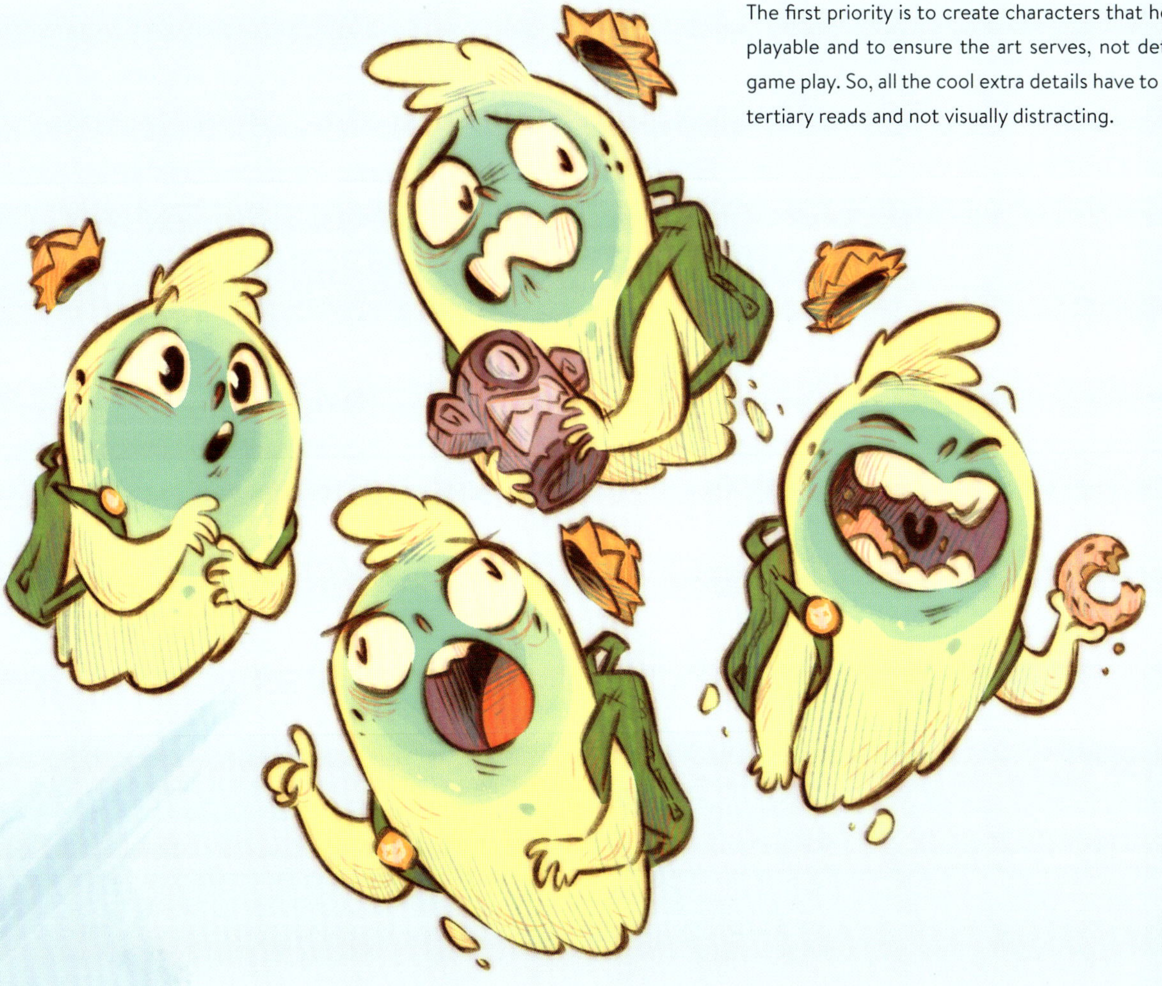

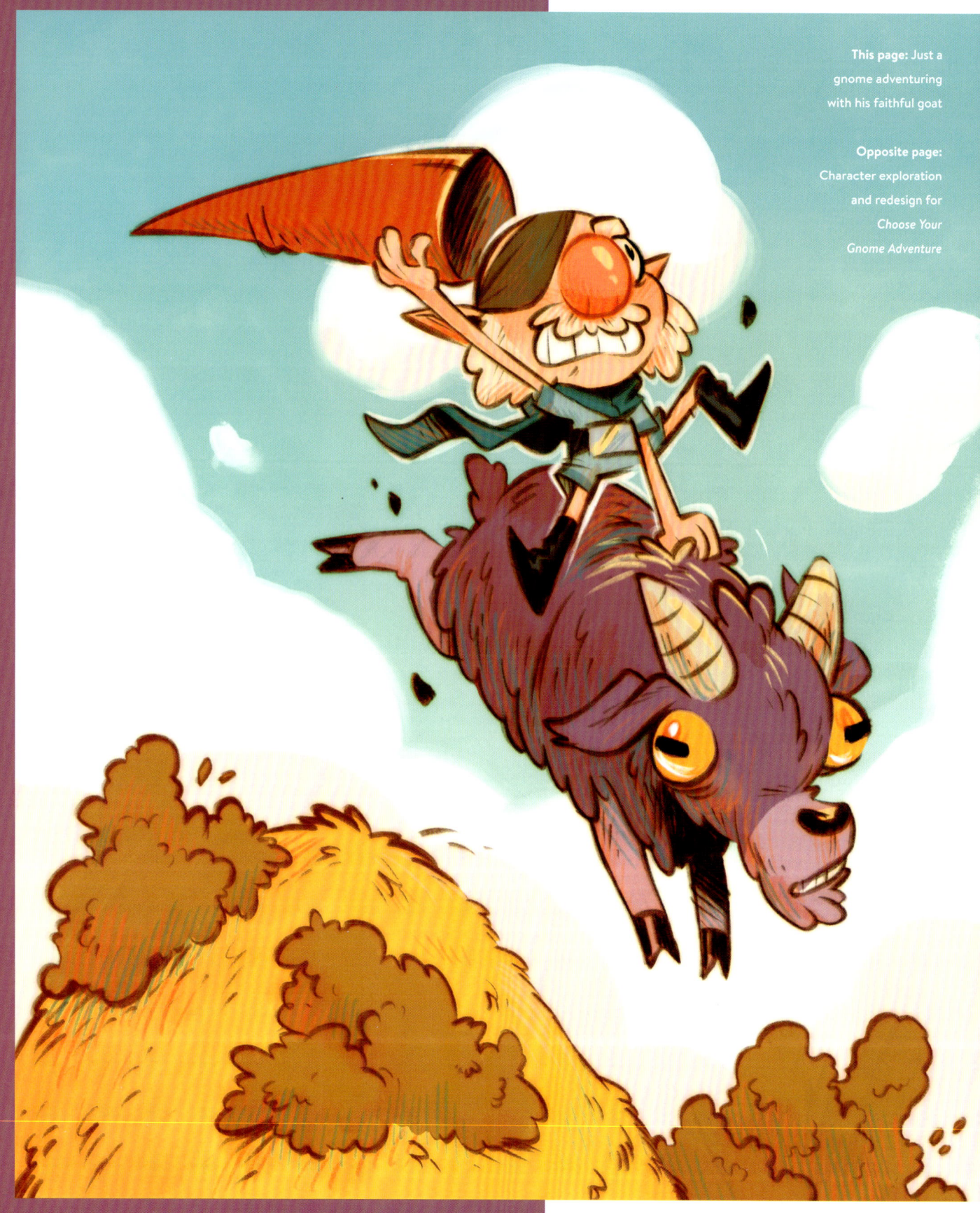

This page: Just a gnome adventuring with his faithful goat

Opposite page: Character exploration and redesign for *Choose Your Gnome Adventure*

Do you have any tips for freelance designers looking to get their name out there and make their hobby a career?

Everyone's situation is different, but I'll share my experience of making it work. First, I had to figure out what I wanted to be doing professionally and be specific about it. If I didn't know what I wanted to do, how I could expect others to know, either? So, decide what you want to draw (Fantasy characters? Mythical creatures?) and what industry you want to be a part of, be it board games, advertising, animation, or something else.

With a direction, then you need to start creating things with your goal in mind. For instance, if you want to illustrate board games, then do just that. You may have to make up your own idea to start with, or maybe do a take on an existing board game (Gnomonopoly, anybody?).

Next, share what you've made! If nobody knows what you're doing, then how can they ask you to make more?

I tend to share the process and, most importantly, completed projects. This could mean sharing on social media, your own website or blog, a forum, a booth at a convention, or reaching out to other artists and directors in the industry.

To be successful in these endeavors, you need three things: skill, motivation, and opportunity. Skill is just a matter of time – the more you repeat the above steps, the more you will improve and get better at the process. I think motivation naturally waxes and wanes for most people – at least, I know it does for me. Realizing that my drive will return helps me get through the times I'm less inspired to work.

Opportunity comes from others, whether it's in the form of a job offer or support for a self-published project. I think receiving such opportunities is largely a matter of time, as well. The two biggest things that have helped me were getting to know people in the industry and sharing projects I'd completed with as many people as I could, until the right people saw them.

That was a lot of information, and it's not the complete picture, but hopefully it's helpful!

"SHARE WHAT YOU'VE MADE! IF NOBODY KNOWS WHAT YOU'RE DOING, THEN HOW CAN THEY ASK YOU TO MAKE MORE?"

"I TRY TO ENGAGE IN AS MANY VARIED EXPERIENCES AS I CAN"

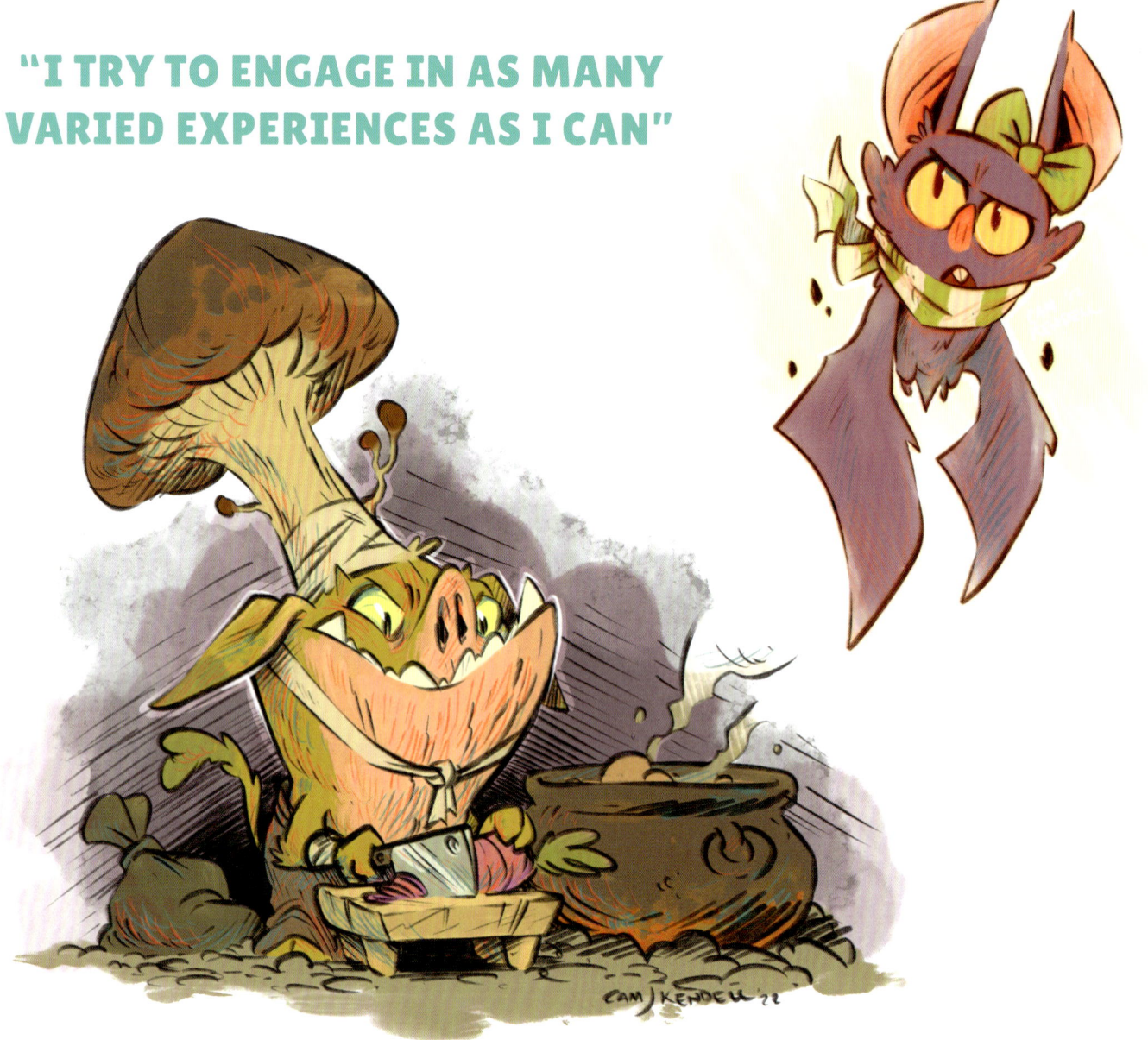

Where do you find inspiration for your character designs?

Inspiration can come from so many different sources, but for me it's all about life experiences: the world and people around me, my childhood passions, inspiring artists, and great stories in video game, movie, or book form. I try to engage in as many varied experiences as I can and I love learning about obscure things, like urban planning, sheep herding, and different religions of the world.

All of these things have an influence on my character designs and can often spark ideas for a character I never would have had on my own.

Some of my greatest childhood influences would be all the media I consumed back then. Movies like *Labyrinth*, *Legend*, *The Dark Crystal*, *The NeverEnding Story*, and the Rankin/Bass animated *Hobbit*. Also, comics such as *Garfield*, *Calvin and Hobbes*, *Mother Goose & Grimm*, and cartoons like *Teenage Mutant Ninja Turtles*, *Thundercats*, and *He-Man*. And I've played a

lot of Warhammer and other tabletop games throughout the years – without a doubt the art in all those rule books has had a huge influence on my artistic sensibilities.

More recent influences have been artists such as Fabien Mense, Skottie Young, and Robb Mommaerts, to name a few, and video games like *Little Nightmares* and *The Legend of Zelda: Breath of the Wild*.

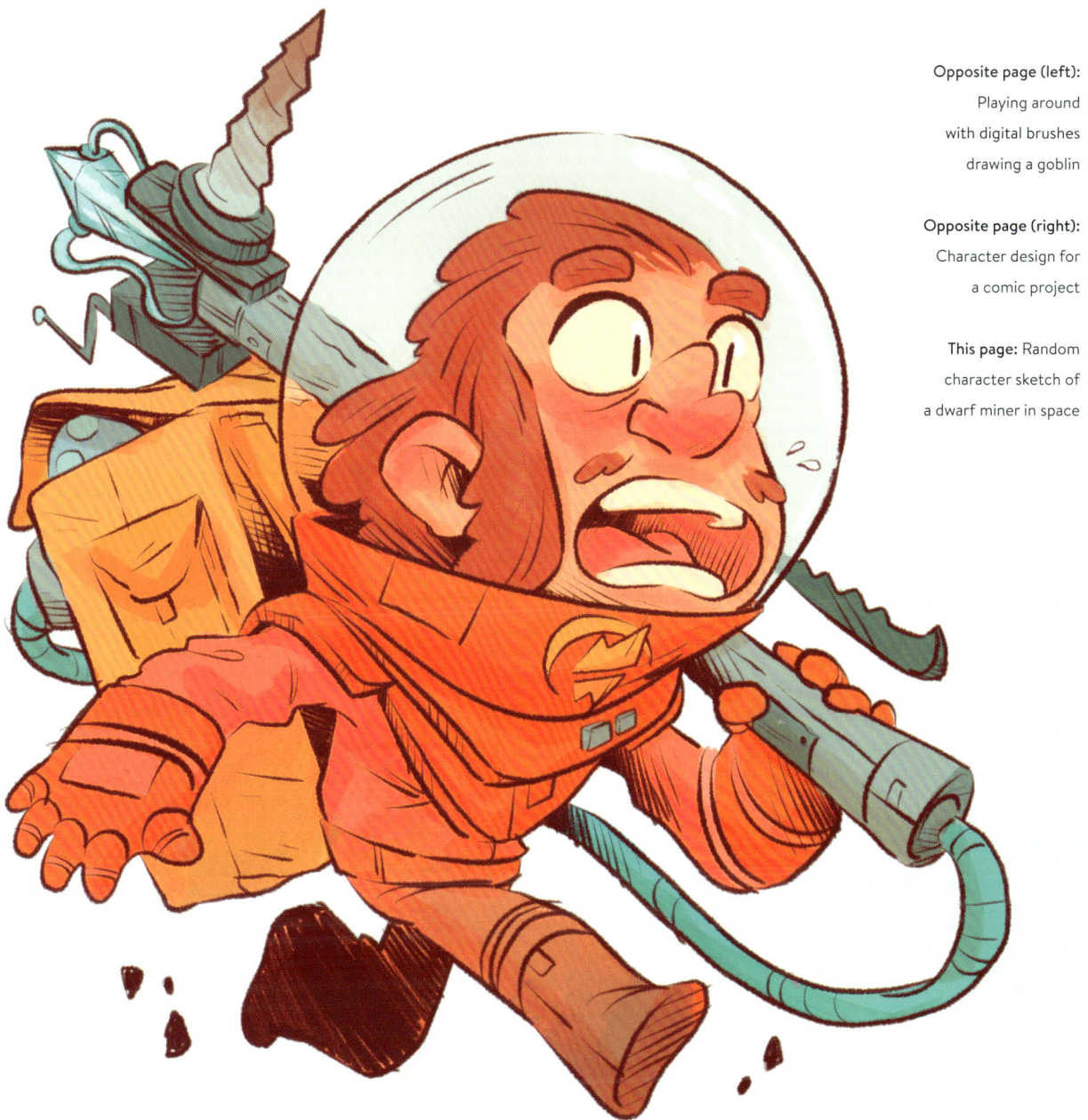

Opposite page (left):
Playing around
with digital brushes
drawing a goblin

Opposite page (right):
Character design for
a comic project

This page: Random
character sketch of
a dwarf miner in space

Thanks for talking with us, Cam! Are there any projects our readers should be looking out for?

Sure thing, the pleasure was all mine! Be sure to stay on the lookout for Marvel's *Rocket and Groot: the Hunt for Star-Lord*, a graphic novel coming in September 2023 from Scholastic, illustrated by me. Head to my website to sign up for Email Encounters, a creativity newsletter, and keep an eye on my social media accounts for sketches, news, and other nonsense.

SETTING THE MOOD
AURÉLIE LISE-ANNE

This tutorial will explain how to change the emotions of a character and narrative mood simply by adjusting lighting. I made sure to use a fairly simple character, keeping its pose the same throughout the different examples to show that lighting goes a very long way to convey a mood and tell a story. This specific tutorial was made in Photoshop, but the same method will work in Procreate. In general, the layer modes in this tutorial are: Multiply for shadows, Overlay for main lights, and Normal for ambient and bounce.

START WITH FLAT COLORS

When painting multiple lighting set-ups of the same character, paint the flat local colors first. Then, on top of these, paint the lighting using Adjustment layers. That way, the lighting will always be easy to change.

SUNNY SIDE UP

Use hard shadows and warm, saturated light to create a sunny look. Add a warm bounce light on the downward-facing shadow parts and a cold light on the upward-facing sections. This is the ambient light that – in this case – is coming from the blue sky above.

MORE THAN A FEELING

When lighting your character, keep in mind their backstory and intentions. In this step, the expression of the character has been changed without changing the lighting. Notice how the story is much less clear than in the next step, where the lighting has been adapted to suit the story.

"KEEP IN MIND THEIR BACKSTORY AND INTENTIONS"

QUICK SHADING TIP

Keep the flat colors from the first step on different layers to quickly select separate areas for shading, without having to switch back to the flat color layer. To select a certain area, click on the layer thumbnail of your desired area while holding Ctrl (Windows)/Cmd (Mac).

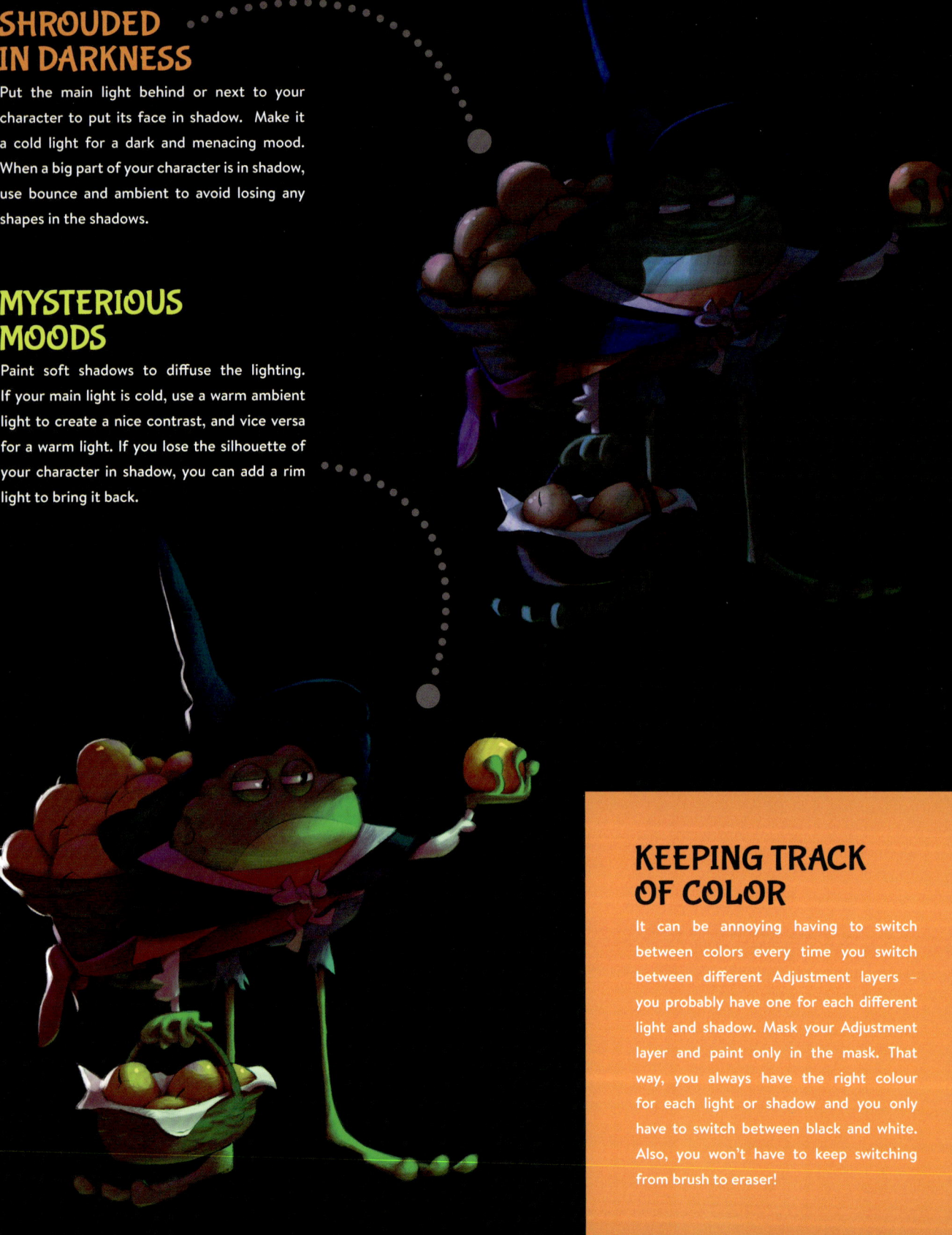

SHROUDED IN DARKNESS

Put the main light behind or next to your character to put its face in shadow. Make it a cold light for a dark and menacing mood. When a big part of your character is in shadow, use bounce and ambient to avoid losing any shapes in the shadows.

MYSTERIOUS MOODS

Paint soft shadows to diffuse the lighting. If your main light is cold, use a warm ambient light to create a nice contrast, and vice versa for a warm light. If you lose the silhouette of your character in shadow, you can add a rim light to bring it back.

KEEPING TRACK OF COLOR

It can be annoying having to switch between colors every time you switch between different Adjustment layers – you probably have one for each different light and shadow. Mask your Adjustment layer and paint only in the mask. That way, you always have the right colour for each light or shadow and you only have to switch between black and white. Also, you won't have to keep switching from brush to eraser!

"BE CAREFUL NOT TO SATURATE YOUR SHADOWS TO AVOID INTRODUCING TOO MUCH COLOR INTO YOUR DRAWING"

SAD IN THE SHADOWS

Use a white light as the main light source to desaturate your drawing altogether. Be careful not to saturate your shadows to avoid introducing too much color into your drawing. However, if you want to add some more color, try to have cold tones as the majority.

LIGHT THE WAY

Have fun experimenting with different lighting situations. For example, try making the main light source a part of your character, or change the light to a very strong, saturated color and see what happens.

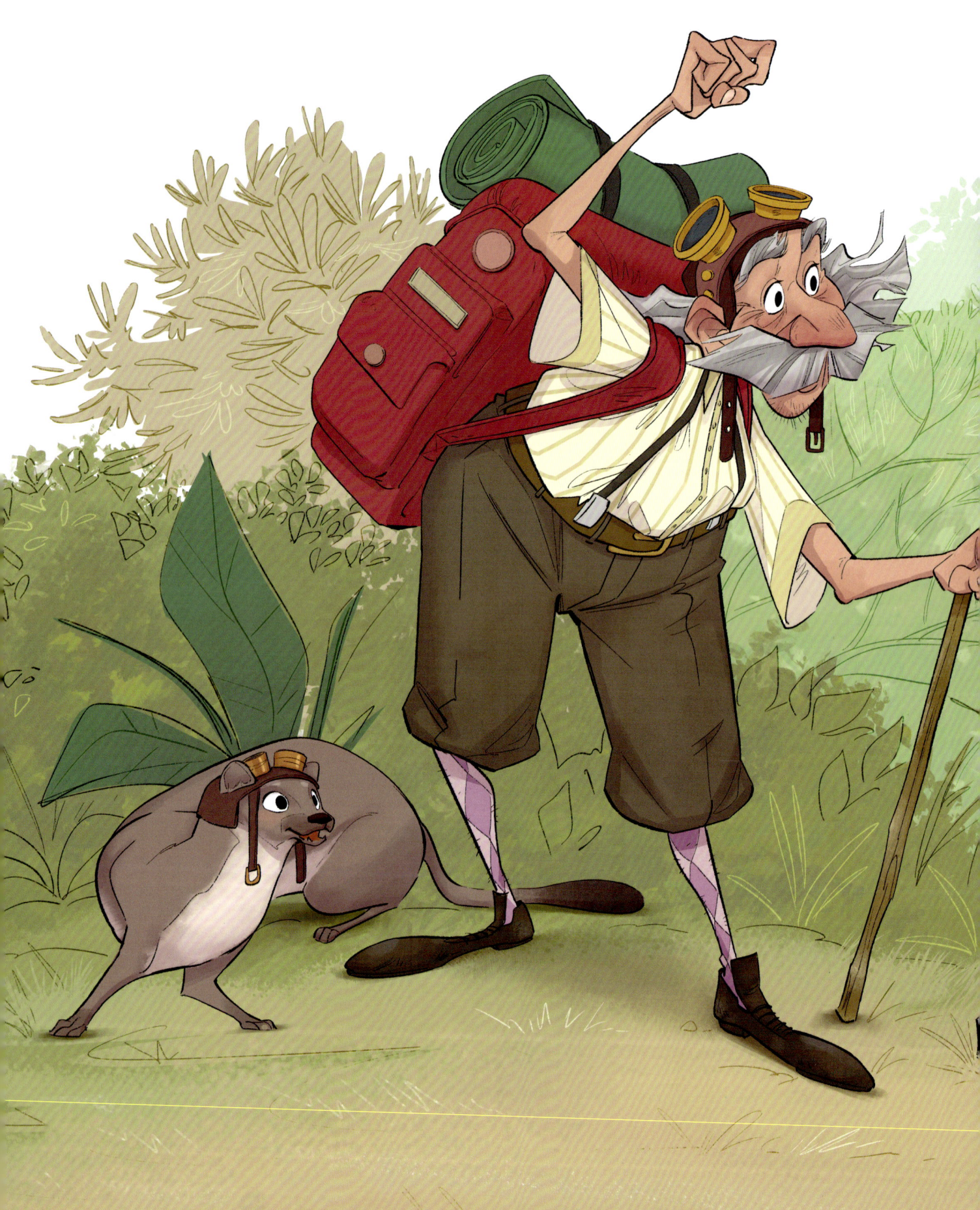

Final image © João Moura

ONE FINAL ADVENTURE

JOÃO MOURA

Hello! In this tutorial we will try to come up with a cool design working to this brief: "An embittered, eccentric old man and his animal sidekick live on the outskirts of society and come across a mysterious object." When I read the pitch I was immediately curious to "meet" this character. There could be so many layers to him, we're going to have fun fleshing him out. I'll start with some traditional sketching with Polychromos colored pencils and my trusty sketchbook, and then move to digital drawing using a Wacom Cintiq and Adobe Photoshop to finalize the design.

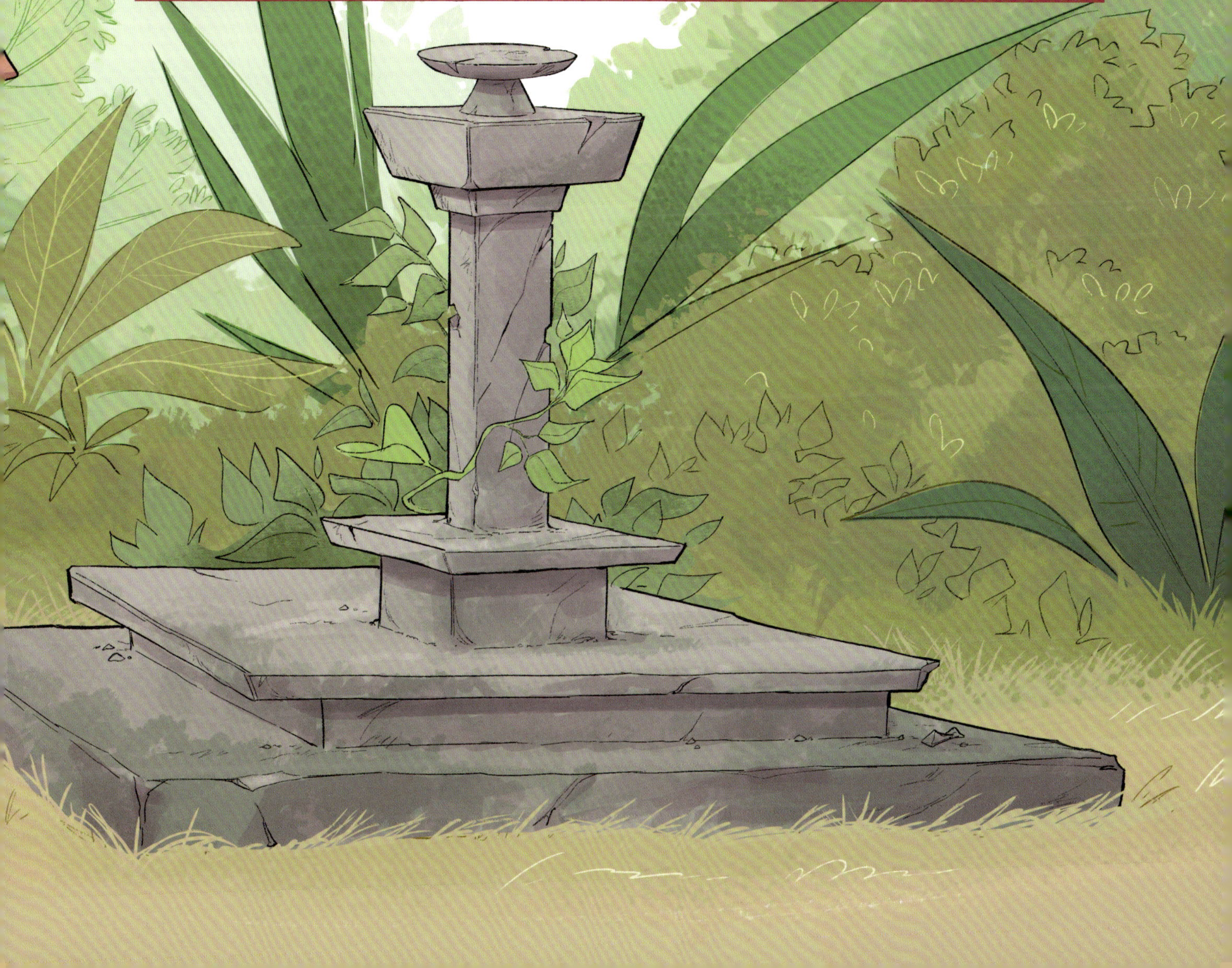

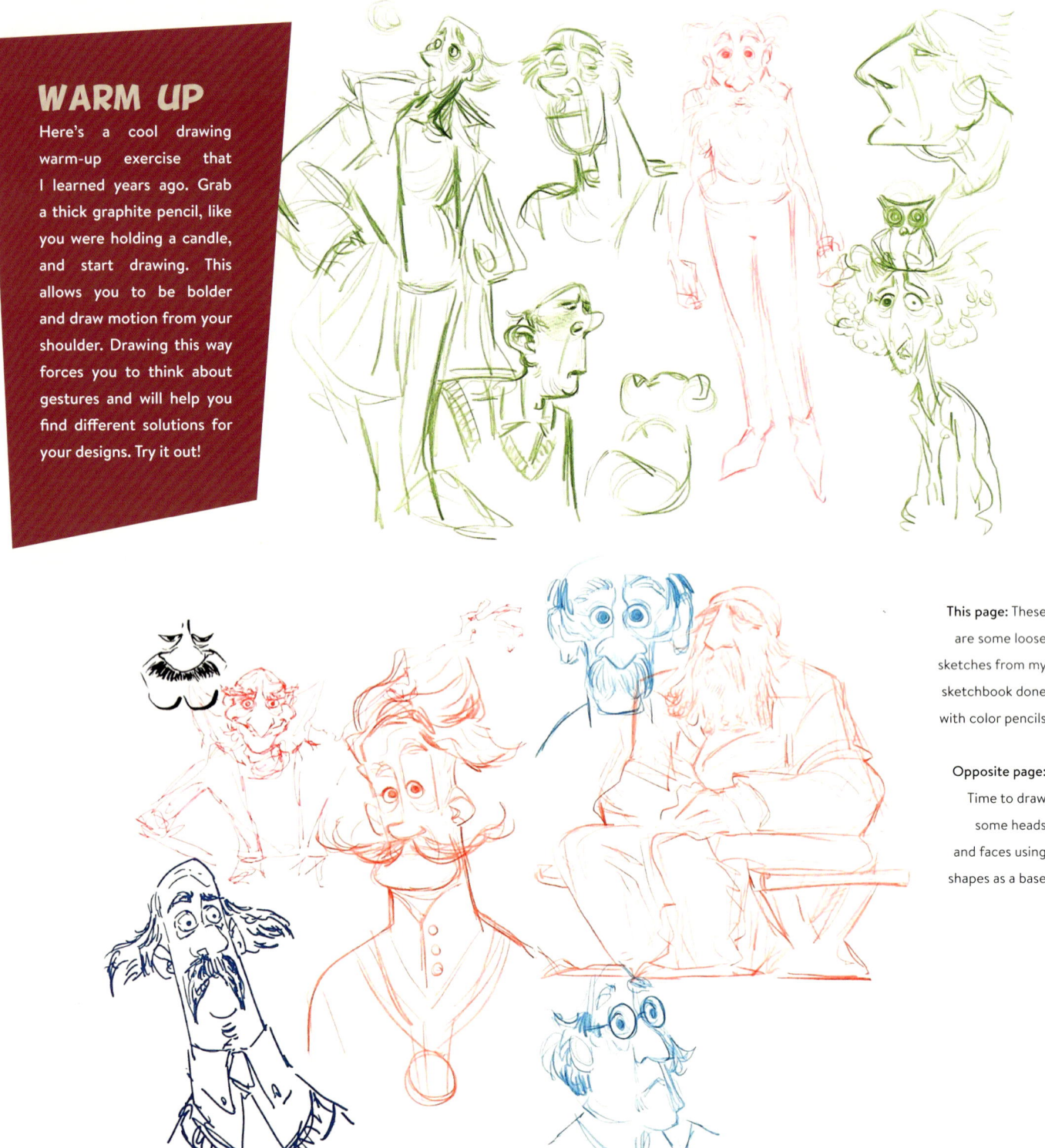

WARM UP

Here's a cool drawing warm-up exercise that I learned years ago. Grab a thick graphite pencil, like you were holding a candle, and start drawing. This allows you to be bolder and draw motion from your shoulder. Drawing this way forces you to think about gestures and will help you find different solutions for your designs. Try it out!

This page: These are some loose sketches from my sketchbook done with color pencils

Opposite page: Time to draw some heads and faces using shapes as a base

LET'S BEGIN!

The first step is the most fun of all. We need to get comfortable with the topic at hand, so what could be more pleasing than to take a sketchbook out for a walk, step into a coffee shop, and sketch old people while having some cake? For this stage, put on your headphones, open some references from Pinterest or similar on your phone or tablet, and start to do some loose sketches. At this point you shouldn't be too focused on finding a specific design. I would recommend trying to always hint at some emotion or "life" in your early sketches. This will help you find what works better for the character you will create.

"YOU SHOULDN'T ONLY BE THINKING ABOUT PROPORTIONS AND VOLUMES, YOU SHOULD BE THINKING ABOUT PERSONALITY AND ACTING, TOO"

HEADS UP!

I start to play with shapes for the face, keeping in mind that "character" is not only in your drawing, it's also in what the drawing conveys. This is a very common exercise, drawing basic shapes and then fleshing them out into a character.

In these drawings you shouldn't only be thinking about proportions and volumes, you should be thinking about personality and acting, too. What is this or that character feeling and why? Ask these questions early and you will be sure to find your character sooner rather than later.

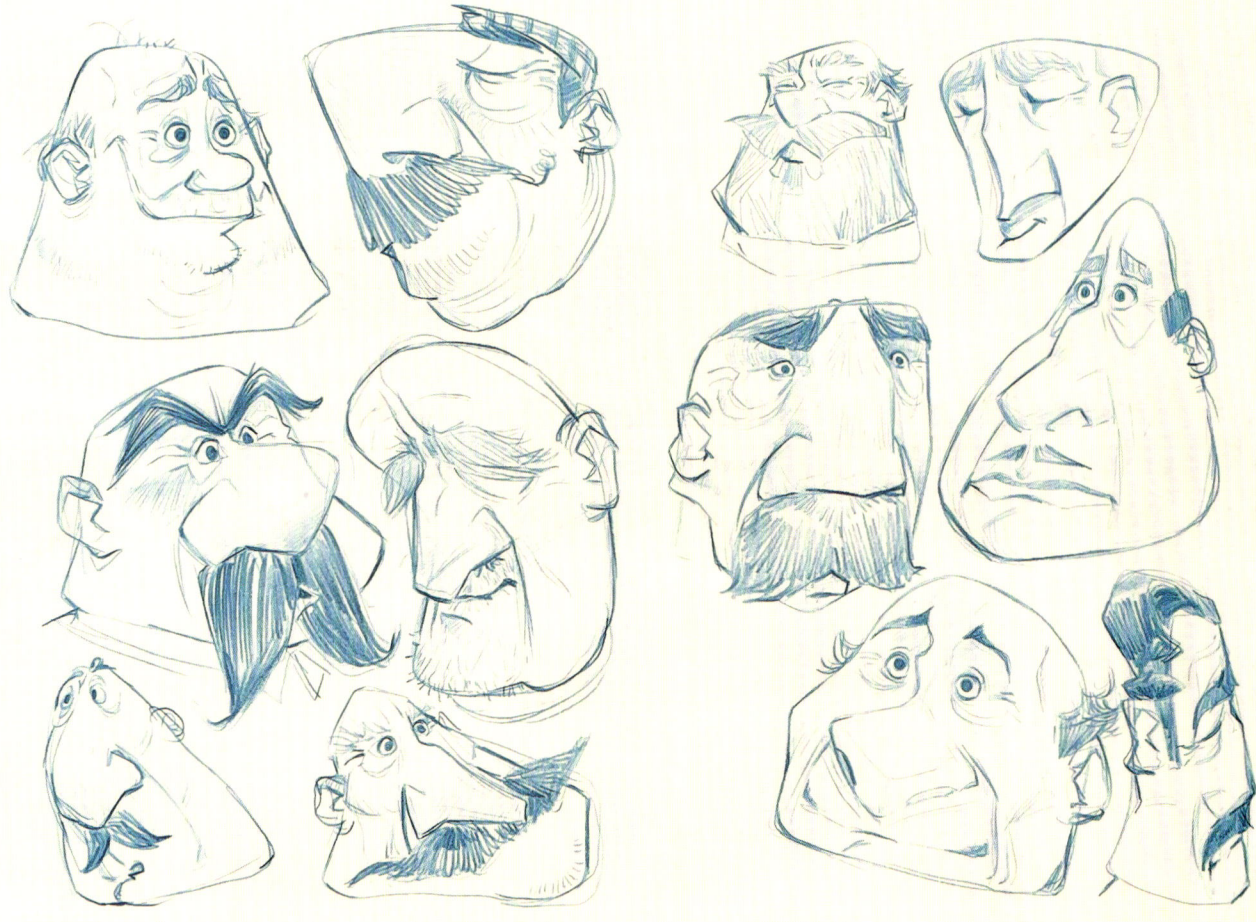

SKETCH QUICKLY

When doing sketch explorations, try to be fast and bold. Don't get too caught up on details – at this point they won't do you much good. The goal here is to have a many options and the looser you are, the cooler designs you can create! I advise you to even try different materials, like brushes or a thick graphite pencil, things that won't allow you to think about details.

STORY TIME

Now that you're feeling a bit more comfortable with the theme, it's time to find the design that fits the character already living in your head. In this case, I already have in mind that instead of being angry, my embittered old man will be sad. I start to develop this spark of an idea into a story, the story of a man who dedicated everything to pursue his career as a biologist and ended up losing the love of his life. He finds out (with the help of a sweet animal companion) that a lifetime of discoveries can't compare to a life filled with love.

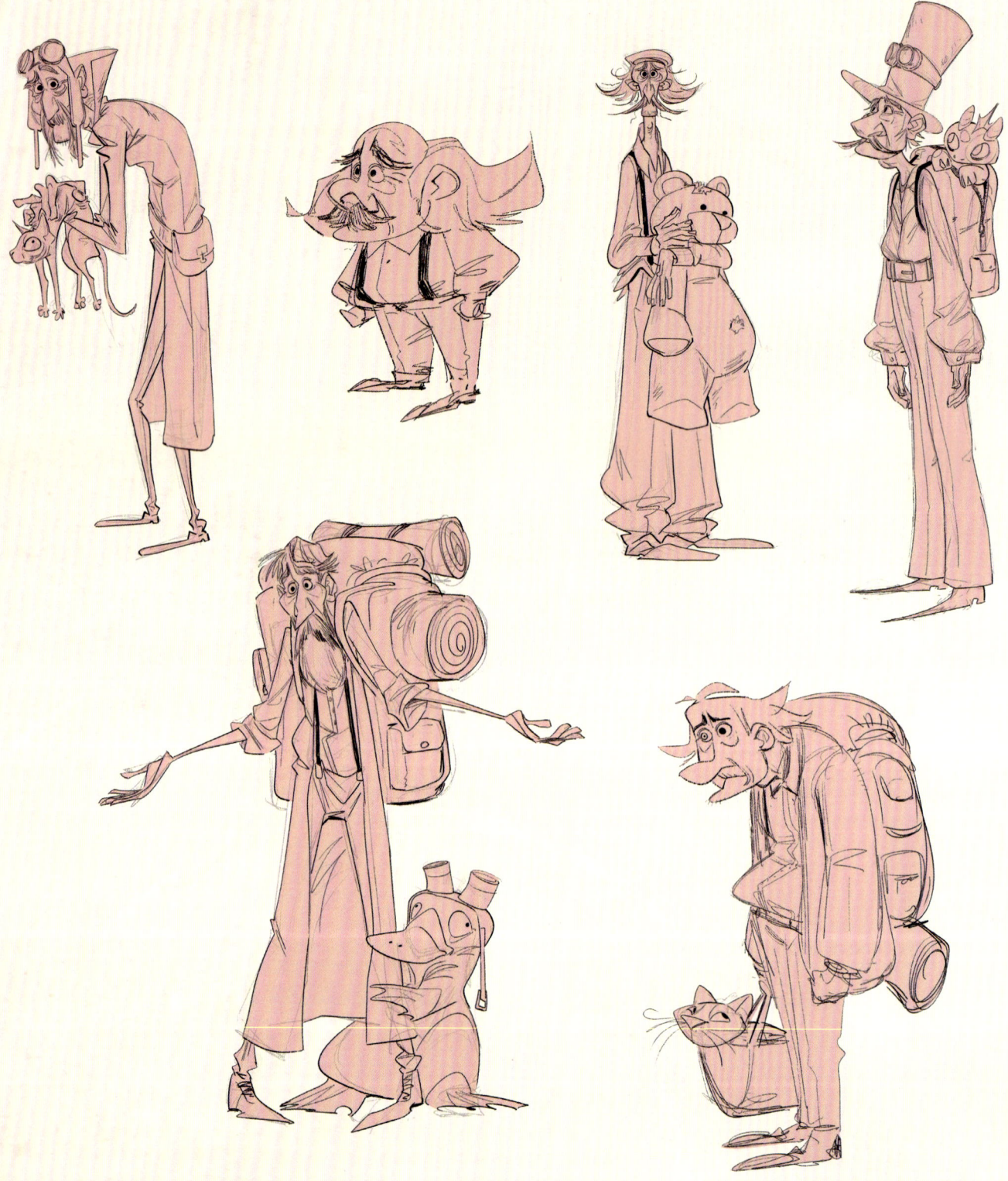

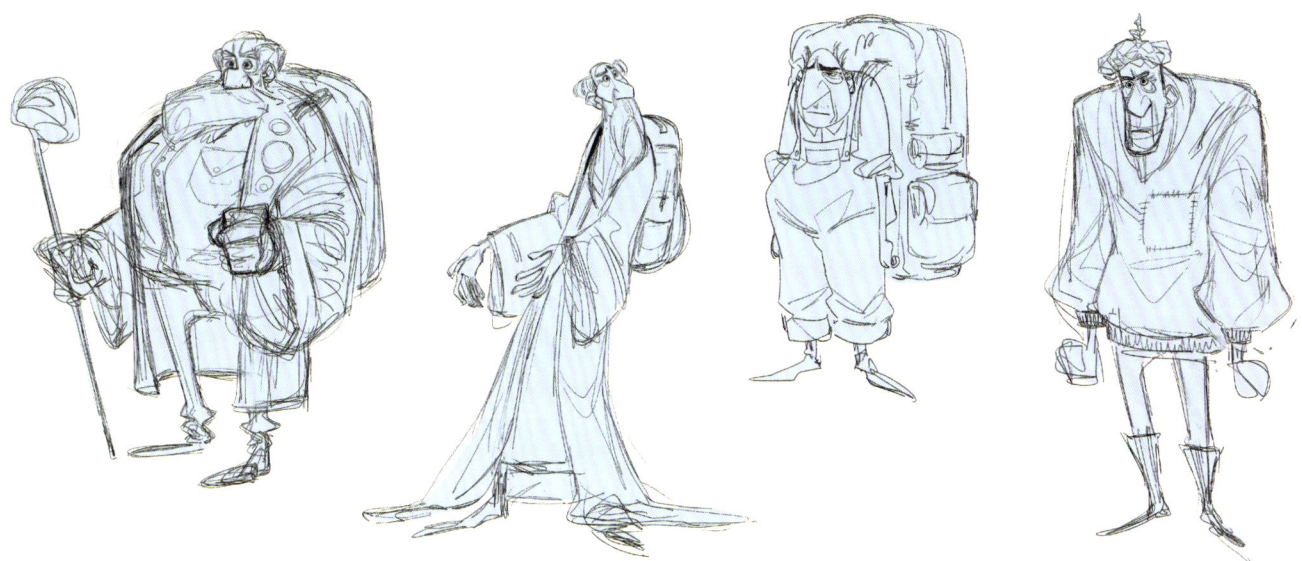

EXPLORING OTHER OPTIONS

Although I am pretty happy with the story I found for my character, I would advise you to try and sketch other ideas, to try and see if there is something that you find more appealing. Exploring other options might develop a stronger path to take, or even give you more confidence in your original plan. I draw some more sketches, studying different types of personalities, like paranoid, mentally unstable, depressed, and even an emotionless state. I'm not too happy with any of these directions – I prefer the frailer appearance of my previous designs.

A WISER ADVISER

Now, let's take a break from the main character design – we mustn't forget about our faithful animal companion. For this character you should consider how they relate to your main protagonist. In my case, as I am searching for a secondary character that would provide guidance to my biologist, I thought immediately of an owl. I invite you to go through the same process as the first step and just go and have fun sketching the topic at hand. This time I decide to sketch digitally in Photoshop, but a sketchbook would have worked just as well.

Opposite page: Let's take our drawings to the digital format and keep exploring

This page (top): It's always good to try different directions to know for sure what works best

This page (bottom): First sketches for our animal companion. Why not an owl?

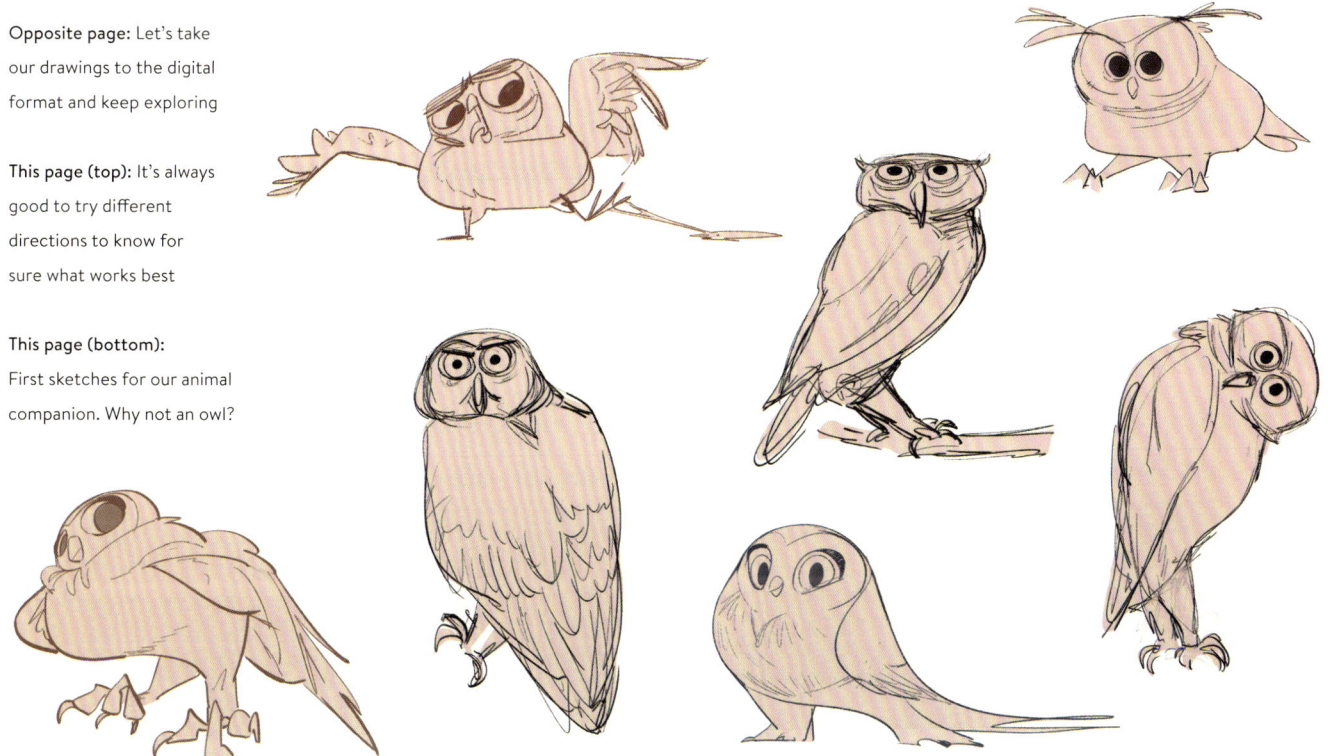

SECOND THOUGHTS

I'm not that happy about my choice of animal. I'm not sure why, but an owl feels like too much of an obvious choice, so I want to try something different – how about a weasel? I'm thinking that the animal is more of an emotional guide for our character, rather than a wise advisor.

The weasel has a cute face, adorable paws, and could wrap itself around our character's neck. This animal will remind the old man of the importance of love and caring for another. So, let's pull our pencils and pens out and sketch some more to find a design that hits the spot.

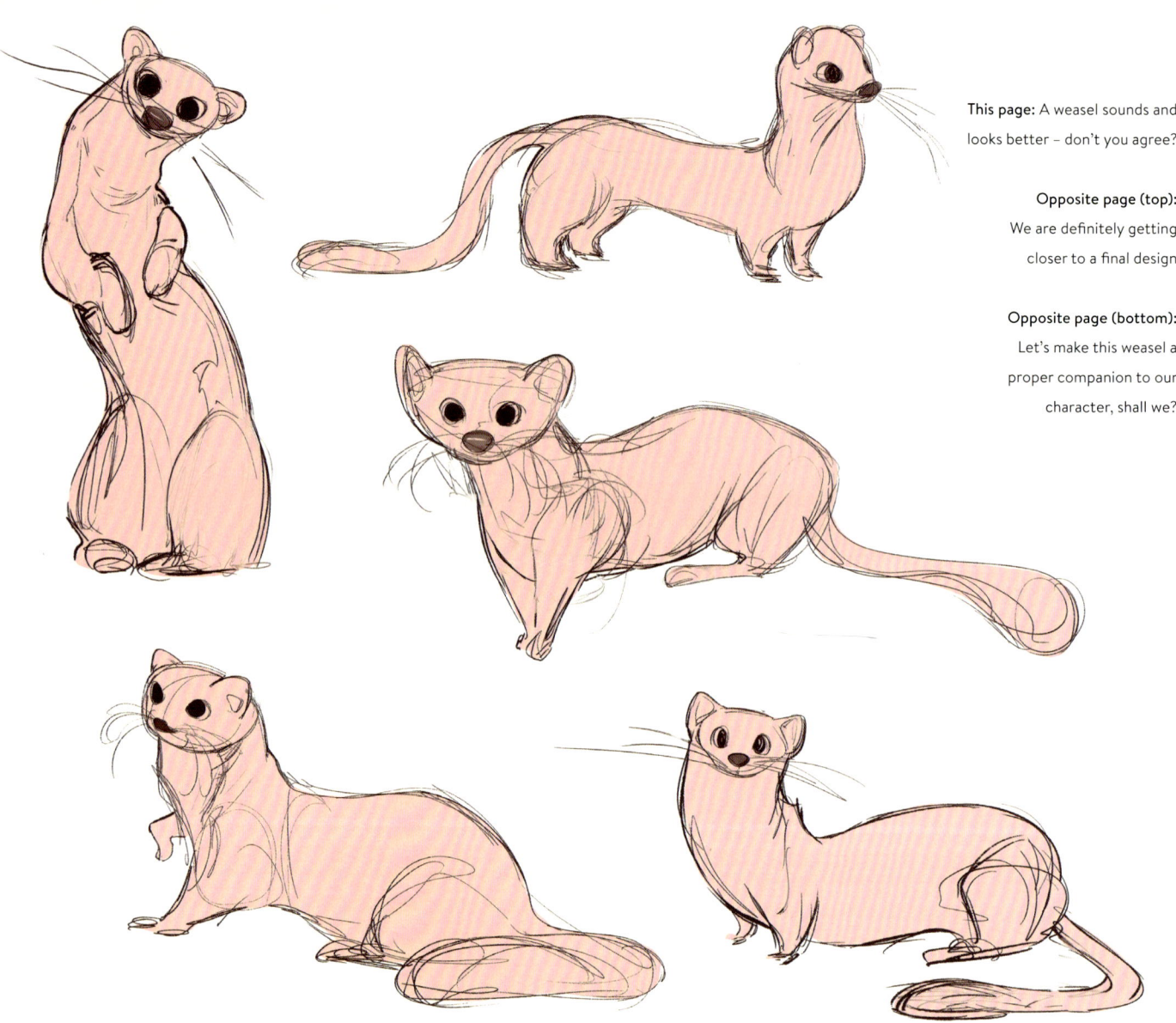

This page: A weasel sounds and looks better – don't you agree?

Opposite page (top): We are definitely getting closer to a final design

Opposite page (bottom): Let's make this weasel a proper companion to our character, shall we?

READING REFERENCES

If you are drawing out of your comfort zone (or even if you are not) it's always helpful to find some great references. By looking for references you are already actively designing, because you are choosing things that make sense for your design explorations. Always be mindful and respectful when using those references, so you don't end up copying. If you do studies from any reference, always credit the author.

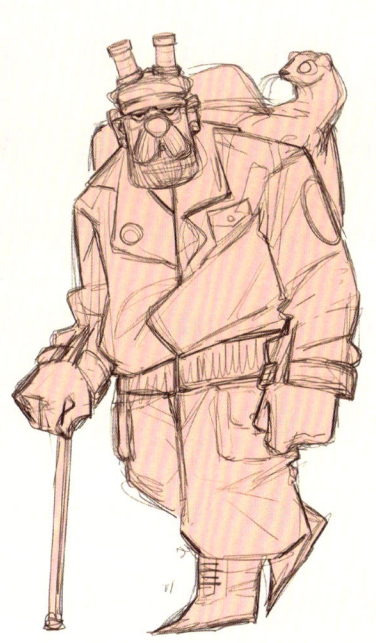
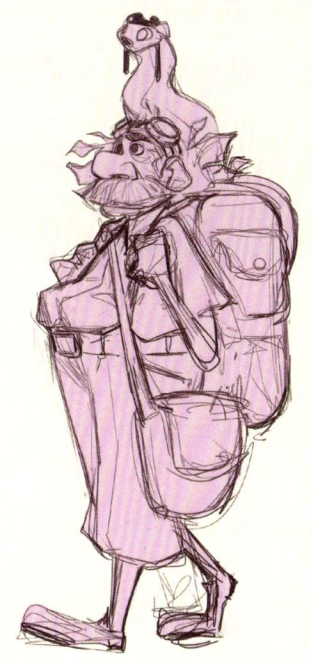
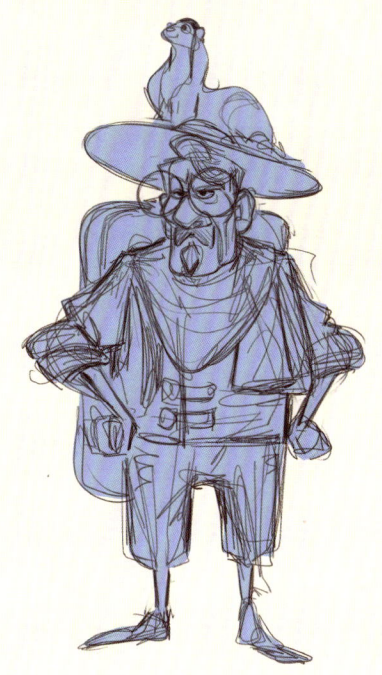

A BRIEF ENCOUNTER

Now I have more confidence in my story and choice of animal companion, I circle back around to the main character design. I still haven't considered the traits "eccentric" and "lives on the outskirts of society" from the brief. To achieve this, I try to give my character some design hints, like goggles and a huge bag, that show this man lives for traveling and doesn't fit in with civilization. As I draw the character here filled in pink, with his quirky, shaggy hair, I immediately feel a strong connection to him – this is the character I had in mind all along! This is the feeling you should be looking for from your own sketches.

REFINING THE SIDEKICK

Now that things are starting to look more defined, we're free to jump from one task to another as we see fit. As I am feeling pleased with the design I found for the main character, I go back to the weasel companion and decide on more aspects of his design, making him cuter and giving him goggles to match with our main character. I'm also thinking about posing, and imagining that the weasel could be the one pointing the way toward our mysterious object. For the story I have in mind, the weasel will find the Aztec gold medallion that our character has been looking for. The medallion has the power to take them back in time, so he can make the right decision to be with the one he loves.

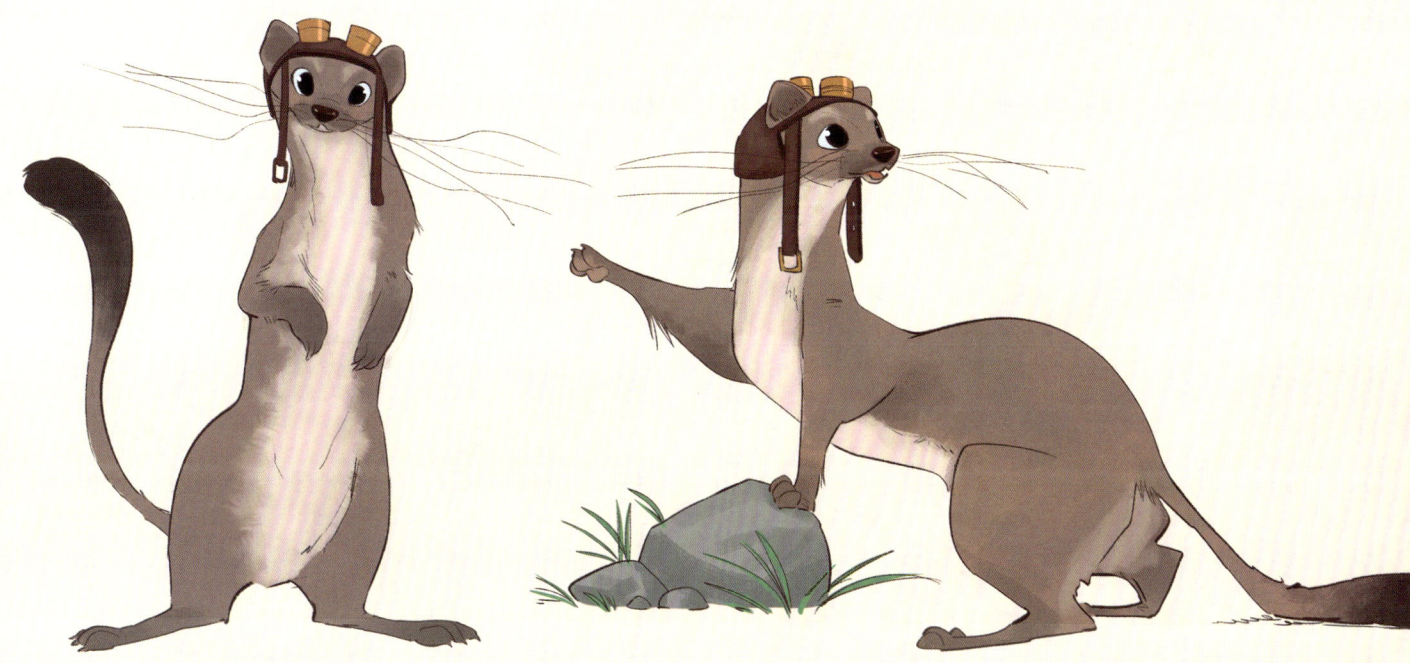

"I TAKE THIS OPPORTUNITY TO GET IN SOME OF THOSE DETAILS, LIKE FOLDS, CREASES, AND WRINKLES THAT CAN ADD TO THE FINAL DESIGN"

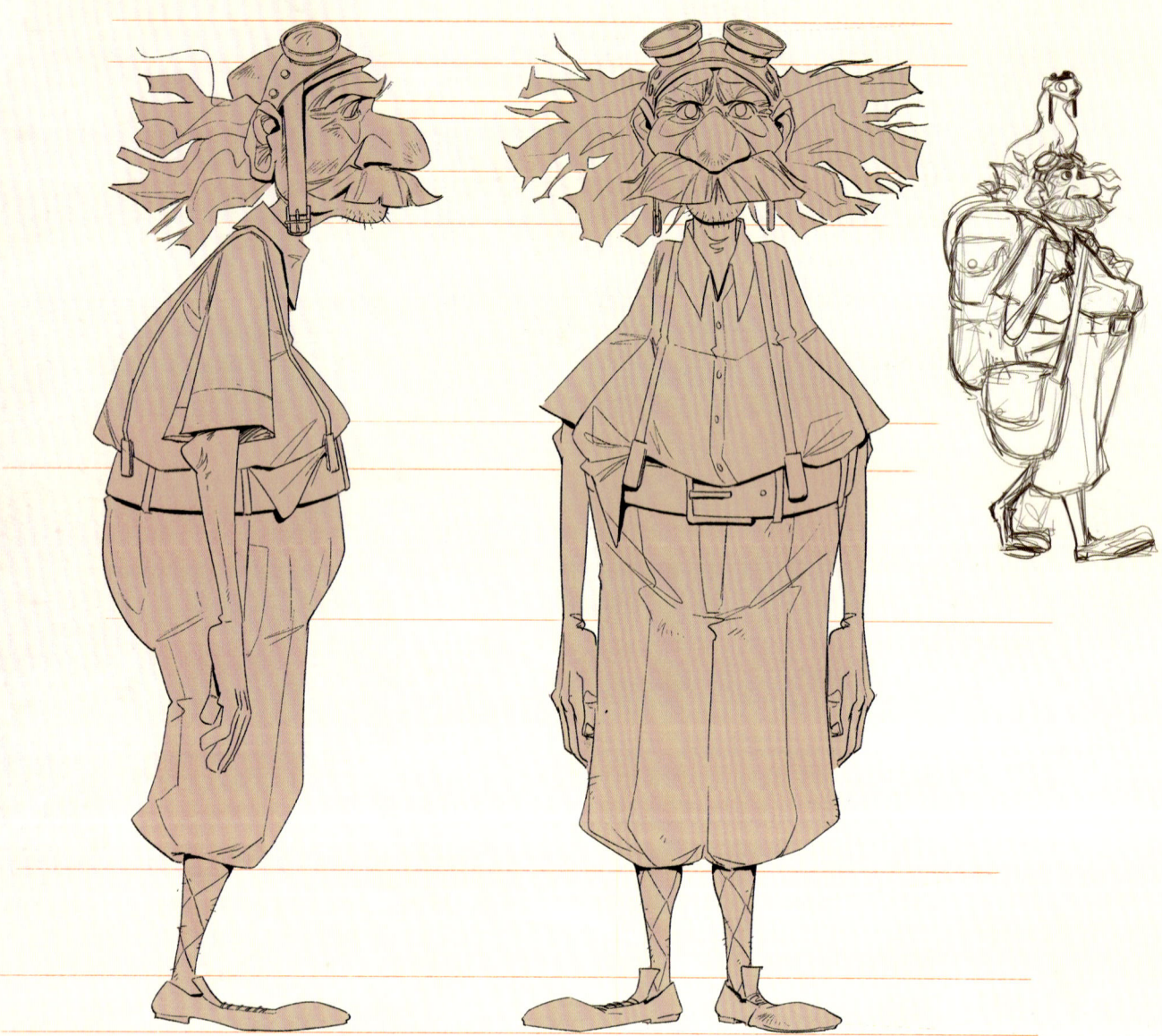

THE TURNAROUND

When I'm feeling confident about a character design, I find it very helpful to do a small turnaround, which in this case is just a front and side view. This helps to visualize your character in three dimensions and consequently they will be much easier to draw in the following steps. I take this opportunity to get in some of those details, like folds, creases, and wrinkles that can add to the final design. You can skip this step if it's not your cup of tea – it's a bit more technical, but super helpful!

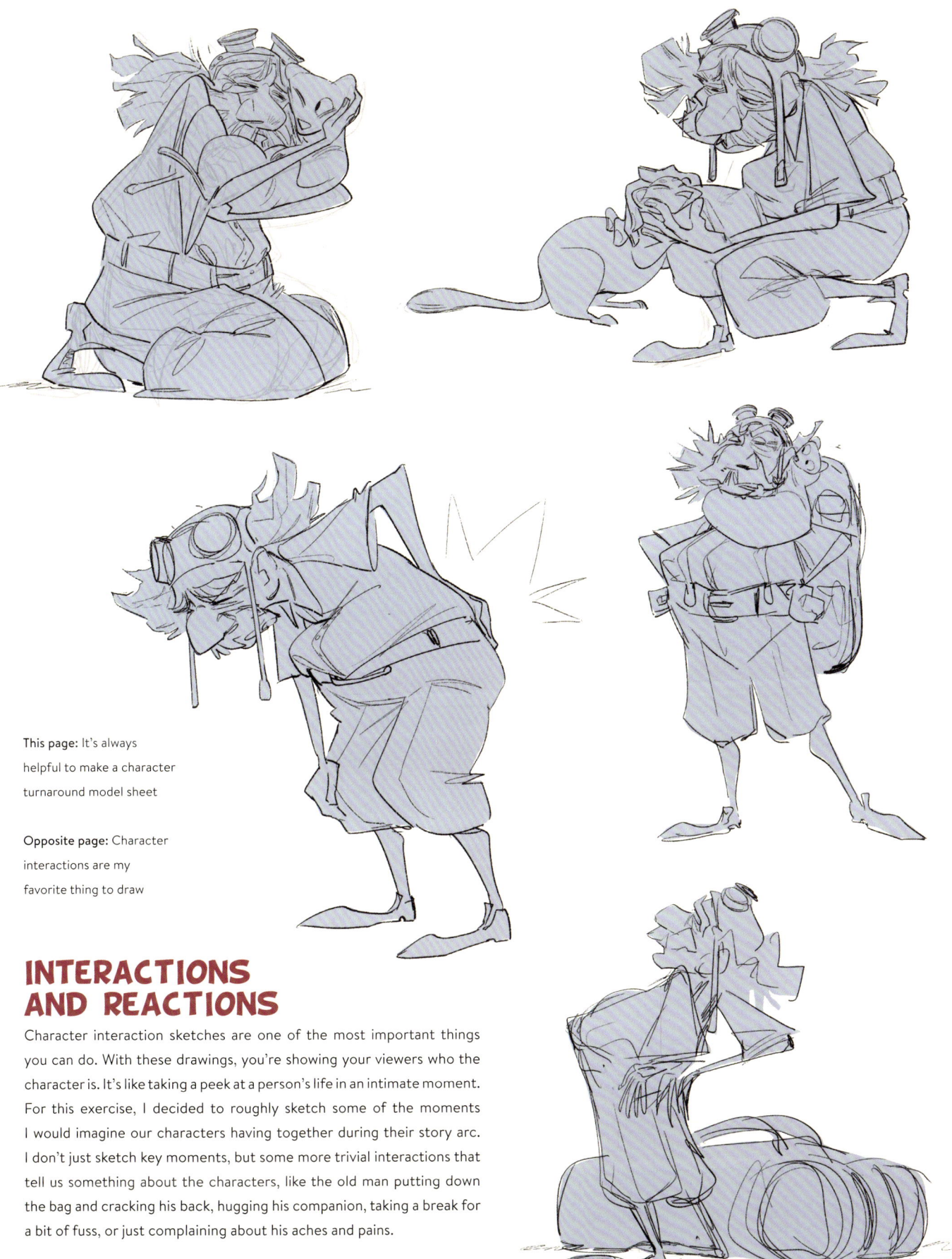

This page: It's always
helpful to make a character
turnaround model sheet

Opposite page: Character
interactions are my
favorite thing to draw

INTERACTIONS
AND REACTIONS

Character interaction sketches are one of the most important things
you can do. With these drawings, you're showing your viewers who the
character is. It's like taking a peek at a person's life in an intimate moment.
For this exercise, I decided to roughly sketch some of the moments
I would imagine our characters having together during their story arc.
I don't just sketch key moments, but some more trivial interactions that
tell us something about the characters, like the old man putting down
the bag and cracking his back, hugging his companion, taking a break for
a bit of fuss, or just complaining about his aches and pains.

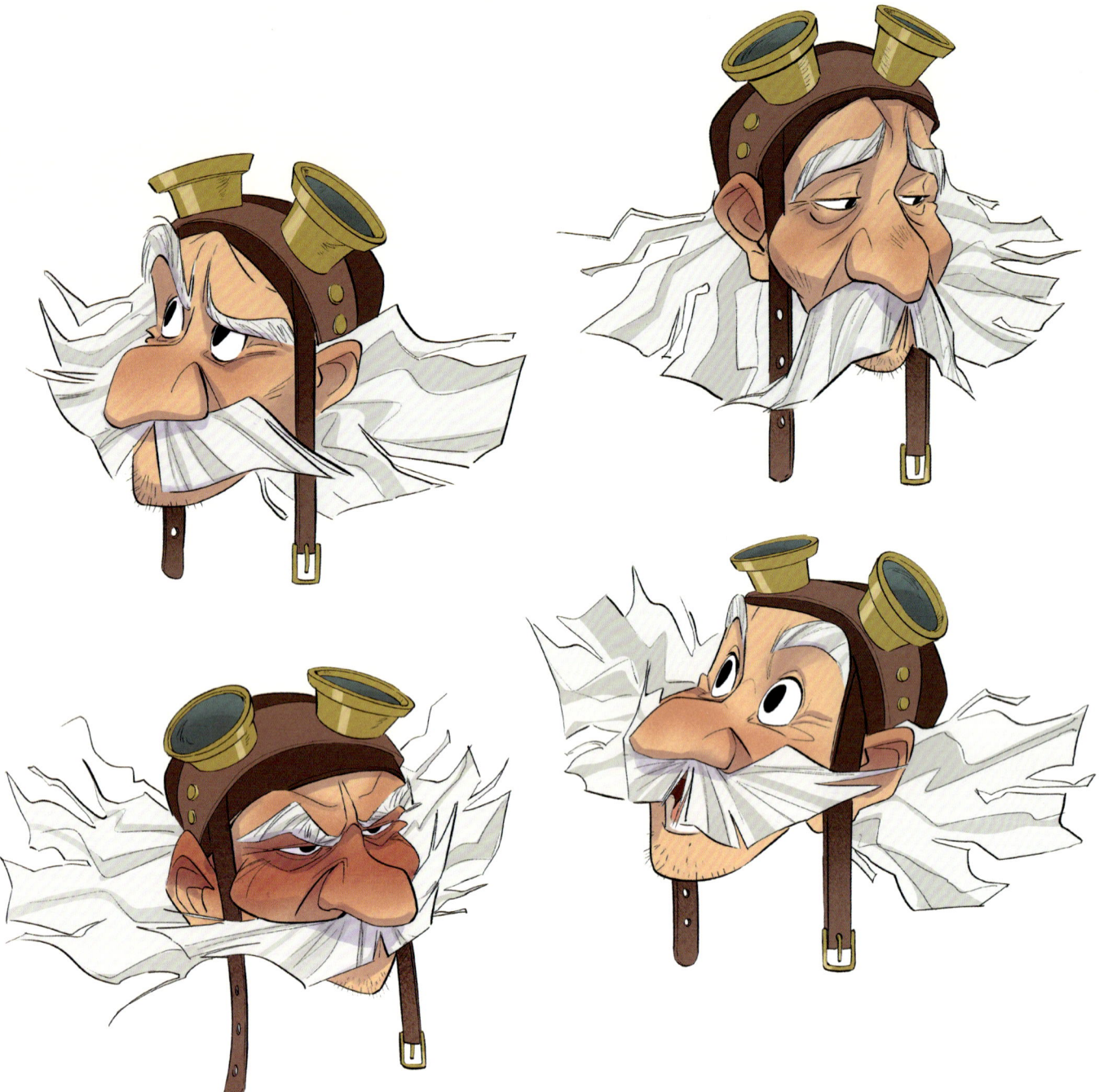

EXPRESSIONS

This step is fun and a favorite of many character designers out there (at least I think it is) – it's time to draw some expressions! This will help to find your characters' personality and emotional range. If you are having trouble, search for some references. There are wonderful resources online from real-life people, doing all sorts of expressions with different kinds of acting. You can also take a cue from other artists' work, but always be mindful to use them only as reference to elevate your work and never to copy.

COMPLEMENTARY COLORS

Now that you have your character and you know a lot more about his journey and personality, it's time to think about colors. For this process, it helps to put yourself in your character's shoes and think "what color shirt would I wear?" Try to think of an interesting palette where elements can pop using the principles of complementary colors. In the example on the next page where the character is wearing a pastel blue shirt, I give him a more saturated red bag so that the blue pops and doesn't look washed out. If we imagine this character in a forest, these colors would make him stand out from all the greens and browns of his surroundings.

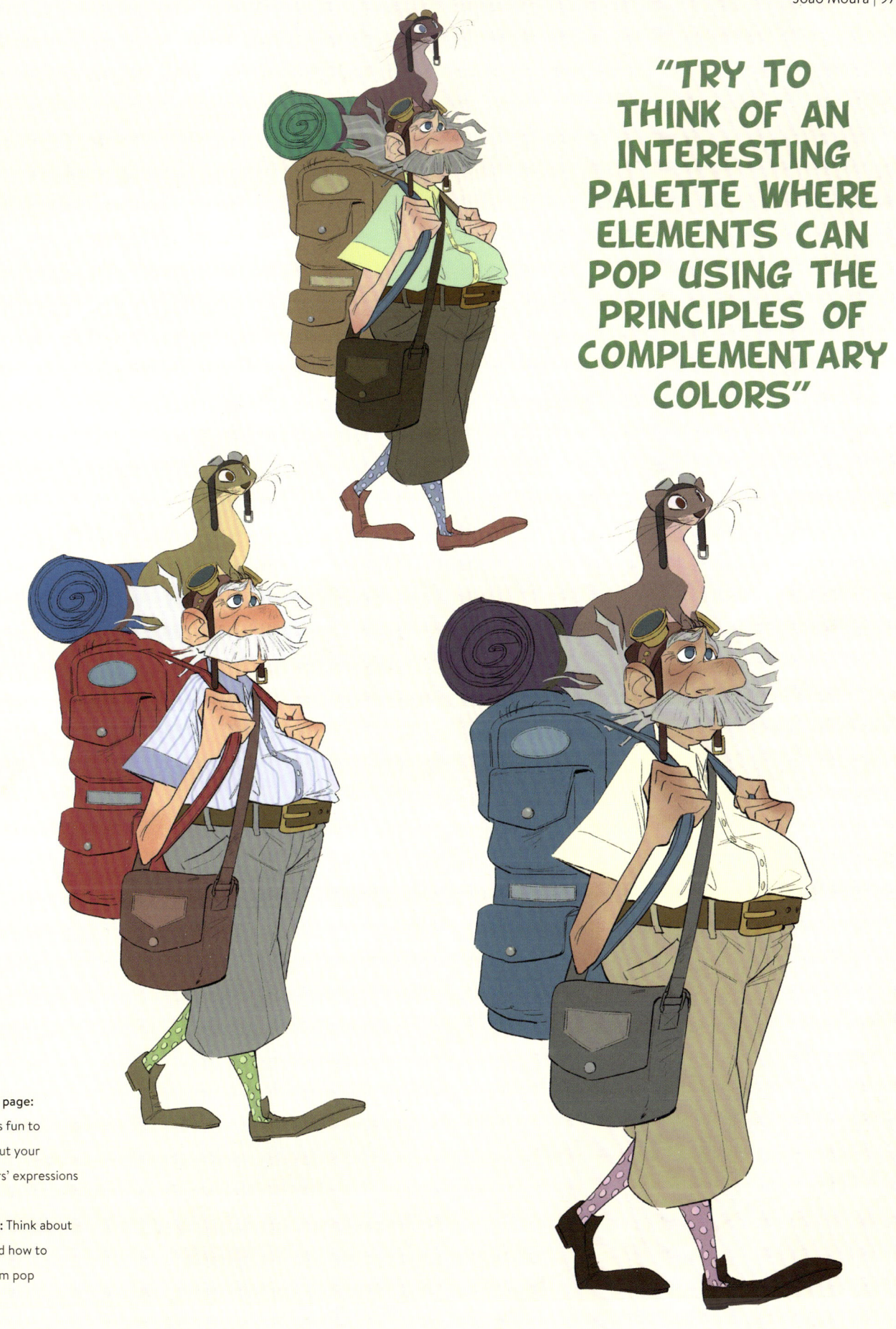

"TRY TO THINK OF AN INTERESTING PALETTE WHERE ELEMENTS CAN POP USING THE PRINCIPLES OF COMPLEMENTARY COLORS"

Opposite page:
It's always fun to think about your characters' expressions

This page: Think about colors and how to make them pop

MAKING INTRODUCTIONS

Finally, we're at the finish line! It's time to think about how you will introduce your character to the world. Will it be at his highest point, or maybe his lowest? There are many options, but in this case, if we consider the prompt, the ideal moment would be when the character finds the mysterious object. I do three very rough sketches to see what feels best to me. Do we want the character to be surprised with his finding (A)? Do we want him to appear victorious and hopeful (B)? Or do we want him to feel suspicious of what he's found (C)?

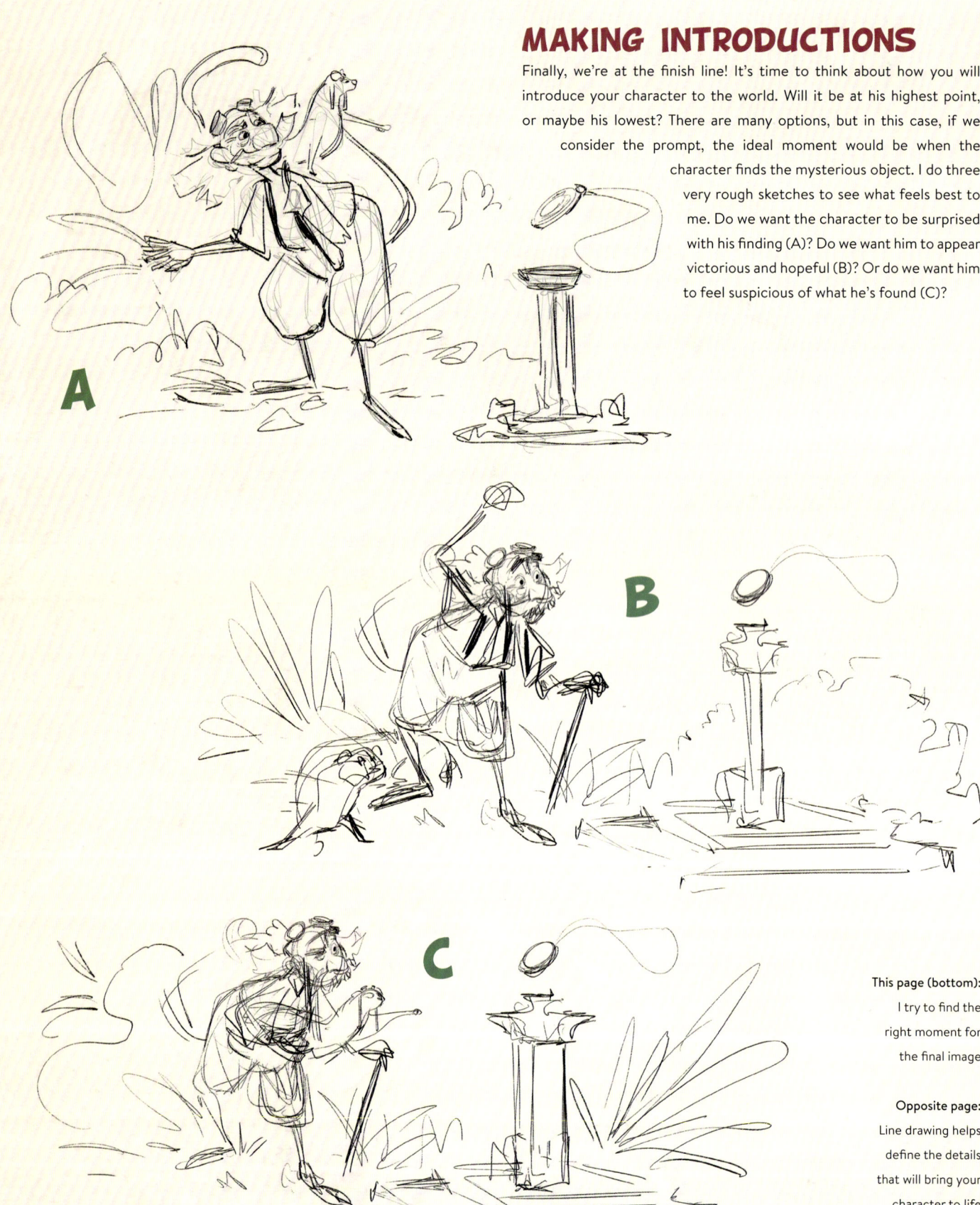

This page (bottom):
I try to find the right moment for the final image

Opposite page:
Line drawing helps define the details that will bring your character to life

THE FINAL PUSH

Choose the sketch that feels most appropriate for your character. In this case, I choose B, where the character is shown as victorious and hopeful. I choose this sketch as I feel it represents him the best. He made a decision he regretted because he let his work get in the way, but deep down he is a sweet old man with a heart that longs for love.

So, now it's time to take the sketch, scale it up, lower the opacity and draw on top of it, correcting it along the way and adding all the details that will help tell your character's story.

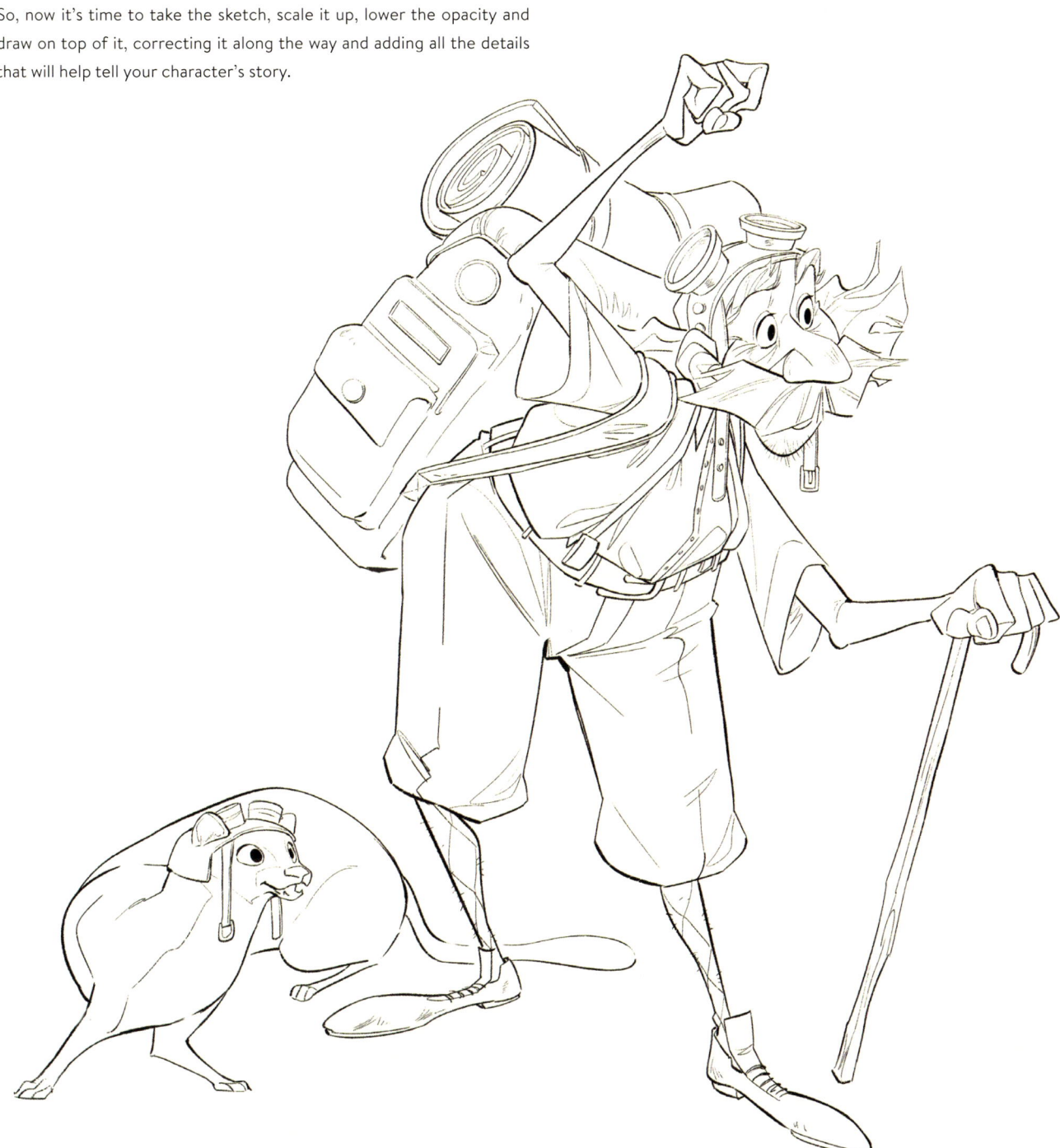

THE ADVENTURE IS COMPLETE

Now that you have your beautiful drawing, it's time to give it life and color. The method I use is to fill the design with the base colors for each element (like blue for the shirt, brown for the pants, and so on) and then paint some volume and texture on top of those. This allows me to go in and change separate element colors without destroying or having to change the rest. I take time to design the prop of the gold medallion and the stone pillar upon which it stands. To bring the whole drawing together, I add some other background elements; trees and bushes so we feel that we are somewhere secluded and wild. Finally, our character will be able to go back in time to feel love again! Or will he? Maybe he already found it along the way?

These page: There we go! Our character comes to the end of his adventure – or is it a new beginning?

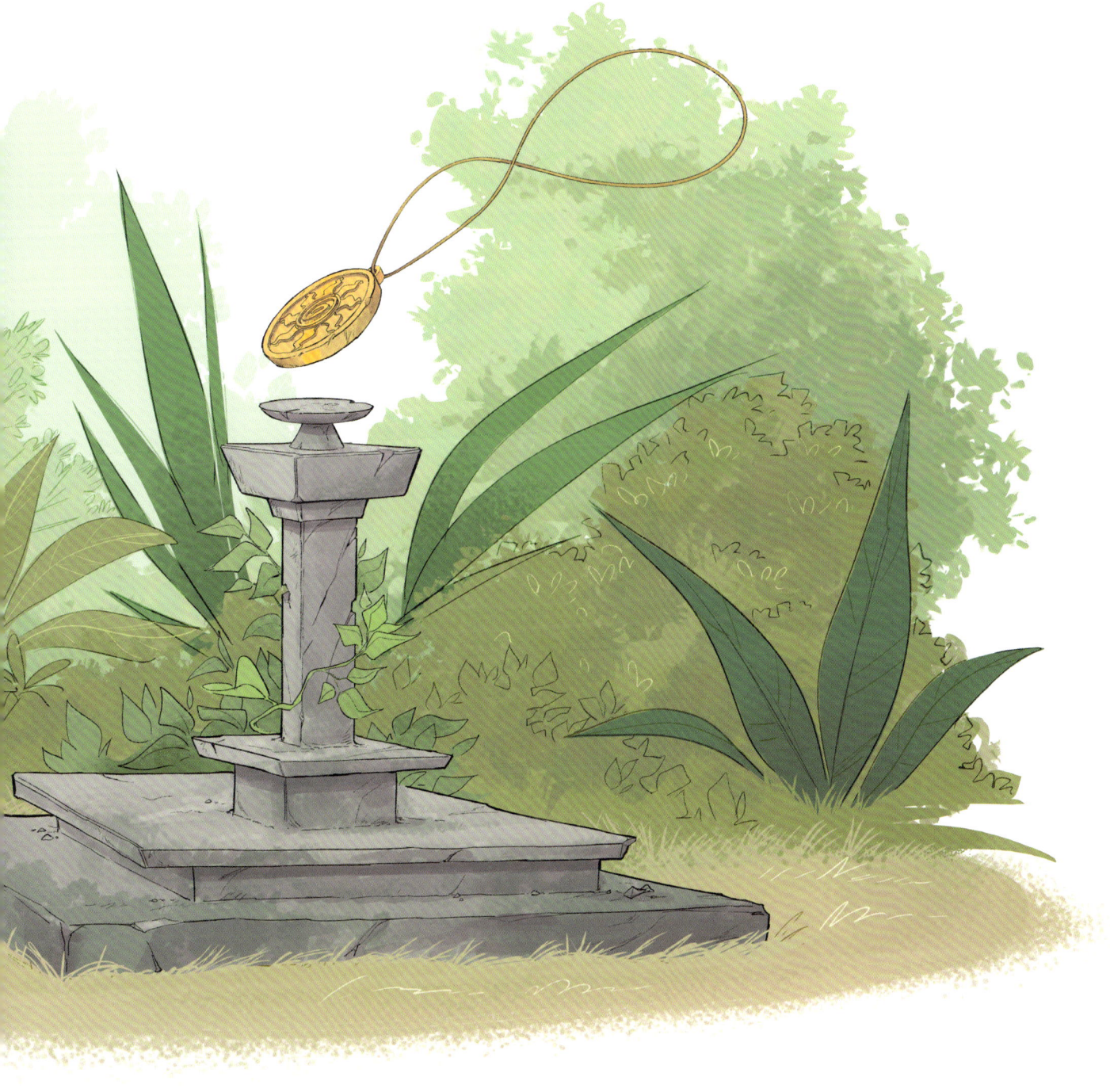

CONTRIBUTORS

LYNN CHEN
Lead game artist
at MoonActive
lynnchenart.com

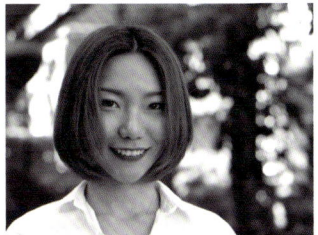

Lynn is a visual development artist working in games and animation. She lives in LA with her family and her studio assistant, Mochi the corgi.

SIMONE GRÜNEWALD
Freelance artist
instagram.com/schmoedraws

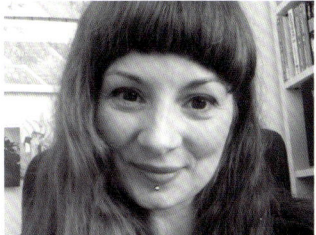

Simone is a story, character, and visual-development artist from Germany. She is happily freelancing and creating tutorials on her Patreon.

CAM KENDELL
Freelance illustrator and author
camkendell.com

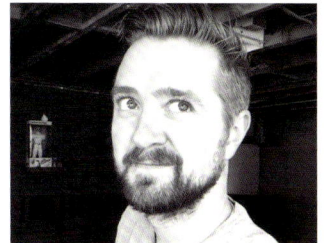

Cam is a freelance illustrator for books, comics, board games, and more. When not drawing, Cam enjoys hiking in the beautiful Utah mountains.

AURÉLIE LISE-ANNE
Art director at Blue Zoo
aurelieliseanne.com

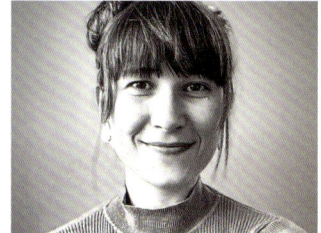

Aurélie is an artist working in the animation and illustration industry. She is happiest whenever she can spend her days drawing.

JOÃO MOURA
Visual-development artist
joaomouraart.com

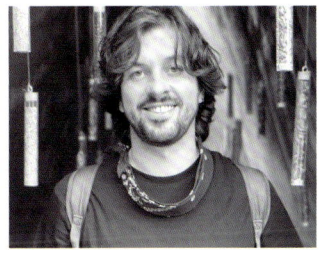

João is a visual development artist from Portugal who works in the animation industry. He loves to draw, especially while eating cake!

DAVID NAVARRO
Freelance illustrator and character designer
instagram.com/danavarrow

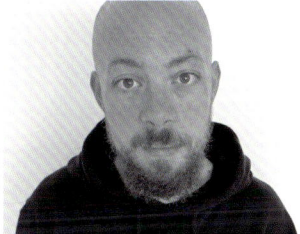

David is a freelance artist who has drawn as long as he can remember. He loves telling stories through his characters.

ROGER PÉREZ
Freelance character designer
instagram.com/thealmightyjerk

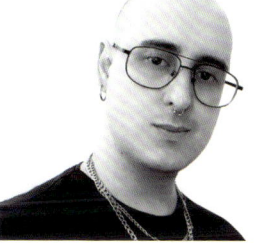

Roger is a character designer who has been working freelance for eight years, creating illustrations, concept art, and character design.

ANASTASIIA PLATOSHYNA
Character designer and visual-development artist
anastasiiaplatoshyna.portfolio.site

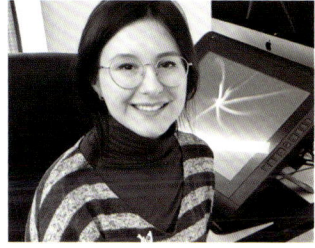

Anastasiia is a Ukrainian-Canadian artist and story-teller, based in Vancouver, working in animation and illustration.

ALEX RELLOSO
Storyboard artist at
The SPA Studios
instagram.com/alexrelloso_art

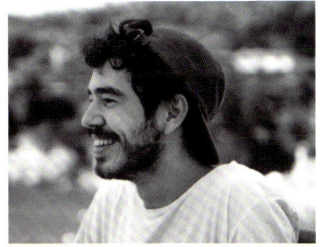

Alex Relloso is a storyboard and character design artist working at The SPA Studios in Madrid. He previously worked for Skydance and Netflix.

JENNIFER VOIGT
Freelance concept artist
vhox.artstation.com

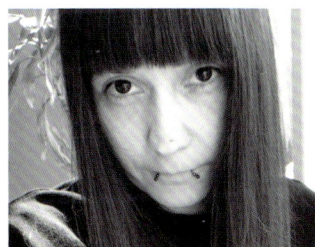

Jennifer is a freelance concept artist from Germany who works in books and games. She loves to draw quirky characters and creatures.

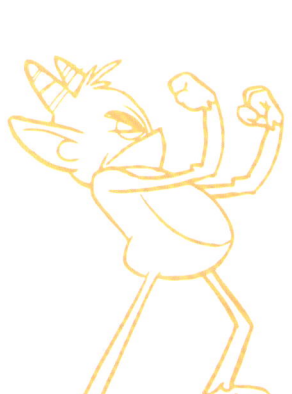

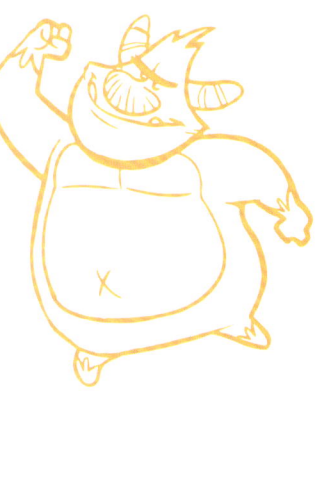

CREATURE TEETH
BY LORENZO ETHERINGTON

REMEMBER – YOUR CREATURE'S TEETH ARE **SURROUNDED** BY **GUMS.**

THINK ABOUT HOW GUMS APPEAR BETWEEN TEETH.

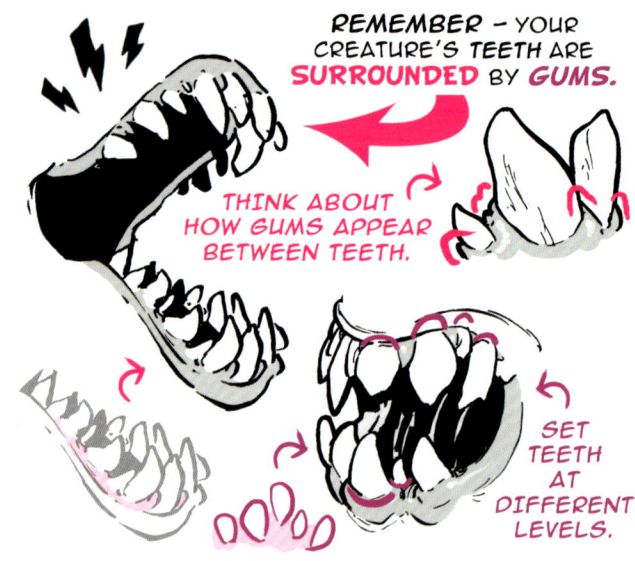

SET TEETH AT DIFFERENT LEVELS.

OF COURSE YOU **CAN** JUST MAKE **EVERY TOOTH TOTALLY DIFFERENT...!**

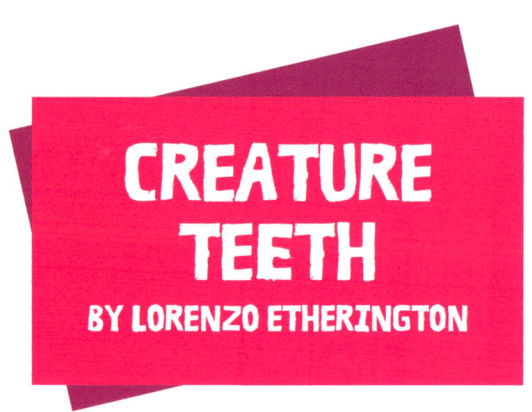

PICK 'N' MIX!

HERE'S **A FEW MORE IDEAS** – YOUR OPTIONS REALLY ARE **ENDLESS!**

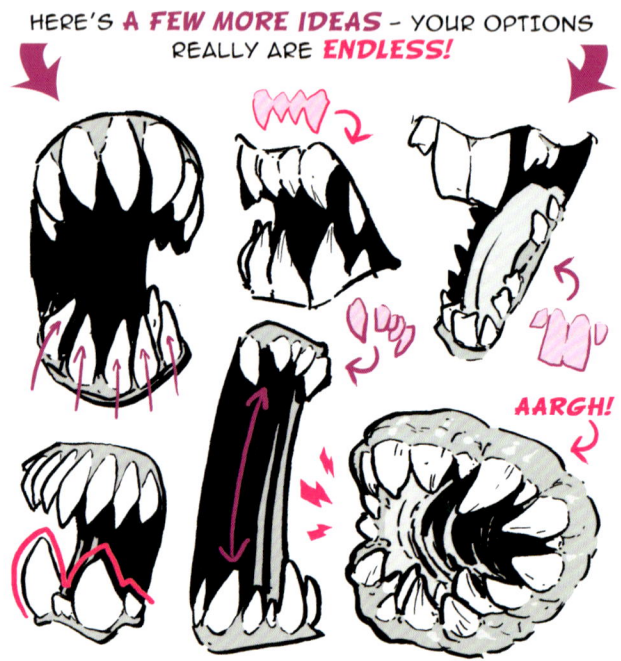

AARGH!

THINK ABOUT **ANGLES** – TRY POINTING TEETH **OUT** OR **IN** AT EXTREMES.

OUT

IN + BUNCH

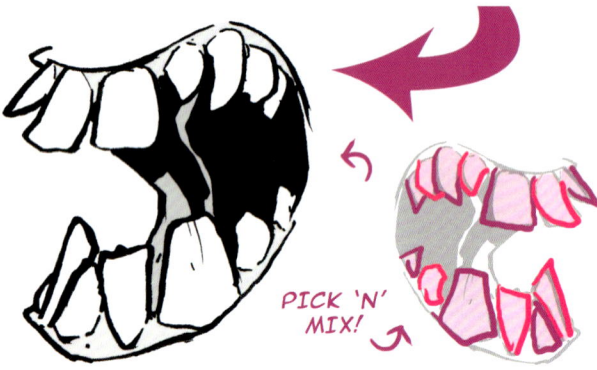

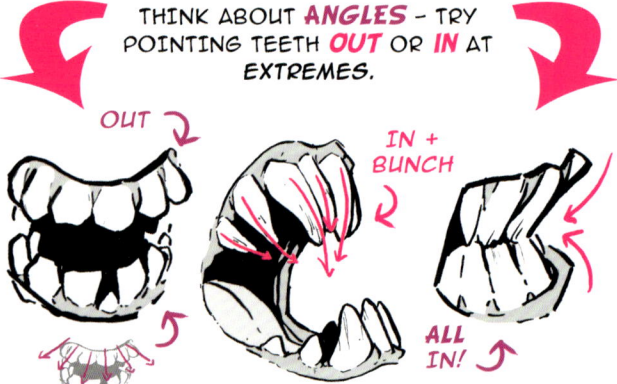

ALL IN!